What a State.

What a State!

IS DEVOLUTION
FOR SCOTLAND
THE END OF BRITAIN?

Edited by
ALAN TAYLOR

HarperCollins*Publishers*

HarperCollins*Publishers*
77–85 Fulham Palace Road,
Hammersmith, London w6 8jb

Published by HarperCollins*Publishers* 2000
1 3 5 7 9 8 6 4 2

Copyright © *The Scotsman* 2000

A catalogue record for this book
is available from the British Library.

ISBN 0 00 653218 7

Set in Linotype PostScript Minion with Photina Display by
Rowland Phototypesetting Ltd,
Bury St Edmunds, Suffolk

Printed in England by Clays Ltd, St Ives plc

CONTENTS

THE ENGLISH

THE BLAIR FACTOR

QUESTIONS OF IDENTITY

FOLLOW MY LEADER

THE DENOUEMENT

INTRODUCTION

On 6 May 1999, Scotland voted for its first parliament in almost three hundred years, an event of huge significance not only for Scots but for people throughout Great Britain. Some two months later, on the first of July, the temporary parliament in the Assembly Hall on the Mound in Edinburgh opened for business. It was a grand occasion, a moment, as Donald Dewar, the parliament's First Minister, said, which was 'anchored in history'.

Sir David Steel, the Presiding Officer, welcomed the Queen, as the 'Queen of Scots'. 'I trust,' said Sir David, 'that the Duke of Edinburgh will not disagree that this ancient capital whose name he bears, with its legal and ecclesiastical headquarters and its world-wide reputation for quality education and financial management has nonetheless until now seemed like a body with its heart missing.'

In the public gallery, Sean Connery, 'dressed as the Laird of Fountainbridge', as Ian Bell observed in *The Scotsman*, beamed like a child at Christmas. It was the greatest day of his life, he said. Another actor, Tom Fleming, read from Iain Crichton Smith's poem, 'The Beginning of a New Song':

> Let our three voiced country
>   Sing in a new world
> joining the other rivers without dogma,
> But with friendliness to all around her
>
> Let her new river shine on a day
> That is fresh and glittering and contemporary;

Let it be true to itself and its origins
inventive, original, philosophical,
its institutions mirror its beauty;
Then without shame we can esteem ourselves.

Then Sheena Wellington sang unaccompanied Robert Burns's universal anthem 'A Man's a Man for a' That', and, in a gesture which brought a lump to most throats, encouraged the throng to join in. 'Ye see yon birkie ca'd a lord/Wha struts, and stares, an a' that?/Tho hundreds worship at his word/He's but a cuff for a' that/His ribband, star, an a' that/The man o independent mind/ He looks and laughs at a' that.'

It was an inspirational gesture which seemed to symbolise the mood of the country on an auspicious day. From the outset, it was hoped that the opening of the parliament would be different to the pomp and circumstance which inevitably accompanies the state opening of that other parliament at Westminster. And so it proved. The atmosphere was relaxed but also dignified and emotional. For many it was the culmination of long years of argument which, after the referendum in 1979, when devolution was denied even after a majority of people voted in its favour, seemed an unrealistic dream. For others, it was a half-way house, a Mickey Mouse compromise that was neither one thing nor another, not full-blown independence or a partner in a union of equals. Still others looked on incredulously, having argued passionately against devolution in the belief that it is a stepping stone to separatism.

But even those whose emotions were mixed had to concede they were witnessing a remarkable event in Scottish history. Come what may, nothing would ever be the same again. Scotland may or may not, as Andrew Neil prophesised, be sleepwalking towards independence, but on 1 July something fundamental changed in a country known for its caution. Crowds lined the streets as the procession wound down the Mound, including children rep-resenting schools from all over Scotland. Parties went on long into the night and bands played in Princes Street gardens. The mood was of celebration, a cathartic expression of joy appropriate to the occasion, as if acknowledging that with the morning the pragmatic business of government would surely begin.

There are those who say the debate for Scottish devolution began when the first article of the Treaty of Union of 1707 proclaimed: 'THAT the Two Kingdoms of England and Scotland shall ... forever after be United into One Kingdom by the name of GREAT BRITAIN.' Like the question of Quebec's divorce from Canada, the debate certainly seems to have been going on interminably. Throughout the 20th century, it has come and gone as the popularity of nationalism waxed and waned. But devolution never remotely looked a possibility until comparatively recently. One landmark was the election of the SNP's Winnie Ewing at the Hamilton by-election in November 1967. In one of the safest Labour seats in the country, in the party's fiefdom in the west of Scotland, Mrs Ewing took 46 per cent of the vote. Suddenly the SNP was a political force to be reckoned with. Nor, it transpired, was the result a freak.

From 1967 onwards, as Professor Tom Devine concludes in *The Scottish Nation: 1700–2000*, 'Scottish politics would never be the same again'. The Nationalists had challenged the Labour Party hegemony in Scotland and the first general election of 1974 confirmed their rise, with the SNP sending seven MPs to Westminster and gaining 22 per cent of the vote. In response, Devine argues, the incoming Labour government embraced devolution as a real commitment despite having fought the election on a platform opposed to it. Just eight months later, in the second general election of the year, the SNP did even better, knocking the Tories into third place in Scotland, achieving 30 per cent of the vote and increasing the number of MPs to eleven.

Between then and now the SNP's fortunes have dipped and climbed but the spectre of devolution, closely followed by the even bigger one of independence, has never gone away. The rise of the SNP was an obvious factor in raising the temperature and profile of the debate on the constitutional question, but it was not the only one. For while the SNP made advances there was no indication that the Scottish people were persuaded by its argument that Scotland should move towards independence. In contrast to the number of people who voted Nationalist, the number who said they favoured independence was significantly lower. Nevertheless other shifts in public mood helped bolster the SNP's cause.

Chief among these, perhaps, was a sense that 'Britishness' held less meaning than it had in centuries when Britain was forging its empire and when these islands were threatened in this century by war. In the post-war period, Britain's declining role as a world power grew ever more apparent. The Empire was in a state of disintegration and Britain no longer could count on its privileged status. The Suez Crisis in 1956 demonstrated America's dominance while the refusal in 1963 of The French President, Charles de Gaulle, to allow Britain into the Common Market underlined our position as a second-class power.

'Ironically,' writes Prof Devine, 'it was the attempt to maintain Britain's status as a world military power that helped to alienate some in the new generation of Scots. In November 1960 Prime Minister Macmillan announced that the country's main nuclear deterrent, the Polaris submarine, would be based in the Holy Loch in Scotland, a decision confirmed in 1964 by the Labour government of Harold Wilson. These controversial moves boosted the membership of the Campaign for Nuclear Disarmament (CND) in Scotland, while opposition north of the border had a particular force because of the realisation that the Scots would be in the front line in the event of nuclear war.'

The introduction of the poll tax in Scotland by Margaret Thatcher's government in 1989 similarly confirmed to many Scots that, from a London perspective, Scotland was being used, as Andrew Marr wrote in *The Battle for Scotland*, 'for political vivisection by the cold-hearted English'. In fact, as Marr points out, it was the Scottish Tories who fought to have the tax quickly. But the perception that this was a heinous levy imposed vindictively on anti-Tory Scotland as an experiment prevailed and helped galvanise the nationalist lobby, with the SNP advocating a mass campaign of non-payment.

Coincidental with this was an upsurge in Scottish culture which seemed to reflect a nation growing in self-confidence. Where previously the noblest sight for a Scot on the make was the high road south, writers, artists and musicians began to explore their homeland without first becoming exiles. In the universities, the study of Scotland grew hugely, particularly in history and literature. Writers such as James Kelman, Alasdair Gray, Iain Banks, William McIlvanney, Janice Galloway and A. L. Kennedy were all part of what the *New Yorker* called 'a Scottish efflorescence.' Scottish painters such as Stephen Conroy, Adrian Wizniewski, Peter Howson, Ken Currie and Steven Campbell enjoyed a vogue among the world's *glitterati*.

Scotland, then, seemed to have shrugged off its enervating inferiority complex, and the new mood in the country was recognised by John Smith, a pro-devolution Labour MP who became leader of the party in 1992. Devolution, he said, was 'the settled will of the Scottish people'. Tragically, he died in 1994 before he could see the project through but when his successor, Tony Blair, came to power in a landslide victory on 1 May 1997 he was not inclined to let his predecessor's promise go by the board. For the new prime minister, devolution was 'unfinished business' and he announced that there would be a referendum on 11 September 1997 when the Scottish people would vote on two questions. Firstly, they were asked whether they wanted a Scottish parliament and, secondly, whether it should have tax varying powers.

The omens, as Prof Devine acknowledges, looked good, given the extent of Labour's election victory and the pro-devolution alliance, Scotland Forward, which brought Labour, the Liberal Democrats and the SNP under the same banner. In comparison the No-No lobby could only boast the Tories, who now had no Westminster representation in Scotland, a controversial frontman in Donald Findlay QC, a director of Rangers football club, and a few high profile businessmen such as Sir Bruce Patullo, Governor of the Bank of Scotland. The result seemed to be a foregone conclusion but the death of Diana, Princess of Wales, in a Paris under pass just 11 days before the date of the election threw the campaigning into turmoil. Some anti-devolutionists even suggested postponing it but were pooh-poohed by Donald Dewar, then Secretary of State for Scotland. After a respectful interregnum the debate was kick-started with the help of Sean Connery and voting went ahead as planned.

The result was an emphatic victory for those in the pro-devolution camp. 74.3 per cent of those who voted supported a Scottish parliament and 63.5 agreed that it should have tax varying powers. The scale of the endorsement astonished many sceptics. Unlike 1979, support for a Scottish parliament was general throughout the country. On the question of tax varying powers only Orkney and Shetland voted against. Thus the Scottish people could vote for their own MSP (Members of the Scottish Parliament) who would have power over all matters apart from foreign policy, defence, macro-economic policy, social security, abortion and broadcasting. The new parliamentarians will also be able to raise or lower the basic rate of tax by 3p, or £450 million in total. Westminster will continue to have responsibility for relations with the European Union, but there will also be a Scottish representative office in Brussels.

The date for what was, in essence, the first purely Scottish general election was set for 6 May 1999 and promised to be a bruising affair, with the question of independence at the forefront. Having campaigned vigorously for devolution, the SNP's leader, Alex Salmond, now had sight of his party's ultimate goal. While Donald Dewar insisted that devolution within the Union could work well, Salmond was ready to pounce on what many saw as its inherent contradictions. But there was more to this election than the eternal constitutional question, what has been dubbed the 'neverendum'. For the first time in a British election, proportional representation was introduced. The trusty first-past-the-post method was redundant and replaced by the additional member system with one vote for a party list, counted on a regional basis, and one for an individual MSP, counted in individual constituencies. In all there would be 129 MSPs sitting in Edinburgh.

But for all the media interest which the debate engendered the campaign, when it finally got under way, was curiously lacking in passion. The Nationalists, in an attempt to garner support from disaffected supporters on the Labour Left, proposed a so-called 'tartan tax', in which they would retain a penny on the basic rate of income tax which the Chancellor of the Exchequer, Gordon Brown, sought to remove in the Budget. But if it was a tactic designed to wrong foot Labour it backfired. Led by Brown himself, Labour went on the offensive, labelling the SNP the party of high taxes.

Yet while it created a lot of noise, the electorate appeared unmoved, with many arguing that Scots, unlike the rest of the British population, are prepared to put up with higher taxes if it leads to improved public services. Be that as it may, the SNP's proposals, though passed almost unanimously at the party's special conference in Aberdeen in March 1999, probably failed to persuade any neutrals to come aboard. In any case, a much more contentious issue was soon to push the tax proposals into the background. While the Scottish general election campaign was proceeding placidly, Britain was engaged in a real war in the Balkans. In reaction to Serbia's brutal programme of ethnic cleansing of Albanians in Kosovo, NATO, backed wholeheartedly by the Labour government, instigated military action. Taking the form of high intensity aerial bombing, British servicemen were part of a sophisticated nightly attack on Serbia's utilities and military bases.

Towards the end of March, before the curtain had been raised on the election campaign proper, Alex Salmond, in an unprecedented party political broadcast, broke the all-party consensus over the Balkans. Addressing the nation on television he accused the prime minister and his NATO allies of pursuing a 'misguided' policy of 'dubious legality and unpardonable folly'. Suddenly, the war became a factor in the Scottish election, with Foreign Secretary, Robin Cook, rounding on Salmond and declaring him to be 'the toast of Belgrade'. The SNP leader, said Cook, now stood 'side by side' with the Serbian leader Slobodan Milosevic.

As an overture to the election it could hardly have been more combustible. While the respective leaders of the four main parties – Donald Dewar for Labour, Alex Salmond for the SNP, David McLetchie, the Tories' recently elected head, and Jim Wallace of the Liberal Democrats – began to tour the country in their cavalcades and battle-buses, a debate raged in the media about where this was all leading. At the outset, *The Scotsman*, which has been a more consistent supporter of devolution down the decades than any of the political parties, decided to take on the role of newspaper of record, covering the campaign in forensic detail, seriously examining the issues but also allowing plenty of space for polemic and humour.

At a time when the nation was potentially at a crossroads, it was, we believed, essential that anyone looking back on this moment in history a hundred or so years hence, should be able, by reading *The Scotsman*, to get a flavour of what actually happened in the fateful days leading up to 6 May. There were, of course, many column inches devoted to considering how we reached this position. Why fix something that ain't broken, argued Unionists, while out and out Nationalists prayed for the majority of seats, which would throw open the whole question of independence. Meanwhile, the Tories hoped that proportional representation would signal the start of their revival north of the border and the Liberal Democrats looked forward, in what the polls seemed to suggest might be a hung parliament, to holding the balance of power.

Though, as in any election, unlikely issues such as student tuition fees came to the fore and dominated for a while, it was the broader picture on which most commentators concentrated their attention. Devolution, despite the insistence of its advocates, is a process not a terminus. Many people, including expatriate Scots, found it difficult to come to grips with it. For them, it was a question of identity. Not surprisingly some returned to explore the roots of the movement for change and left either enlightened or bemused. Some things just cannot be explained; they simply are. Try to take the pulse of a nation and it is not long before you are resorting to snapshots and anecdote, personal history and family upbringing. The economics of devolution are undoubtedly important but they are only part of a mosaic. By voting for it in such heavy numbers Scots seemed to be expressing a desire for change which cannot be easily articulated or dissected. No one, however, should underestimate the strength of feeling and purpose which move the people of this normally reticent nation to exercise their authority at the ballot box.

'There shall be a Scottish Parliament.' These six sonorous words which comprise the first section of the Scotland Act really say it all. Whether the Parliament lives up to dreams and aspirations of the people who voted for it remains to be seen. But these are early days yet and there is a long way to go before it can be judged a success or otherwise. But there are now 129 Members of the Scottish Parliament charged with making it work. After all the hullabaloo of the election Labour, with 56 seats, fell narrowly short of an overall majority and were forced to forge an alliance with the Liberal Democrats who had 17 MSPs, while the SNP are the official opposition with 35 seats. Predictions of the demise of the Tories proved premature as they won 18 seats. Moreover, three minority parties found their way into Scotland's first parliament, including the Greens, the Scottish Socialist Party, and the Labour renegade Dennis Canavan, who confounded his former colleagues who sought to bar him from the first Scottish parliament in nearly three centuries. Thus it is the most diverse of assemblies, the latest episode in this ancient nation's compelling saga.

FALSE UNITY

A feeble and flimsy 'NO'

IAN BELL

It was one of the better confessions in a week of bad faith and unctuous fibs. 'I'm voting Yes,' said the boy in the Paisley street, 'because of the people who want me to vote No.'

You could call it the positive-negative approach, and it is less perverse than it sounds. After all, it is the way most of us have voted for years. Given the dearth of real choice in politics – for whom should a republican vote? or an anti-abortionist? – it is the only way to record an opinion. Keeping the bastards out matters more, to a lot of us, than getting the chancers in.

So with home rule. There is a constituency, and a sizeable one, perfectly capable of working out that the scheme proposed is a gimcrack affair full of holes, illogicalities and problems waiting to happen. What of it, when the alternative is Westminster's parody of participatory democracy and a Scotland run, to all intents and purposes, by five suits in the Scottish Office?

Hence the reticence of the No campaign when it comes to making a case for the status quo. They predict desolation if Scotland has the temerity to approve Labour's modest little scheme. They are a sight less eloquent when attempting to advertise the febrile little world that is Gomorrah by the Thames, with its constitutional fictions, its lobby fodder, puerile debates, absolute insularity, unelected peers, centralized power, and minatory assumptions about a dream-state called Britain.

In their particulars, too, the Tory conventionalists do an entrancing line in gall. Such humility as 1 May taught them has evaporated. The talk, after the deluge, of 'listening to the people' was the passing of wind. The party which submerged itself in sleaze – and was encouraged to do so by Westminster's institutional senility – now damns Scotland's parliament for corruption before it has even been created.

It insists, too, that recent events have concentrated the minds of Scottish voters wonderfully. Yesterday's newspapers were full of headlines announcing that we have been fair put off by Labour's scandals. The fact that last week's *Scotsman*/ICM poll showed the opposite is ignored as an inconvenient detail, just as the unqualified rejection of the Tory case at the general election is shuffled over in silence.

They are a visionary lot, nevertheless, the Nay-sayers. They know, as for a fact, and in every detail, what a devolved Scotland will be like. They have seen the taxes go up and the inward investment fall, the Nationalists rampant and the socialists (as they still call Scotland's centre-right) with their hands in the till. They understand the nature and ambitions of the new parliament even before its members are elected.

Curiously, the Tories urging a No vote also seem to have absolutely no expectation of winning power in that parliament. Why might that be? In their every description of life after home rule Labour (calamity) is in power, perhaps with Liberal Democrat help. Tories have seen the future. Clearly, this in no way affects the disinterested advice they are dispensing.

But hold on, they say. How can Labour and the Scottish National Party be in alliance against us? One wants the Union preserved; one wants it dissolved. A contradiction: they can't both be right. This is logical. It is as logical, indeed, as the dissolution of a Conservative Party that has accepted the irreconcilability of its Eurosceptic and Europhile wings. No?

In reality, of course, the Tories will stick together until they are in the position (back in government) to fight out their differences. So it is with Labour and the SNP. The Edinburgh parliament is their chosen arena and they will work together only until it exists. And where better to argue over the last fundamental issue concerning Scotland's future than in Scotland itself?

In the end, the real problem with home rule might be termed the insolent minority, the ones who tolerate the people's will only when it coincides with their own. The general election ought to have daunted them just a little, but not a bit of it. They have a new hero in the governor of the Bank of Scotland, who has decided that in this case the customer cannot possibly be allowed to be right.

Sadly for him, Sir Bruce Pattulo's customers might have other ideas. They might wish to inform him that there is a standing charge for bankers who dabble in politics. They might even ask how a bank with international ambitions copes with local tax variations abroad but cannot manage such a thing at home. They might even remember that tax cuts and tax increases will depend, at the last, on their votes, not on his advice.

For all that, Sir Bruce remains a curiosity in a curious No campaign. It has been, for the most part, both disingenuous and feeble. It seems incapable of defending the merits of the settlement it is trying to defend. It pins its few hopes on apathy and fear. It is comprised of people with an oddly hostile attitude towards their fellow Scots. Meanwhile, its desperation – why is no one listening? – grows more obvious each day, its protestations more shrill.

The No lobby is less a campaign than the tantrum of a political group accustomed to getting its own way. The old arrangement suited. Under the old settlement, sustained by governments England had chosen, it was possible to pretend that Conservatism still mattered in Scotland. Now a paradox – Labour, elected by English votes, offering home rule to Scotland – means that Scottish Tories must stand on their own feet. This is not life as they understand it.

They will calm down, of course, once the Edinburgh parliament is a reality and the British constitution begins to reform itself around that fact. Having said No for so long some among the Conservatives of Scotland will say Yes to election quickly enough when the time comes. Then they, too, will speak the language of identity with a new fluency and a new confidence. It being the purpose of the project, home rule might even give them back their self-respect.

For now, it looks as though they must be taught another lesson. The brutal pragmatism that was once the distinguishing mark of the Conservative Party has deserted it. Tories insist, it appears, on doing this thing the hard way, like a wilful Canute building sand castles while the tide comes in. So be it: some of us remember 1 May with a certain fondness.

In the end, though, the attacks of the No campaigners matter less than the utter flimsiness of their defence. At a time when the old Westminster system commands little by way of respect, far less of loyalty, all that remain are tales told to frighten children. No change, as even the hardened losers among them have been heard to advise, no chance.

It should be fun to watch, in any case.

25 August 1997

West Lothian answer is to cut number of MPs

PETER JONES

One fact, above all, needs to be clearly understood and accepted by all those who will gather in Edinburgh's Assembly Rooms tomorrow to launch the campaign for a 'Yes, Yes' vote in the autumn referendum on a Scottish parliament. It will be a meeting of high excitement and enthusiasm. The participants will have the evidence of the Referendum Bill, published yesterday, before them. The thrill of knowing that the home rule bandwagon, stalled for eighteen years, is now rolling will be intoxicating. But there is that one hard fact needing to be recognized.

This business is not about independence. It is not about nationalism. Braveheart talk needs to be left where it properly belongs in the fantasy world of cinema. This is about devolution. It is about rearranging the internal constitutional machinery of the United Kingdom while leaving it intact and united.

Many times in the last eighteen years, supporters of devolution have tended to ignore this and have been tempted to use the language of nationalism in pursuit of what remains a unionist cause. An odd belief has grown up among the Labour and Liberal Democrat devolution supporters – and in some parts of the media. It is that whatever Scotland wants, Scotland will get whenever, as has now happened, the Tories were swept away and Labour took power.

Hence the fury when Tony Blair announced the decision (taken not by him, but by a committee comprising Donald Dewar,

George Robertson, Ann Taylor, Jack Straw, Gordon Brown, and Lord Irvine of Lairg) that there should be a referendum. Hence, also the rage when he said during the election that the Scottish parliament would not be sovereign. These are things which are offensive to Nationalists, but not to Unionists, even pro-devolution Unionists.

Devolution is a United Kingdom business. It cannot be unilaterally declared, it has to be passed through the United Kingdom parliament. All parts of Britain have an interest in this. If the MP for Plymouth or Ramsgate feels that what is happening far to the north will nonetheless affect his or her constituents, that concern should, and will, be raised. If the concern is serious enough, it might even lead to the MP voting against devolution. This must be recognized.

It must also be dealt with. It is no good presupposing that Labour's thunderous majority of 178, backed with the moral authority of a 'yes, yes' referendum vote, can be used to bulldoze through such concerns. Left ignored, such concerns will turn into resentments and poisonous grievances, leading to destructive revenge action when the political tide eventually turns, as turn it will.

One such concern is the West Lothian question. Yes, it sounds tedious. It is complicated when put in parliamentary terms. Why should English and Welsh MPs not be able to vote on Scotland's domestic business when Scottish MPs will still be able to vote on English and Welsh home affairs? In the blunter language of the English pub, the problem is more obvious: 'These bloody Jocks, they've got their own bloody parliament, so how come they still boss us around?'

The favoured solution of *The Scotsman*, that Scottish MPs should not vote on English business, would work in the circumstances that now prevail. Labour has a massive majority of 129 in England. But in a different parliament, where Labour, or any other party, had a small overall majority, but a minority of English seats, the opposition parties would run England. English devolution would become a fact, whether or not the voters wanted it, and the signs are they don't want it.

But the Labour landslide means another solution can work. Scotland is over-represented in Parliament. If Scottish constituencies were as big as those in England, Scotland should only have 57 MPs, not the 72 as now. Cutting the number back to that level would help, but it is not enough. The Scottish contingent in the Commons would have nothing like the constituency or committee work of English MPs.

When Ulster had its devolved parliament for fifty years this century, it sent only 12 MPs to Westminster. Because of devolution, Ulster was under-represented. If the same principle of under-representation was applied to Scotland, there should be only 42 Scottish MPs. Before 1 May, when Labour fretted that its majority would be 30–40 seats, this was unthinkable. The loss of 30 seats, most of which would be Labour, could obviously scupper the party's chances of re-election to Westminster.

But now the political landscape has been changed in unforeseen ways, the West Lothian answer that Scotland should accept under-representation at Westminster in return for devolution of power to Edinburgh is not only thinkable, but on ministerial agendas as they draw up the devolution white paper for publication in early July.

There is a consequence which will upset devolution supporters. The Constitutional Convention's plan envisages that the Scottish parliament will have the same number of seats elected by first-past-the-post means as there are at Westminster, with the provision that Orkney & Shetland is split, i.e. 73. But if the 72 Scottish Westminster seats are cut to 42, it follows that the number of Scottish parliament constituency seats will fall to 43. Assuming the number of Scottish parliament seats elected by PR remains at the 56 set by the convention, then the total number of Scottish parliament seats will be 99, not the 129 seats planned by the convention.

Far from shrieking foul, the convention supporters should welcome this. It will make winning a 'yes, yes' vote much easier. As well as answering the West Lothian question, it answers those who fear a top-heavy and costly parliament in Edinburgh. It will make the devolution legislation easier to get through Westminster. It will also make a 'yes' vote in the Welsh referendum easier to achieve since the Westminster under-representation price the Scots are paying for maximum devolution would be obvious to those who currently complain that the Scots seem to be getting a much juicer slice of the cake than the Welsh, who are promised only a minimum devolution assembly.

In the same vein, the critics who claim that Mr Blair is only seeking party advantage from devolution would be answered. Those who want Scotland to move forward should, if they accept that devolution is Unionist business, pay the price of under-representation at Westminster, and leave injured nationalist feelings to be felt and voiced by nationalists.

16 May 1997

Salmond and Dewar can't both be right. A Yes, Yes vote for devolution will reduce Scotland to the granny flat of Britain

ALLAN MASSIE

It is not a question of patriotism. Bravehearts have nothing to do with it. It is easy to accuse Scots who intend to vote against the creation of a Scottish parliament of a lack of patriotism, just as it is easy to accuse those who favour the incorporation of the United Kingdom, or indeed of an otherwise independent Scotland, in a European federation, of being unpatriotic. In neither case is the accusation just. It is better to accept that people want what they think is best for their country, but don't agree as to what it is.

It appears to me no more anti-Scottish or un-Scottish – though we don't yet have a parliamentary committee on un-Scottish activities – to favour the continuation of the Union as it is now, than it is un-Scottish for Alex Salmond to look forward to Scottish membership of the ever-closer union of European States provided for in the Treaty of Rome.

There are several reasons for voting No, No on Thursday. First, a natural reluctance to abandon the home in which we have lived, on the whole comfortably and successfully, for almost three hundred years. Those who are campaigning for a Yes, Yes vote, as distinct from the Nationalists, who are (temporarily) their allies in the campaign, will have it of course that we are not leaving the home, but merely readjusting our position within it. That is undoubtedly what Donald Dewar believes. Perhaps he is right. So let us admit that we are not definitely, and certainly not immediately, being invited to leave what has been our settled dwelling; we are merely, as it were, being asked to move into a granny flat. I am not convinced that we shall be happy there.

This first reason for voting No is powerful and simple: many of us feel an affection for the Union in its present form and for the constitution as we know it. This was exemplified in a letter to a national newspaper last week. The writer was Frank Coutts, formerly of the King's Own Scottish Borderers and a past president of the Scottish Rugby Union. He said that, as a soldier, he had always 'eschewed politics', believing it was his duty 'to owe allegiance only to the government of the day, of whatever hue. The British Government, that is.' He continued: 'I am a Scot by birth, schooling, residence and regiment – and a piper to boot – but I could not possibly vote yes for anything that challenges my loyalty to Britain and the Commonwealth.'

Some will no doubt call this view old-fashioned, but a couple of television programmes on Sunday, Stephen Magee's admirable *The Ghost of '79* and the Kirsty Wark-hosted *The People's Debate*, featured a number of young people displaying a similar lack of enthusiasm for a constitutional change that puts the integrity of the UK at risk. Loyalty to Britain runs deeper than many Yes campaigners will allow, and does not imply disloyalty to Scotland. It is possible to love both, just as it is possible to love both your mother and your wife.

The second reason for voting No, No is that this referendum is fundamentally and doubly dishonest.

It is dishonest because we are being asked to vote on a white paper and not on an act of parliament. A parliamentary bill will follow a Yes vote, and, while the Government will undoubtedly introduce a bill which replicates the proposals of the white paper, we do not know how that bill will emerge from scrutiny in both Houses of Parliament.

Of course, if we vote Yes, No there will be some confusion,

and it will be necessary to amend Chapter 7 of the white paper. We can't tell just what form that amendment will take, but it is unlikely it will merely see the dropping of those paragraphs of the chapter which relate to tax-varying powers.

The second reason why it is dishonest is that the referendum is being promoted by political parties with clear contrary aims. Donald Dewar and the Labour Party tell us that devolution will strengthen the United Kingdom. Mr Salmond and the Scottish National Party are confident that it will lead to the end of Union. They can't both be right. This point was put very forcibly in *The People's Debate* by a young man, a student, who described himself as a Labour Party activist. His attempt to extract a satisfactory answer from Dewar and Salmond was – shall we say – politely evaded. Yet it is worth pointing out that it is not so long since Mr Salmond was saying that the only honest referendum was a multi-option one, offering a chance to declare for independence.

There is another dishonesty in the devolutionary cause. Throughout the years of Tory government, we became accustomed to hearing about 'the democratic deficit': Scotland voted Labour and got a Tory government. The Conservative argument, valid but unsatisfactory to many Scots, was that we were playing by Unionist rules and that England could conceivably get a Labour government though returning a majority of Conservative MPs. (This actually looked very probable in 1992.)

Devolution is supposed to correct that democratic deficit. It does not, and cannot, do so, because the argument based on the democratic deficit is an argument for independence, not for devolution. Set up a Scottish parliament as proposed in the white paper and then look at the list of powers reserved to Westminster. You will see that next time we have a Westminster government which does not command majority support in Scotland, it will still take decisions on a wide range of affairs which concern us; and these decisions will affect us and the way we live just as surely as if there was no Scottish parliament or its members had been banished to St Kilda.

That doesn't worry me as a Unionist any more than it worries me that the present Labour Government doesn't command majority support in the two parts of Scotland I know best: the Borders and the North-East.

If we had had a Scottish parliament since 1979 it could have done nothing to prevent the shift from direct to indirect taxation or the cuts in the rates of income tax. It could not have stopped Margaret Thatcher's trade union legislation. It could not have prevented the closure of Linwood or Ravenscraig, or the Ministry of Defence from choosing Devonport rather than Rosyth as the base for refitting Trident. It would have had no influence over the level of the state pension or indeed over anything to do with social security, the department which now disposes of one-third of the UK Government's revenue.

It could of course have prevented the imposition of the poll tax, and kept the old household rates, which were as deeply unpopular, though only of course with the minority who paid them, shouldering an unfair share of the cost of local government. It could have prevented the sale of council houses to tenants, and, in the temper of the Labour Party throughout the 1980s, would probably have done so.

Of course, then as proposed now, the parliament would have had responsibility for health and education in Scotland, two areas of government where the Scottish identity has been respected, and Scottish individuality preserved: two areas of government also where spending, per head of population, is, and has been for years, very much higher in Scotland than in England. The truth is that the Conservative governments since 1979 moved very cautiously in these areas, and respected ways in which we do things differently from the English. That is not surprising, since policy was formed by Scots in the Scottish Office. But the extent of the differences was brought home to me recently by a meeting with an old friend, a Scot, who works as a schools inspector in London. He complained to me that the last government had pursued diametrically opposed policies on schools inspection in Scotland and England; and that the Scottish way was much better.

Even if this was not so, it is reasonable to question whether health and education, important as they are, are so important that they should make essential the creation of a Scottish parliament with all the additional costs and the likelihood that it will provoke, rather than allay, ill-feeling between different parts of the Union.

Be that as it may, the fact remains that 'democratic deficit' is, if you accept it, an argument for independence, not devolution. It is something that mere devolution will not remove or correct.

There are other reasons for voting No, No. The financial provisions for the parliament are ridiculous. It is not healthy for a supposedly responsible body to be so dependant on another superior body for its revenue. Writing recently about the malaise of local government, Iain MacWhirter suggested we should restore the local tax base. 'Part of the problem,' he said, 'is that local councils no longer raise the money they spend. Nothing could be better calculated to undermine civic responsibility. The balance should be restored with more tax raised locally and less raised centrally. Councils would then be answerable to their local electorate.'

We are being offered, in the first instance, a parody of a parliament with small powers and little responsibility. A student of South African politics told me recently the powers given in the White Paper to the Scottish parliament are almost exactly those which the South African apartheid regime gave to the Bantustans. Vote on Thursday for 'Scotland – the new Transkei.

Those who believe this will lead to a 'fair and just settlement for Scotland within the framework of the UK' assure us that something similar works elsewhere and that there are not precedents for devolution leading to the break-up of a Union, a view that would surprise Czechs, Slovaks and Yugoslavs. In any case, they rarely compare like with like.

Most of the examples they give are of federations, like the US, Canada or Germany, or confederations like Switzerland, all built from the ground up. Spain is a more relevant favoured example, and devolution is held to be a success, at least to Catalonia. But the example is recent, the history brief. The much-respected newspaper, *El Pais*, recently complained that the integrity of Spain had been put at risk, the idea of Spain was withering in the face of manifestations of local selfishness.

There is, of course, a case for devolution as proposed, just as there is a case for independence, a case for the Union in its present form, and a case for a federal UK. Nothing has been said in the course of this campaign to persuade me that the case for devolution is a good one. Indeed, of the four possible constitutional arrangements listed above, it appears to me the least satisfactory, offering only an illusion of self-government and consigning us, as I say, to a granny flat within the UK. Scotland deserves better than that. So it is, in my view, an act of patriotism to vote No; even while I accept that other patriots will vote Yes. We are talking about a difference of opinion, not a different degree of commitment to Scotland.

9 September 1997

CAN BRITAIN SURVIVE?

Unto the breach

ROBIN HARRIS

The continued existence of Britain as a medium-sized power with a more than medium-sized role has long been one of the given assumptions of international affairs. But what if all that were to change? What if not just the institutions but the allegiances and even the identity of Britain were fundamentally to alter? Until recently such a hypothesis would have seemed risible. But suddenly it is not. The rest of the world has not yet grasped it, but Britain is Balkanizing and, as elsewhere, the dynamic imperative in the process is changing national awareness.

The British, and especially the English, have traditionally considered themselves above nationalism. The Right has understood that as well as the Left. For example, in his *Dictionary of Political Thought*, Roger Scruton, Britain's leading conservative political philosopher, notes: 'In the United Kingdom nationalism is confined to the Celtic fringes, where it has been associated with movements for home rule in Ireland, Scotland and – to some extent – Wales. English nationalism is virtually unknown, at least under that description.'

When Britain's Empire bestrode the globe and the schoolroom maps were largely coloured red, London was a vantage point for overseas advance, not a refuge for a threatened society in retreat. In such circumstances, it was only natural that the constituent components of the British state – English, Scots, Welsh, and even on occasion Irish – were generally prepared to ignore their national differences. Britain thus became that very rare entity – a multinational nation-state.

Of course, it was never entirely harmonious. Not just Scots but even some die-hard English objected to subordinating their primary national identity in the wake of the 1707 Act of Union. But the economic benefits arising from the removal of internal trade barriers reconciled all those actively prepared to exploit the new opportunities. The Welsh, having been formally united with England since Henry VIII's reign, are accordingly even better integrated into the British framework. The Irish were always, of course, in a different category. To a greater extent than either Scotland or Wales, Ireland was subdued and colonized through the brutal assertion of English power. Yet even so, today's Irish nationalists are wrong to portray the relationship between the Irish and English as exclusively one of struggle and repression. In truth, Ireland can as little shake off its English connection as the English can disentangle themselves from the fate of Ireland.

But the inhabitants of the United Kingdom today feel less British because they have been systematically persuaded that all of the more recognizable features of Britishness – language, history, tradition, ethnic homogeneity – are suspect. This is a long process with parallels in other modern nation-states. But recently it has taken a new twist with the election of Tony Blair's New Labour Government, which has managed to provide a fresh challenge to the concept of British nationhood by making it seem at once rebarbative and ridiculous. Mr Blair and his colleagues have declared war on British history. The Prime Minister confessed early on to feeling that 'British pageantry is great, but it does not define what Britain is today'. The process of 'rebranding' Britain then proceeded apace. Initially, four grey plastic 'space-age pods', created by a well-known exhibitor of erotic designs, were installed on Horse Guards Parade in London and were used to display 'cool' British products. Then a video was circulated among Commonwealth leaders improbably depicting 'Britain: The Young Country'.

But most effort to design a new politically correct Britain has gone into the £800 million Millennium Dome. The creative director of the project has made it clear he sees no place in the dome for the Union Flag, or for 'other nationalistic' features that would 'give the wrong signals'.

Both the complex historical and the crass contemporary reasons for a decline in the sense of being British affect the English, as well as the Scots, Welsh and Irish, but necessarily in somewhat different ways. This is because for most of our history as a politically united island no clear distinction was drawn between Englishness and Britishness.

In this matter, assumptions tell their own story. When Nelson signalled before the Battle of Trafalgar that 'England expects every man will do his duty' he was not thereby excusing the fleet's Scottish, Welsh and Irish sailors from doing theirs. When John Buchan wrote that '[British] Imperialism is ... a sense of the destiny of England', he was not thus implicitly excluding his fellow Scots from the Imperial enterprise.

The identification of the British with the English was in fact quite understandable. After all, the language spoken in the British Isles, outside of a part of the (ethnically misnamed) Celtic fringe, was quite definitely and properly described as English. And language, then as now, was one of the principal accepted determinants of nationhood.

Moreover, English economic, political and cultural dominance of Britain is the central fact of British history. Both opponents and defenders of the Union often feel unhappy about accepting that – the former because it puts into sober historical perspective the grandiose claims for Scottish, Welsh and Irish separateness, the latter because it provides an all too brutal reminder of what the Union of the United Kingdom in fact signifies. It is rare for nations to challenge political structures that they already dominate. But there are exceptions. It was the Russians, to whom all other inmates of the 'Prisonhouse of Nations' had to defer, who finally overthrew the Soviet Union. The English may, in very different circumstances but with equal lack of reflection, be starting to drift along the same route.

A kind of English nationalism is now astir in Britain. Those two over-used words, 'kind of', are however required, for English nationalism is underdeveloped. It puts in a regular appearance at middle-class English dinner tables, invoked by grumbles about the Scots. It is speculated about by Tory politicians anxious for a cause and worried about by Labour strategists.

But the change is perhaps clearest at the bottom of the social pile – and it is difficult to get much lower in any heap of humanity than the English football hooligan. When, in 1966, England played in the final of the World Cup, Wembley stadium was a waving forest of Union Flags. But in the summer of 1998, it was all quite different. The Union Flag was now replaced by the Cross of St George. Streaming from giant banners, painted on the faces of lager-louts in a hundred English urban centres, finally worn by chanting mobs in the streets of Marseilles, the Cross of St George was omnipresent. In such circumstances the genie of a kind of English nationalism burst from its bottle, which was then smashed in some Frenchman's face.

Nor did the new flag disappear with the termination of England's participation. For a full two months the Cross of St George flew from London taxis, was draped outside pubs and became the all-purpose motif for T-shirts. Indeed, only a chilly, drizzly English autumn proved sufficient to break the spell of English fervour: by October the red-white bunting had at last been taken in. But by now the middle classes and the chattering classes had woken up to the phenomenon.

It is tempting to consider the behaviour of the English fans as an unfortunate but essentially insignificant reflection of the wider problem of the underclass. But there is a special reason why the fans gathered for mayhem under the Cross of St George in such numbers last summer. They had lost – or more accurately had been deprived of – a sufficiently compelling British national identity and they wanted to flaunt, in the way they best knew how, a new identity that they had made their own. In this, the English condition has something in common with the next most frequent offenders among World Cup fans, the Germans, whom English hooligans now apparently regard as their most worthy opponents. The Germans are expected to channel their national self-interest through the European Union, and the English through the Union of the United Kingdom. And in neither case is it now enough.

Meanwhile, the Labour Party is ever more painfully impaled on its Scottish policy. Labour has, after all, long depended upon its strength in Scotland in order to be a viable British party of government. Some of the Government's most senior – and, not coincidentally in English eyes, least popular – members are Scotsmen, including Gordon Brown, the Chancellor of the Exchequer; Robin Cook, the Foreign Secretary; and Lord Irvine, the Lord Chancellor. Labour initially imagined that its promise of a Scottish parliament would win it the lasting gratitude of the Scots. But Scottish voters have turned against Labour for a variety of reasons, the desire to punish Scottish Labour Party corruption and misbehaviour being among them. But essentially they have done so because they have turned against the English – and 'English' is what Labour in power in Westminster now seems.

Mr Blair may be forgiven for being mystified. His problem is that, though he was born and went to school in Scotland, the Scots have detected in him a leader as English as their traditional *bête noire*, Margaret Thatcher. His claim that he would draw support from a 'Middle [i.e., middle-class] Scotland', as he had from 'Middle England', was subject to particularly waspish criticism, for even the Scottish middle classes now think that they have nothing in common with their English equivalents. That poses New Labour an insurmountable problem: it can neither satisfy the obstreperous Scots, nor reassure the English who resent their manners.

The Liberal Party, relatively strong in Scotland and priding itself on its commitment to devolved government, is equally incapable of articulating English national sentiments. Which leaves the Conservatives. Shell-shocked by the worst defeat in their history, enmeshed in complicated structural party reform, led by an unpopular and still insecure leader, the Conservative Party was initially reluctant to embark on any such controversial strategy as trying to exploit English national exasperation. But Tory toes are now being tentatively dipped into these troubled waters. The occasion is the need to resolve the so-called 'West Lothian Question'. One response to this would be for English MPs to meet and vote separately on English matters. But some leading Conservatives want to go further and have begun to argue for a new institution, an 'English parliament'. The new Tory leader, William Hague, is apparently attracted by the politics of this option.

Of course, the Conservative Party would not be true to its current reputation if it were not split on the issue. Those most fearful of European federalism believe that a separatist England would be more vulnerable to the European project of turning the country into a glorified Euro-region. For their part, some expatriate Scottish Tories now representing English seats at Westminster fear that such talk might amount to giving up on the Union altogether. However, if there are votes in English nationalism, the Tories will surely find a way to reconcile it with their traditional constitutionalism. It is naive to expect otherwise. But for the country as a whole there are also drawbacks. The first is obvious: the more that explicitly English grievances are stated and English interests declared paramount, the more opportunity the Scottish nationalists will have to fuel separatist passions.

But what of the position of the English within truncated Britain? Because of the historical congruity between Englishness and Britishness, there is a real loss to England if a part of Britain secedes. Retreats easily become routs. The retreat from Empire made perfectly good sense, and was reasonably well managed, but it left scars on the nation's psyche. Even the unavoidable retreat from Hong Kong prompted nostalgic regrets. Collective psycho-analysis may be even more uncertain a science than the individual kind, but a nation does need to retain the will to hold on to what it is and has – and perhaps even suffer the occasional temptation to expand – if it is not to become dysfunctional.

There are also risks of more tangible English losses. There has been little serious discussion of the military implications of separation, but they are large. For example, the British submarine-based nuclear deterrent has for many years been stationed on the Clyde. It would quickly have to be relocated in an English port. The business would be costly and disruptive, and it might open up all sorts of unpleasantness between the two countries.

Then there is the matter of Britain's permanent membership of the United Nations Security Council. In theory this should not be affected, for in fact and in law it will be clear that English Britain is the successor state of the United Kingdom. But that may be over-optimistic. British Security Council membership is already a source of resentment among a variety of powers and might be subject to renewed challenge.

The truncation of Britain would also have implications for the already difficult relationship with Europe. If Scotland achieved membership of the European Union, English resentment would undoubtedly increase as the English taxpayer made a substantial net contribution to the EU annual budget, benefiting the Scots.

But, all that said, by any realistic assessment the status quo is no longer a long-term option. If the United Kingdom has lost the support not only of the Scots but of a substantial section of the English too, it is only sensible to recognize the fact and act upon it. English nationalism then begins to make sense. And there are some compensations. A better articulated English nationhood might help to heal the inevitable psychological scars of separation. It would certainly make easier a clean break on terms that give neither side lingering cause for regret. The transition period to independence will, above all, be one for clear thinking and hard bargaining. A strong dose of English nationalism could avoid the sort of compromises over rights of citizenship, access to social security and possession of military hardware that would lead to endless wrangling in the future between two neighbours with a mutual need to co-operate.

In the longer term, there are other potential gains for England's own governance. The present Scottish left-wing socialist base of the Labour Party would at a stroke be excised from the new body politic. That would be highly beneficial for England. Mr Blair would have to press ahead faster with his programme of making New Labour free-market-friendly so as to continue to attract the support of middle-class England, if he were to remain in government. But if he failed in that task, the disappearance of viscerally anti-Tory Scotland from the political equation would allow the return of a Conservative administration. Either option would open the way for the radical action that all parties accept is needed, but none dare currently carry out: to curb welfare spending and the dependency culture.

Still unanswered questions about the country's international orientation and role could also at last be openly addressed. A fundamental reassessment of English Britain's relationship with Europe, and even integration within an Atlantic Free Trade Area, would become possibilities once the mirage of Scottish 'Independence in Europe' had disappeared from the horizon. All of which suggests that with sickly states as with stricken individuals, victims both of prolonged misdiagnosis and maltreatment, amputation, though painful and inherently undesirable, may ultimately be part of the remedy – as long as the patient is strong in heart and mind and retains the will to live.

30 January 1999

Sleep-walk to devolution

ANDREW NEIL

Devolution has long been an obsession with all modes of fashionable Scottish political opinion, backed by their unquestioning (and usually unthinking) allies in the Scottish media and the blethering classes in general. But it has yet to become the consuming concern of the Scottish people. One of the most remarkable features of the general election north of the Border is how little devolution has featured in the campaign.

Except for Tony Blair's gaffe in *The Scotsman* at the start of the election, (during an interview, he compared the Scottish parliament to an English parish council) it has barely merited a mention. It is, of course, discussed *ad nauseam* in television and radio studios, though enlightenment on the matter is usually elusive. But that reveals more about the agenda and preferences of the broadcasters than it does about the priorities of the people. Candidates of all political parties report that it is hardly ever brought up on the doorstep.

Nobody should be surprised by that. A poll in this newspaper last month showed that, when asked to name the most important issues facing Scotland, devolution ranked a miserable eighth, trailing far behind education, health and unemployment and even coming after the ragbag of issues gathered under the 'others' category! The airwaves and the public prints may be thick with devolution chatter. It is largely passing the Scottish people by.

This is not to claim that Scotland does not want devolution. When prompted by pollsters with a question which specifically

mentions devolution, a clear majority of Scots express support
for some form of home rule (though the numbers drop when
independence is also included as an option). They also vote in
large numbers for two devolutionist parties (Labour and the Liberal Democrats) and another (the Nationalists) which also sup-
ports devolution, but only as a pit-stop on the way to separation.

The evidence suggests that Scots are actually pretty lukewarm
about devolution, that it ranks low in plain folk's priorities – but
that, if it is on offer, they are going to have it. One reason many
of them say they want it is because it is Labour Party policy: as
loyal voters of Scotland's predominant party, they are content to
toe the party line. Another reason many Scots want devolution
is because the Tories are against it: the Scottish Tory Party is
such an enfeebled, disliked and discredited political force that its
opposition to devolution has done much to undermine the case
for something like the status quo.

The result of this somewhat negative, less-than-enthusiastic
mood, however, is that Scotland is sleep-walking towards devolution. The case against has gone largely by default because of the
lack of credible voices prepared to oppose it. The Scottish business
and financial community, for example, is overwhelmingly against
a parliament in Edinburgh, often for sound reasons; but most of
its leading lights say so only in private, behind closed doors.

This is not a sensible method of approaching major, radical
change. It has meant, above all, that Labour's plans for home
rule have not been subject to searching scrutiny, despite their
far-reaching constitutional consequences. The Tories are wrong
to claim that devolution in itself will inevitably lead to the
break-up of the United Kingdom. There are plenty of international precedents to indicate that some forms of devolution
can actually strengthen existing nation-states. Sadly, Labour's
scheme is not one of them.

Unless you are a Nationalist anxious for a separatist Scotland,
there is only one fundamental test by which to judge the efficacy
of any devolution plan: will it help keep the United Kingdom
together? Judged by that yardstick, Labour's proposals are fatally

flawed. They are being presented as a new constitutional settlement which will make the Scots feel more comfortable about staying within the Union while doing nothing to antagonize the English about Scotland's place in that Union. In fact, they have been unwittingly designed to achieve the exact opposite.

There are two fundamental weaknesses in Labour's home-rule blueprint which seriously undermine its purpose. The first is the intention to finance the Edinburgh parliament almost entirely by a block grant from London; the second is the failure (refusal would be more accurate) to answer the West Lothian question. The first flaw will fan Scottish nationalism, the second English nationalism. Together, they will make for a heady, unstable brew which will indeed undermine the Union.

Any Scottish parliament which is not responsible itself for raising from the Scottish people through taxes and other imposts all the money it intends to spend on our behalf will only perpetuate the unhealthy myth which has dominated Scottish political culture for too long, that big government is a free ride. Worse, when the overwhelming source of that parliament's funds (even if the tartan tax were to be levied at full whack) is a grant from Westminster, then you have a system tailor-made for exploitation to Nationalist advantage.

An Edinburgh parliament will be run by the outdated collectivist consensus that still dominates Scottish politics. It will want to spend, spend, spend. But instead of having to go to the Scottish people to raise the money, it will rattle the begging bowl loudly in London; and when Westminster refuses to stump up any more cash, the Nationalists will have a field day. Imagine the rumpus when a Scottish parliament has to preside over the closure of some school or hospital or bankrupt company because London was too mean to come up with the cash to save it. A system more designed to exacerbate tensions between London and Edinburgh would be hard to conceive. The Nationalists must already be licking their lips. The only way to avoid a bust-up would be to make the Edinburgh parliament responsible for raising every penny it plans to spend. It would add a dose of realism to the

Scottish political debate. But it is not even on Labour's radar.

Nor is an answer to the West Lothian question. The Scottish people have an answer: they accept that, if English MPs no longer have a say on Scottish domestic affairs, then Scottish MPs should be unable to vote on purely English matters. But for its own self-serving reasons (fear that it will need its Scottish cadres to sustain a Westminster majority), that is not an answer Labour is inclined to give. This failure could be catastrophic for the Union.

Imagine the headlines in the *Daily Mail* or *Telegraph* the day after some grammar school in Kent is closed on the casting votes of Scottish Labour MPs. That may never happen; but there are a host of other issues dear to Middle England's heart in which Scottish Labour votes could be decisive.

Devolution in its proposed form risks lighting the blue touch-paper of English nationalism. If it explodes at the same time as a new resentful Scottish nationalism becomes the prevailing mood of the Edinburgh parliament, then the Union is unlikely to last. At the very least, Labour's home rule plans will be only an interim stage and early in the next decade Scots are likely to face, even with our own parliament, the more fundamental question of union or separation.

18 April 1997

Coming home

GAVIN ESLER

My working life has been as a foreign correspondent investigating the world's strangest places, from darkest Peru to Brazil, Cuba, China and Saudi Arabia. I have been up the Orinoco without a paddle and on the edge of the earth in the Aleutian islands of the north Pacific. I thought my homecoming from my last posting in America would be a chance at last to hang up the 'our man in' hat and put Washington and the world behind me. But once back in my rapidly changing native land I was soon a foreign correspondent again, exploring Scotland on the eve of the election of its first parliament in three hundred years as a stranger would, trying to discover who we are now and who we might become.

Like thousands of expatriates, I belong to the Go-Go Scottish tradition which believed that to Get On you had to Get Out. It is arrogant to think any expatriate can adequately explain anything of Scotland to those who live here. But I thought I might see the obvious with fresh eyes. And since we are a practical people let me begin at the end, with some conclusions. Every Scot I have talked to in recent weeks – men, women, old, young, Nationalist or Unionist in outlook – seems convinced we are at a great turning point in our history. The catch is whether we have the wit to seize it.

Businessmen in Edinburgh, football supporters, Asian Scots in Glasgow, intellectuals, English residents, political commentators and an SNP campaigner in a remote glen in the western Highlands all repeated the same refrain: the Scottish parliament must do something. The Scottish parliament will Be, they all said. But that is not enough. It also has to Do – do something, do almost anything, to live up to the twin burdens of our hopes and our history. And, as I discovered by the end of my journey, the challenges facing the new Scotland may be great but they are nothing in comparison to the identity crisis facing England as it reluctantly comes to terms with the possible reinvention of a new Britain.

My journey of exploration began as it would in the Amazon or the Arabian desert. I bought maps and a guidebook, I talked to anyone who could spare me time, from Ross-shire to Gourock, from Govan to Edinburgh's New Town, looking for clues to how a new Scotland was sprouting from a very old Scotland.

The guidebook warned that the country has an unreliable and inhospitable climate, but that it is a land of unique beauty and glorious empty wilderness. Geography, of course, was never our worry. History was the problem. The guidebook noted this history centred around Scotland's problematic relationship with England. Oh, yes, I remembered. That. Our daft vice of seeing ourselves only in relation to them. The best of Scotland has always been when – from Andrew Carnegie to Alexander Graham Bell or Alexander Fleming – we measure ourselves against the greatest in the world. When we do that, this small part of an insignificant archipelago in a remote corner of Europe can claim an outstanding record of achievement utterly out of proportion to its size or apparent strength.

But the worst of Scotland, I always thought, was when we only measured ourselves against the elephant in our bed: the English themselves. Did we beat them at Hampden? At Murrayfield? At Flodden? I wondered whether our Scottish split personality had changed, our bizarre ability simultaneously to think ourselves both superior to the English and yet inferior, the belief that we Scots are more blessed than they are despite our irritation that England is richer, more powerful and more successful. Had we the confidence to get over all that, I wondered? And what does being Scottish, or British, or both, mean to us now?

Edinburgh, where I grew up, offers the first clues to our national dilemma. Drive down Princes Street and look to the north from John Lewis's to Marks & Spencer to Burger King, Waterstones and Boots. You are in any town, anywhere in Britain, the same shops, same products, same prices. But look to the other side of the street, to the south, and you could only be in one place in the entire world, the most beautiful capital city imaginable, Edinburgh castle, the gardens, the Scott monument and the Mound. For three hundred years since the peculiar invention of Great Britain Scots have been walking down a street with two sides and two views of ourselves.

On one side we are Rule Britannia British, like Bristol or Cardiff or Newcastle. On the other side we are distinctive, proud, unique and a different nation altogether. I was driving down Princes Street looking both ways, going to meet a remarkable guide to the new Scotland, a man in the mould of Carnegie and Bell, a Scot who has taken on the best in the world and won. David Murray, the owner of Rangers Football Club, is a self-made millionaire many times over, in command of business interests from Norway to New Zealand, metals and mining to property development, sports management and even a restaurant.

'I'm proud to be British,' Murray booms, his brain working nineteen to the dozen, 'but I'm Scottish first. It's a great country, there are great opportunities in Scotland, but the problem you've got with Scots in Scotland is that they are unwilling to take risks. We are something of a whingeing nation.'

Murray is one archetype of who we Scots would like to think we are, a big man in every sense of the phrase, affable, intense, canny, and quick-as-a-whip intelligent. He does not suffer fools gladly. As the numerous telephone calls he took as I chatted with him in his offices show, he really does not suffer fools at all. Go-Go Scots like David Murray once made their fortunes in the British Empire, but Murray has taken on the world while remaining based at home.

Schooled for a time at Fettes, where his Scottish accent was so unusual he was nicknamed Jock, Murray left school at sixteen and started in the metals business at £7 a week. He has recently moved to an office in the heart of Edinburgh's New Town, a building which was once the home of another great Scot, Lord Lister, the originator of antiseptic surgery. Murray proudly showed me around, showed me the best view in the world of Edinburgh castle, and a magnificent painting of the crowds of supporters gathering at Ibrox for a Rangers game. Scots, he said, in Africa, north America, the Pacific, invented the world. Now we've got to reinvent Scotland. The Scottish parliament has got to do something – that phrase again – to rekindle Scottish innovation and risk-taking. 'Dae something, dae something,' he repeated with even greater intensity, 'do something to rekindle a spirit of enterprise.'

Murray is well known for attacking the SNP's policy on taxes as a killer of business spirit. But, I wondered, if Scotland is so full of talent, how come the Rangers team reads like the United Nations – Klos, Porrini, Amoruso, Kanchelskis, Albertz, Guivarc'h. Where was all the home-grown talent, the Jim Baxters and Brands and Waddells in among the barely pronounceable names?

In a perfect world, Murray responded, only half joking, Rangers would field a team comprised of eleven Scotsmen earning £50 a week like Celtic did when they won the European Cup. But now, if Rangers, or Scotland, want to compete against world-class opposition, they have to take the best from wherever they can get it. Rangers, like Scotland, Murray asserted, had changed rapidly in the 1990s and would have to change even more in the future. His big fear was of an anti-climax, that the new Scottish parliament could become a disappointing clone of Westminster, filled with pasteurized politicians obsessed with political trivia. We cannot miss this opportunity, Murray insisted repeatedly, like a businessman watching a big deal about to turn sour, because if the parliament does not work, Scots have run out of excuses.

On the way to my next appointment I drove round the streets of the New Town, constructed as a monument to Scotland's Britishness – Charlotte Square, Hanover Street, George Street, Frederick Street – still this old duality about who we are. It was obvious from talking to David Murray that national identity is not like a hat. You can wear more than one at a time. David Murray, like most Scots, manages to be effortlessly Scottish plus British plus a man of the world.

In Glasgow, Bashir Ahmed, from the group Scots Asians for Independence, has even more layers of identity. Ahmed, an SNP candidate for the Scottish parliament, is, after a long life's journey which began thirty-eight years ago when he left a village in rural Pakistan, now able to be simultaneously a Scot, an Asian, a Glaswegian, a Muslim and a member of the Scottish National Party. When pressed to give himself a label he opts for Asian-Scottish, proud of his traditions even if he describes himself now as a stranger in his former village in Pakistan. 'Is there anything British about you?' I wondered. 'My passport,' Ahmed responded, though he quickly said he looked forward to holding a Scottish one, following independence.

'Scotland to me is everything,' he says, with the enthusiasm you hear from new immigrants to the United States, as he talked of Scotland as the land of opportunity. What was especially revealing was the easy-going way he used the word 'we' to describe the new Scottish national mosaic of which he is a part. 'After three hundred years,' Bashir Ahmed said, 'we are getting our Scottish parliament back. A short time ago we got our Stone of Destiny back. So we are getting everything back.'

By now, of course, your foreign correspondent exploring Scotland is in trouble. I had more questions than answers about who we really are and what we are about to become. I had talked to many Scots who showed a weariness or a disappointment about the election campaign. But everybody seemed to share a kind of relaxed, settled sense that this moment is more than a series of niggling debates about education, healthcare and tax; that it is a watershed even if we cannot quite see clearly to the other side.

I was planning to meet a number of intellectuals and thinkers, including the SNP leader Alex Salmond and some English expatriates to gauge whether the English felt uncomfortable in the new Scotland. I thought together they might help me to join the dots and produce a clearer picture. I also wanted to have a look at the site of the Scottish parliament, but on the way I decided to have some fun. One trick of all foreign correspondents is to come up with a kind of national cliché and see how relevant it might be to a changing country. There being no convenient whisky distilleries, I decided to check in on the national dress. Are kilts, to put it crudely, Up or Down? Up, it seems. Very, very up.

I dropped in to a number of kilt and tartan shops selling a full set of our national dress for around £600 a time, and they all heaved with customers. Rona Cornwall who manages the Celtic Craft Centre in a close off Edinburgh's High Street pointed to customers almost falling over each other and said: 'We are busier than we have ever been.' Half the customers were local Scots, she guessed, half expatriates determined somehow to re-establish part of their Scottish identity at an exciting time in our history. The couple Rona was serving when I struck up our conversation had English accents.

The four seamstresses the Celtic Craft Centre employs were working at maximum capacity on thirty kilts each, and this is still the supposedly quiet season before the summer rush. As I watched the man with the English accent carefully look through the choice of sporrans it occurred to me that we Scots have many reasons to be grateful. You would never, P. G. Wodehouse once remarked, mistake a Scot for a ray of sunshine. But we remain a polite, rational and, I found, an extremely helpful people.

We whinge, as David Murray says, but in a world where nationalism often means reaching for the Kalashnikov, Scots are slowly and peacefully working through where we might fit in relation to England, to Europe and to the rest of the world.

I turned from the High Street to look at the site of the new Scottish parliament. In the spring sunshine it was a desolate hole in the ground surrounded by rubble, but as I continued my journey as an explorer by walking around the building works, I realized a simple truth. It does not take much imagination to see that something good can be built here.

20 April 1999

Is Britain dead?

GAVIN ESLER

Drive from Glasgow south for six hours and you reach London. Drive from Glasgow north for six hours and you reach Ullapool, one of the beautiful towns of Wester Ross, the Scotland that is always closest to our sentimental hearts.

One of the arguments against an independent Scotland has always been this simple piece of human geography. Do Glaswegians have more in common with the people of London or Belfast or Cardiff than they do with rural Scots in Ross-shire or Shetland or Orkney? And aren't the lives of the people of, say, Sutherland much closer to those of folk in mid Wales or Cornwall or County Antrim than those in Airdrie or Dundee?

On the next stage of my journey as a foreign correspondent exploring my native country I wanted to find out how far the Scots are truly different from the English. I also wanted to meet the man whose solution to our national dilemma is the most radical, the Scottish National Party convener, Alex Salmond.

There was a phrase I kept hearing again and again. 'Maybe we Scots,' people whispered, 'are too feart for independence.' Are we frightened? Or are we too canny? And there was another whisper – don't tell the English – that we are over-represented in Westminster, over-powerful in Tony Blair's Cabinet and over-subsidized by English taxpayers. Shoosh! Loose lips cost subsidies.

On the way to meet the SNP leader I also wanted, in Burns' phrase, to see ourselves as others see us, to talk to 'returners',

Scots who had come home after living abroad, and also to English immigrants.

Dennis MacLeod is a returner, a refreshingly off-message SNP supporter living in a glen in Ross-shire. He spent thirty years seeking his fortune in Africa and Canada. In 1995 he returned home and describes himself as 'always instinctively nationalist'. He continues: 'I was always Scottish. I did indeed have a British passport and still do. I am a Canadian citizen as well.'

So what does being British mean? 'A very convenient passport,' he replied, 'a wondrous history and many achievements. But like all empires it is near its end.'

MacLeod is now chairman of Business for Scotland, encouraging businesses to support independence. Given the tartan tax and some forecasts that oil will dip below $10 a barrel, this sounds a hard sell.

'Scots have a tremendous entrepreneurial spirit,' MacLeod said of the supposed fear of independence. 'But there's this negative side that says we can't even run our own country, that we have to have an apprenticeship,' meaning the devolved parliament, though independence is 'only a matter of time'.

The western Highlands are so attractive I have met many English people running pubs, guesthouses and hotels from Torridon down to Loch Sunart and even on Barra. How might MacLeod's English neighbours fit in? 'I have no negative feelings towards English people,' MacLeod said, another constant refrain of almost every conversation I had in Scotland. 'Around the world you stick to your own, and my own are Scots and English.'

Then why break up the United Kingdom? 'I would like to see us retain the monarchy so the UK remains still a United Kingdom,' MacLeod said, off-message again.

It has been a long marriage with the English, I was thinking. Can't live with them. Can't live without them. Then I checked with half a dozen English acquaintances living in Scotland and, surprisingly, not one had experienced anti-English racism. They all knew some highly publicized cases but one summed up the common view. 'It's a class thing,' she said. Not nationalism at all. She found as much hostility towards her educated London accent in Newcastle, say, as in Scotland.

Bernard Crick, the biographer of George Orwell and emeritus professor at Birkbeck College, London University, is an eminent English intellectual who chose deliberately to live in Scotland. He showed me around the glorious garden of his flat in Edinburgh as I pressed him on whether leaving London meant merely swapping one British city for another. 'No,' he said. 'Scotland is a very different country.' How? 'History. The behaviour of ordinary people. The things that intellectuals talk about. A more convivial and hospitable atmosphere than the south-east of England.' Crick said he was even welcomed at council meetings of the SNP as 'a rather strange novelty' while English colleagues thought he had been 'addled by the Celtic twilight' for his peculiar obsession with the growing Scottish national consciousness.

'We held a celebration party after the [devolution] referendum,' he quotes as an example of change. 'Three Scots turned up in kilts.' A decade ago, that would not have happened. Traditionally, he says, the English repressed their Englishness for the sake of the Union, until Margaret Thatcher came along. English Tories always knew 'the Great Game of politics was to hold the Union together'. Queen Victoria cultivated Scotland. Tory leaders did likewise.

But while the Royal Family still play the Great Game, Thatcher, in Crick's view, was midwife of the Scottish parliament thanks to her 'ineptness, insensitivity, with no sense of history'.

And, curiously, I was beginning to conclude that the new Scottish parliament posed far more severe challenges for England than for Scotland. As I left Crick's flat, Salmond's office confirmed he would he happy to break away from the election campaign to talk about national identity. I was slightly surprised and feared he would be in a glum mood. SNP opinion polls were cratering, the press was hostile, there were reports of internal feuds, rows over his statements on Kosovo and attacks from business on tax policy. But I was still no nearer answering the central identity question. Is Glasgow closer to London than to Ullapool? How different are we?

David McCrone, a sociology professor at Edinburgh University, has analysed the results of Scottish voter opinion surveys going back to the 1970s on precisely this point. 'Are the Scots different from the English?' he repeats my question. 'The answer is, by and large, no.' If you ask: 'Should the government put more money into the NHS?' 96 percent of Scots say yes, as do 95 percent of English people. Should criminals get tough sentences? English agree 84 percent, Scots 83 percent and so on. But the more subtle point, McCrone argues, is that we interpret common values in different ways. In the case of the NHS many Scots concluded that Thatcherite England was out of touch with Scottish values and punished the Tories accordingly. 'Scots were always nationalist but it suited us to be British,' McCrone argues. 'We are not frightened of independence, just hard-headed about the pros and cons, living up to our canny image.'

McCrone was optimistic about the new parliament, but pessimistic on one point. 'About England. Is there going to be a mentality change, that they live in a multinational state?'

This was proving the most awkward twist in my journey. I had set out to rediscover Scotland and had found, broadly, that we are quietly optimistic, comfortable in our national consciousness without being overwhelmed by it, and calm about independence even though we seem set to reject it.

But conversations repeatedly turned to those who did seem confused and frightened of change: the English political class and the English press, with their strange obsession with rows about the Queen's head on pound notes, rivalry with Germany, resentment against Scots in the Cabinet, irritation over subsidies and confusion over devolution. McCrone's work shows some Scottish affection for Britain, though a belief that Westminster is too small for the big things in life, like macro-economic policy and defence, and too big for the small things like local schools, social services and the NHS. So what then of Britain, I wondered, this nation invented out of Protestantism, Empire and war? With Britain squeezed between giving more power to Brussels and to Edinburgh, Belfast and Cardiff, is Britain dead?

'I don't know if you can reinvent Britishness,' McCrone responded thoughtfully. 'But the only way to hold on to Britishness is to be relaxed about it. Don't try too hard.' He laughed as he suggested that nowadays 'To be a Scot is a matter of the head. To be British is a matter of the heart.'

Maybe for the English it is the other way around. By the time I got to see Salmond my own head was stuffed with opinions about who Scots are and where we might be going, but I thought he might be in a bad mood. Salmond was in an election strategy meeting. Maybe his colleagues were torturing him with bamboo shoots up his fingernails? Apparently not. He emerged from the meeting wearing a maroon Hearts supporters pullover and a generous smile, as relaxed as a man leaving a golf course after a good game.

Whatever you think of his views, Salmond passes the two most important tests of American politics. First, he demonstrates grace under pressure. Second, you would let him baby-sit your children. He remains defiantly unscary in what could be a scary time, when the word 'nationalism' conjures up scenes of Balkan depravity. I mention that during my years living in the United States two out of three British ambassadors were Scots. 'Oh?' he says, joking about the Scots' ability to turn the Union to their advantage. 'Maybe I'll have to rethink this whole independence thing after all.'

Is any part of you British? He rephrases the question. 'The definition of a nation is when people believe themselves a nation, and by that test Scotland clearly is a nation. But it is quite reasonable for people to have a multi-layered identity.'

Salmond talks proudly of Scots Asians who support him and objects to Norman Tebbit's infamous cricket test, the idea that Asian immigrants are not English if they do not support the English cricket team. For Salmond, if Scots Asians support Pakistan at cricket, that is a matter of celebration. But if we really are multi-layered Scottish, British and European, then is independence impossible to sell?

Salmond relaxes into an anecdote about the Rangers–Hearts Scottish Cup final, last year when he was teased by Rangers fans who sang 'Rule Britannia'. He talked to the fans and was besieged by autograph hunters who said they would vote SNP. The club that most symbolized Britishness in Scotland, from Union Flags to British anthems, included SNP supporters who saw no contradiction between their various identities.

I had spoken to John MacMillan, the general secretary of the Rangers Supporters' Association, who agreed that some of the club's fans support the SNP, though he was himself extremely concerned about the costs of independence. 'If the Scot Nats gain power it could be a disaster for us,' MacMillan said. 'I'm both Scottish and British and I'm proud to be both. I have a gut feeling independence would be a disaster financially for this country.'

So, I persisted with Salmond, was there any part of Salmond himself that was British? He again said some SNP supporters retain a sense of Britishness while still wanting independence within Europe. I was about to say 'Name one', when he beat me too it.

'Like my mum.'

'Your mum?'

'Yes, my mum. Many older Scots have a sense of British identity,' he insisted, 'but still can vote for independence.'

Well, some of that comes from shared sacrifice in wars, so was it a tactical blunder for the SNP convener to attack British policy in Kosovo when British lives were at risk?

'I made those remarks because I believed them, not for tactical purposes,' Salmond responds energetically. 'I was well aware that the remarks were not immediately popular, but I would do it again.' The extent of what he calls the 'smear campaign' that followed surprised him, but he continues: 'I passionately believe that they have made an enormous mistake'.

The conversation turned to the attempts by the Chancellor, Gordon Brown, to reinvent Britishness for the millennium. Salmond was particularly scathing. 'To paraphrase Steinbeck, I'm fighting a cause which is unwon. He is fighting a lost cause.'

Brown's naked ambition, Salmond claimed, was to become prime minister. 'If I succeed then he can't become prime minister. If he becomes prime minister, then I haven't succeeded ... [though] this'll be the last election where there'll be the ability of the Westminster cavalry to ride to the rescue of the beleaguered Scottish fortress.'

He agreed that there was a growing English dilemma over their identity and the future. There was a 'great opportunity for a new Englishness', but 'it would be presumptuous to lecture the English on how to develop their sense of identity'.

Oh, go on, I said. Do it anyway.

'The English have a great ability to catch up. There is a new debate starting about English identity. It ranges from the sublime to the ridiculous, from Billy Bragg to Simon Heffer' – Heffer being the author of a new book on the subject.*

Despite the dismal Stephen Lawrence affair and other evidence of racism, Salmond talked approvingly of how England has coped with becoming a multi-cultural community, with inter-racial marriage so common it is not even remarked upon. But while the English people have changed rapidly, their institutions have not. The House of Lords, the press, the police, the establishment remain 'geriatric, aristocratic, frozen in time'. English people will cope with whatever their troublesome northern neighbour decides on 6 May while those geriatric institutions will creak, groan and complain.

When I left Alex Salmond he was still smiling, like the cat hopeful of getting to the cream whatever the opinion polls may say. He was off to more meetings. I turned south to resume the life of an expatriate Scot. As the plane took off into a blue spring sky, I was profoundly optimistic that the struggle of competing nationalisms on these islands is being fought not with Kalashnikovs but with ideas, talk of taxes and civilized discussions of national identity. Boring, some Scots told me. Well, be grateful.

* Simon Heffer, *Nor Shall My Sword: The Reinvention of England*, Weidenfeld & Nicolson, 1999.

I have spent my life as a foreign correspondent reporting on interesting conflicts and interesting monsters. Boring is good. Very good indeed. My journey ended where it began, in London, a great imperial capital, in the middle of a war against the extremely interesting Slobodan Milosevic.

Scots have spent years figuring out our many layers of identity, working at this strange marriage of convenience called Britain. I was surprised how relaxed we are about the future. Then it hit me. It is here, in England, that the shock waves will be most profound. There is an undercurrent of bewilderment. Salmond's last words were ringing in my ears. All this great political debate, he joked, 'and not even one bloody nose'. Whatever we do, whatever we decide, I was thinking, let's keep it as boring as possible, and no bloody noses.

26 April 1999

The tearing point

SIR MALCOLM RIFKIND

'It was the best of times, it was the worst of times, it was the age of wisdom, it was the age of foolishness, it was the epoch of belief, it was the epoch of incredulity, it was the season of Light, it was the season of Darkness, it was the spring of hope, it was the winter of despair, we had everything before us, we had nothing before us, we were all going to Heaven, we were all going direct the other way.'

Thus wrote Charles Dickens of revolutionary France in the 1790s. Should we write the same of turbulent Scotland in the 1990s?

There is, indeed, an excitement in the air, from Shetland to Hawick, from Stornoway to St Andrews, and it is not just felt by those who voted for an Edinburgh parliament in the referendum. Hardened Unionists, including some not yet intellectually convinced, confess to sharing the belief that a new Scotland is being born and that it provides an opportunity to look at old problems in a new way.

For the time being, understandably, all the attention is on the first elections to the new parliament, whether Labour will rule, whether the SNP will challenge, whether the Tories will revive, whether the Liberal Democrats will coalesce. These are all crucial questions, but it is worth remembering that the parliament will be a means to an end, not an end in itself. Yes, its presence will stir our pride and make many walk a little taller, but the ultimate justification for the constitutional turmoil both here and in Wales will be if these changes lead to more successful, confident and prosperous countries.

Even the most enthusiastic supporters of devolution recognize that there are serious risks in disturbing a United Kingdom that, for the most part, has worked remarkably well for almost three hundred years. I wish to highlight three problems and opportunities, all of which can be successfully resolved, but which will need mature common sense and judgement rather than Braveheart-style sentimentalism.

Firstly, is Scotland going to relax and give devolution time to work or are we going to lurch into a new, damaging and divisive debate about separatism? I can think of nothing worse, whatever the final decision, than for Scotland to spend the next ten or twenty years arguing about whether it is going to remain in the United Kingdom or whether it should become a separate state, divorcing from England and Wales.

Such a period of indecision would be a massive distraction from dealing with residual poverty, unemployment, improving our schools and modernizing the NHS. It would also be a massive switch-off for existing and potential new investors in Scotland. This would not be because the investment community wants to intervene in our political debate or is anti-Scottish. It is because investors seek stability and if Scotland seems incapable of deciding its constitutional status for the foreseeable future they will go elsewhere. That is what has happened in Quebec with disastrous results for that unhappy province.

I would like to believe that the solution would be to have an early referendum on independence to resolve the issue once and for all. I am confident that Scots, by a large majority, would vote against it but that, I fear, would not resolve the issue. The culprit is the SNP. It would simply acknowledge the result and indicate that it would like to try again in five years. That is precisely what has happened in Quebec where the Nationalists have lost referendum after referendum and simply demand another. They now call them 'never-endums'.

What is needed is for the Nationalists to do what the Scots

Tories did. We recognized that the last referendum was an over-whelming statement that Scots wanted a parliament within a reformed United Kingdom. We have accepted that and pledged to help to make devolution work and create a new political stability. The Nationalists should do likewise. They should learn from the Catalan Nationalists who, despite being in power in Barcelona, have not used their position to try to tear Catalonia out of Spain. As a result investment has flowed in and prosperity has soared.

The second issue that needs to be resolved is Scotland in Europe. Whatever the future holds, it is clear that, for the whole of Great Britain, the European dimension will loom large. To some extent the European and separatism issues have merged. That, at least, is what the Nationalists would have us believe. Our future, they say, is as a separate state in the European Union. That will ensure all the benefits of international co-operation while divorcing us from the dreaded English. Whenever the Tories are being teased for having fought against devolution I am tempted to remind the SNP that Europe was anathema to it until only a few years ago.

The reality is that Europe and its aspirations are a powerful argument for the Union and not the clinching reason against it. I say that for strong idealistic reasons as well as the practical considerations. The practical aspects are not irrelevant. It is not Portugal, Denmark or Ireland that are crucial to the main decisions of the EU but Germany, France and the United Kingdom. My own experience of the Council of Ministers over several years convinced me that while Greece or Ireland sometimes won a sweetener to get them to vote in the right way, they were marginal to the central debates. I don't want that to be Scotland's fate.

Nor can it be assumed that a separate Scotland would be admitted immediately to the EU. It would have to negotiate its membership and, while no Continental country is hostile to Scotland, each would have its own reasons for ensuring that the process took a long time. France, Germany, Italy and Spain all have their own nationalist and separatist movements. They would want to send a clear signal to Catalans, Bretons, Flemings, Bavarians and Basques that automatic re-entry as separate states was not on.

But the most powerful argument against breaking up Britain and having separate membership of the European Union is an idealistic one. The whole point of the European Union is to resolve conflict, war and hatred by creating shared political institutions, common loyalties and interests, and a single destiny.

What hope would there be for Europe at the early stages of this historic process if England and Scotland, having shared a nation-state for three hundred years and a monarch for four hundred years, now decided that they had so little in common with one another that they had to go their own separate ways?

The United Kingdom has given its peoples exactly what Europe is trying to do on a larger scale. Countries which fought each other for centuries have enjoyed peace, stability and representative government. They have achieved this by sharing a parliament and a government, creating a single market and endorsing common values. The break-up of Britain would be a disaster for Europe, not just for Scotland and England. The best way to achieve a united Europe cannot be to dismantle the United Kingdom.

The third theme as we approach the Holyrood parliament is a more domestic one. How will it help to create a modern, dynamic, prosperous and fair Scotland that will be an example, not a rival, to England and Wales? Crucial to that objective will be the growth of a confident and successful middle class helping to run a modern, competitive market economy. Scotland must become a country that believes in low taxation, personal responsibility, reward for effort and the merit of excellence.

In the 1980s many of these values were associated with Margaret Thatcher and, because she was anathema to many Scots, Scotland allowed itself to be convinced that it believed in high taxation, government subsidies and the imposition of an artificial equality.

The truth, as usual, was with neither of these propositions. Thatcherism was not the repository of economic selfishness and the Scots were not subsidy junkies. But the political connotations have made it more difficult for many Scots to embrace the need for competitiveness and entrepreneurship with enthusiasm. That will be a prime challenge for the Scots Tories in the New Scotland. As well as accepting the need to craft a new language of unionism for a reborn United Kingdom the Tories will be Scotland's only self-professed moderate centre-right party. Without them there would be a dangerous and unhealthy vacuum in the Scottish body politic.

Donald Dewar and his colleagues may present themselves as New Labour and some of their policies are identical to those of their Tory predecessors. But the mass of the Labour Party, including dozens of Labour-controlled councils, still looks to the state, the taxpayer and the unions rather than to the private sector and the free market.

The Liberal Democrats and the SNP are, by their own admission and aspiration, to the left of even the Labour Party. There is all to play for if the centre-right is moderate, fair and pragmatic. On the whole I am optimistic about the new Scotland. I was once told that a pessimist is someone who believes things couldn't be worse while an optimist is someone who knows that they could be. But that's not the only reason. Scotland and the Scots are cautious, sensible people who distrust ideology, learn from experience and have a deep sense of what is fair and unfair. In many ways a devolved Scotland with its own parliament within a United Kingdom is the kind of Union the Scots would have preferred in 1707.

Now as we approach 2000, Scotland, England and Wales can be an example for Europe. We can produce a UK able to meet the aspirations of all its people; a Union that continues to be proud of its British identity while enhancing our Scottishness and Englishness as well. Nothing that is worth doing is easy. But it is a challenge we can all look forward to and our children will be grateful if we succeed. What is often not realized is that Europe will be delighted too.

20 March 1999

Cool heads, not brave hearts

ALLAN MASSIE

When I was eight or nine, my favourite book was a novel entitled *In Freedom's Cause*. It drew heavily (though I didn't of course know this then) on the stories collected by Blind Harry and John Barbour, and then told again by Scott in his *Tales of a Grandfather*. Its hero was a young man who fought by the side of Wallace and Bruce and the Black Douglas, and the book inspired a strong sense of Scottish patriotism. It didn't strike me as odd that the author was an Englishman, G. A. Henty, even though the Scots were unqualified good guys and the English the villains.

It still doesn't. Henty, a former war correspondent, was the author of more than seventy action novels for boys, and also edited a patriotic boys' magazine, *Union Jack*. He could write admiringly of Wallace and Bruce as heroic fighters in the cause of freedom precisely because it seemed then, just over a hundred years ago, that the Union of Scotland and England was so firmly founded that discord was impossible. So Scots and English could accept each other's national heroes comfortably and with pride. Being for Wallace or Edward Longshanks in the Wars of Independence was like being for Charles I or Cromwell in the Civil War. You might take sides, and even be strongly partisan, but, when you thought about it, you admitted that you were in a sense the heirs of both parties in the struggle. So English historians like G. M. Trevelyan could also honour Wallace and Bruce, and conclude that the Wars of Independence were a good thing because they ensured that the eventual Union was achieved by agreement and not by conquest. Scotland was, in this way, very different from Wales and Ireland, especially Ireland.

Yet today, we stand at a fork in the road of history. The Union in its old form is behind us. One road ahead leads to a reformed Union; the other to its dissolution. Is the partnership between Scotland and England to survive, reconstructed on Scottish terms? Or is there to be a demerger?

The constitutional history of Great Britain has been, in comparison with the history of, say, France or Germany, so tranquil, such a story of mere adjustment rather than being interrupted by violent revolution that the gravity of the choice before us still escapes many. Yet nobody should doubt that if we take the road towards independence, we should be tearing up much that is familiar, abandoning much with which we have been comfortable, and setting out for a future even less certain than any future must be.

Something would be gained; only the most blinkered Unionist can deny that. Conversely something would be lost; only the most blinkered Nationalist can pretend otherwise.

For almost three hundred years now we Scots have possessed – it might be too provocative to say enjoyed – a dual nationality. We have been Scots and British. Sometimes one identity has been uppermost, sometimes the other. Defining what we mean by British has rarely been easy, except in time of war when the foreign enemy has been clear.

Recently, an attempt to define just this has been made by Gordon Brown and Douglas Alexander, in a pamphlet, *New Scotland, New Britain*. In examining 'the values and then the common endeavours that bind us together', they write: 'In 1603 it may just have been a joint Monarch, and in 1707 a common Parliament and little else. Today it is not simply that we share a common island, and a common language, but that we also share a commitment to openness and internationalism, to public service and to justice, to creativity and inventiveness, to democracy and to tolerance.'

This is doubtless all true, and the sentiments are admirable.

Who would dissent from them? But it doesn't take us very far. Nationalist Scots might point out, correctly, that, except for the common island, we also share all these things with the citizens of the Republic of Ireland.

Yet Messrs Brown and Alexander are on more interesting ground when they consider Tom Nairn's argument 'for supporting a Scottish breakaway'. They write: 'For him, the key to nationalist renaissance lies not so much in ethnic and linguistic factors, "but in the slow foundering of the British state" ... In other words, for Tom Nairn, the strongest argument for a Scottish state is neither the strength of a Scottish culture nor the threat to Scottish identity but the failure of the British state.'

This is why Labour has embarked on what Mr Brown and Mr Alexander call the 'fundamental constitutional changes' of which we are the recipients this week.

We have been a long time arriving at this point. Scottish home rule has been on some people's agenda for more than a hundred years. It was adopted by the Liberal Party as a companion to the Irish home rule proposed by Gladstone, though in office from 1906–14 the Liberals did nothing effective to further it. It was the policy of the Labour Party in its early days, and of the Independent Labour Party. There was a Scottish Home Rule Association between the wars.

In his huge novel *The Four Winds of Love*, Compton Mackenzie, a founder member of the SNP, worked out an elaborate (and absurd) constitution and programme for a Scotland with dominion status.

In the 1940s, John McCormick's Covenant Movement won widespread support, though that support did not go very deep. In opposition, at different times, both Labour and the Conservatives favoured some degree of self-government for Scotland.

But it was the rise of the SNP twenty-five years ago that persuaded Labour to bring forward a bill that would have given Scotland an assembly. Its purpose was clear: to arrest the march of nationalism, and there were almost as many doubters as enthusiasts in Labour's ranks. Public support for that bill was inadequate, according to the conditions laid down for the 1979 referendum. Its opponents campaigned under the slogan 'Scotland is British' – which the Scotland Act had never denied.

If Labour's first attempt at effecting devolution was provoked by fear of nationalism, its second, successful one was prompted by resentment of Margaret Thatcher's brand of Toryism. It was the long years of government by a Conservative Party with only minority support in Scotland that convinced Labour of the validity of Tom Nairn's argument that the old institutions of the British state were working badly, and required reform.

Those of us who opposed that reform failed to persuade others of its dangers. We were out of step with the march of history. Tam Dalyell may have been right when he called devolution 'a motorway to independence with no exits'; time will tell. Alex Salmond certainly agrees with his judgement.

Yet if the Brown–Alexander analysis of Nairn's argument is correct and if their remedy proves adequate to the disease, if, that is to say, the problem is merely institutional, then those of us who saw devolution as a mere stepping-stone to independence may, again, be proved wrong.

There is, however, reason to think that the disaffection is cultural. What is happening in Scotland is not unique, not peculiar to Scotland. It is not that Scotland is oppressed by England; there is no evidence for that at all. It is not that it is becoming more different from England; the contrary is the case. If you read, for instance, Stevenson's essay 'The Foreigner at Home' you will find him listing differences between the Scots and the English which have all but disappeared today. Where today is that severe Scots Presbyterianism which once marked and defined our character? Gone altogether. Like the English, we today are a people who live for the moment. Could anyone say, as Stevenson did of his own time, that 'about the very cradle of the Scot there goes a hum of metaphysical divinity'? I think not. Scots slip into English life, and English into Scots life, with no great strain or difficulty. It is because we are growing more alike that we feel the need to declare our difference.

And this, as I say, is not peculiar to us, or to the relations between Scots and English. The same need is felt in other European countries. The more culture becomes international, supra-national and uniform, the more urgently people seek whatever in their own history and inheritance can distinguish them from others.

Devolution, which is upon us tomorrow, may be seen as a political device intended to repair the institutions of the United Kingdom in a manner satisfactory to us Scots, may indeed be that, and may – who can tell? – serve that purpose. But it also expresses a deeper yearning: to make something which is specifi-cally and distinctively ours, which will allow us to devise our own answers to our own domestic problems, to find a native Scottish way to better education and a better health service; and at the same time to allow us to contribute to the well-being of the United Kingdom.

I thought this would be possible without constitutional change. I thought Scottish identity and everything that is meant by Scot-tish culture could be preserved and developed within the old statute. The electorate judged otherwise, and its judgement has to be accepted.

The fear is that the spirit of devolution will be primarily defens-ive; that it will be used to resist change rather than to enable us to shape it; that it will lead us to withdraw into ourselves and become introspective, self-absorbed, content to cultivate only our own kailyard, indifferent to the rest of the United Kingdom, parochial and myopic.

That danger is real. It will become threatening if we think of the administration to be set up at Holyrood as the government of Scotland, forgetting that it has fewer powers than the governor and legislature of any state in the American Union, and forgetting also the large part that the parliament at Westminster and the Government of the United Kingdom will still have to play in Scotland.

But it can be avoided if we accept devolution for what it is: a middle way between the unitary state and independence. It will not be easy to manage. In his latest novel, *November 1916*, Solzhenitsyn writes: 'Nothing is more difficult than drawing a middle line for social development. The loud mouth, the big fist, the bomb, the prison bars are of no help to you, as they are to those at the two extremes. Following the middle line demands the utmost self-control, the most inflexible courage, the most patient calculation, the most precise knowledge.'

I would add something else: the utmost generosity of spirit. Scotland makes a new start, takes a new road, this week; and that generosity of spirit, which requires you to concede that you are not always right but that those who disagree with you may have something of value in their argument, which requires you to acknowledge that others have interests as legitimate as yours, will be necessary if we are to make a success of it.

There was a generosity of spirit in that book of Henty's which enthralled me as a child; and there has been a generosity of spirit, a give-and-take, in the history of British democracy. Devolution may work as intended if we remember that cool heads are as necessary as brave hearts. If we don't, and if we lose generosity of spirit, then the project is doomed and we are indeed on that motorway of which Tam Dalyell spoke.

5 May 1999

Mr Dewar feeds the tiger

ALLAN MASSIE

The story begins more than twenty years ago, when the abandoned Royal High School on the Calton Hill was chosen to be the home of the Scottish assembly. But the result of the 1979 referendum meant that there was no Scottish assembly. Nevertheless, the Royal High School remained the likely home for any assembly or parliament that might ever come into being. It was outside its gates that some hardy spirits established their vigil after the 1992 election. Some time in the next few years nationalistically minded folk started calling it 'New Parliament House'.

This is perhaps why one of Donald Dewar's aides let it be known that one reason for rejecting the Royal High as the home of the parliament that is actually going to be created was that the Calton Hill site might become 'a nationalist shibboleth'. This objection makes very little sense, and not only because none of the dictionary definitions of 'shibboleth' makes sense in that context.

One assumes that Mr Dewar's aide meant that the choice of the Calton Hill would encourage nationalist sentiments, while the choice of the Holyrood site would depress them. Really?

Orwell once remarked that there were more than a dozen, perhaps twenty, ways of expressing incredulity in English. Any, and all, would seem appropriate in this instance. 'Pull the other one' would do fine. But we might say: 'And now you tell us.'

For it is worth remembering that all through the summer Mr Dewar and his colleagues were assuring us that the establishment of a Scottish parliament was the surest way of quelling enthusiasm for nationalism. It was the way of preserving the Union. It is true of course that this message was muted during the referendum campaign itself, because Labour found that it needed to get the SNP onside to ensure a convincing majority for its proposals. Nevertheless, the underlying message was still that it was seeking, as Mr Dewar put it himself, 'a fair and just settlement for Scotland within the framework of the United Kingdom'. 'Scotland,' he assures us, 'will remain firmly a part of the United Kingdom.' Dear me, yes.

Now it is suggested that all this would have been put at risk if it was decided to plant the parliament on the Calton Hill, because this would encourage that strange beast, 'a nationalist shibboleth'.

This is pathetic. It is, in the language of the football fanzines, mince. It is not the location of the parliament which will encourage nationalism, and the move towards separatism. It is the very fact of its existence. Baron 'Big Donald' Frankenstein has breathed life into his creation, and he will not be able to control his monster. The notion that it will be less dangerous if chained to the Holyrood site than if left to roam the Calton Hill is, to put it as politely as possible, baloney.

> There was a young lady of Riga
> Who went for a ride on a tiger;
> They returned from the ride
> With the lady inside
> And a smile on the face of the tiger.

Mr Dewar is the young lady, and nationalism the tiger; and he has no one to blame but himself for his uncomfortable situation.

He has fed the tiger raw meat. Labour's commitment to devolution was the first course; the collaboration with the SNP in the referendum the second; the arguments about the building and the site a rich pudding. As soon as Mr Dewar decided that the Royal High School, which had been thought quite adequate by the last Labour government, was now too small and insufficiently grand, he encouraged the tiger's appetite. (The suggestion that the First Minister would require an official residence was just another tit-bit.) All this encouraged the idea that what we are going to get is a national parliament rather than a subsiduary legislative body with very restricted powers.

The reality is that the Scotland Bill, if it passes without major revision, will create a parliament, and executive deriving from it, with fewer powers than are possessed by any of the states of the US. Politically, the new Scotland will be more like a lesser Virginia than the Republic of Ireland – lesser because the government of Virginia has, for instance, extensive tax-raising powers denied the Scottish parliament. Theoretically indeed, it will be weaker still, for the powers possessed by the federal government of the US were originally ceded to it by the states, while the powers of the Scottish parliament are to be ceded by the UK parliament.

But this is not how things are commonly seen. All the talk of a new Scotland, encouraged by Mr Dewar, must lead people to suppose that we are entering into a state of quasi-independence. Mr Dewar, and the Labour Party, are still engaged in trying to have it both ways. It seems improbable that they can do so for long.

Ironically, the chosen site for the parliament may do precisely the opposite of what (apparently) Mr Dewar hopes the rejection of Calton Hill will achieve. Far from dousing nationalism, it should rather inflame it. Symbolically, the Royal High School may have seemed an appropriate site, because it is perched up on the hill above the city; yet the symbolism of the Holyrood site runs deeper and is more compelling.

It provides a far stronger link between the 'new Scotland' and the old independent kingdom. It may not be exactly in the heart of Old Edinburgh, as the real Parliament House is, but it is nevertheless in the Old Town, in what was the capital of pre-Union Scotland, before the Nor' Loch was drained and Edinburgh expanded in the north into the New Town.

The parliament of pre-Union Scotland did not always meet in Edinburgh, for parliaments were also held in Stirling and Perth and probably other towns also; but when it did meet in Edinburgh it met in the Royal Mile; and now the new parliament will do so also. It would be hard to give a clearer signal to the encouragement of nationalism.

There are different reasons for thinking the choice of site a good one. A new building may be marginally cheaper than the reconstruction of existing ones. It will revive the lower end of the Royal Mile. The physical restoration of the Canongate has been a success, but the street still seems a drab, dead place – and Holyrood Road is worse. So siting the parliament there should liven it up.

Yet, whatever the reasons that have prompted Mr Dewar's decision, the outcome is likely to be the reverse of what he must be assumed to hope for: that is, the stimulation of nationalism. But since this is the likely result of his creation of the parliament itself, this may not matter too much. All the same, I should not be surprised to learn that Alex Salmond is really quite happy with the decision. Indeed, he may have pulled off a smart one. By letting it be known that the SNP favoured Calton Hill, he has lured Mr Dewar into selecting a site that has richer historical associations with the old, independent kingdom. Game, set and match to Alex.

14 January 1998

PHONEY WAR

The long, winding road from ballads to ballots

ANGUS CALDER

Well, was the Union of Parliaments in 1707 really the 'end of an auld sang', as Lord Seafield famously said at the time?

An equally famous *bon mot* of the same period was Andrew Fletcher of Saltoun's statement that if he could make the nation's ballads, he did not care who made its laws. As a law-making body, the Scottish parliament had not done much to sing about before its final sessions, which were graced by storming speeches from Fletcher and others against the idea of Union with England. Like other such institutions in Europe, the Scottish parliament had represented the propertied elite, not the people at large.

Scotland kept its ballads in spades. The century after Union saw marvellous efforts by Ramsay, Burns, Scott and others to preserve and extend the nation's heritage of song. Lairds and titled ladies, who wrote excellent lyrics, sang along, as it were, with their tenants and servants. By treaty, Scotland preserved its own Established Church, governed since 1689 on Presbyterian lines which sharply differentiated it from England's, as did the character of its four old universities, open to all-comers and ready to teach modern, practical subjects.

Crucially, Scots law remained separate. While Scots rose to the highest positions in the English legal system, no Englishman practised in Scottish courts. Scots found parliamentary seats in England – there was no traffic the other way.

Our sense of history has been muddled by the picturesque

Jacobite rebellions of 1715 and 1745. Bonnie Prince Charlie, who aimed to make his father king of England, was opposed by most Highland, as well as Lowland, Scots. His defeat came to symbolize the collapse of the old Gaelic order, but this was well under way before he arrived. Culloden was a victory for Presbyterian, Whiggish Scotland, which was still in practical terms its own nation after 1707, dominated by great landowners of old family and by clever lawyers of landowning stock.

Politically, it was 'managed' for London governments by Scots who controlled the flow of crown patronage in return for delivering the votes of Scottish MPs in support of English prime ministers. From the mid 1720s, John Campbell, Duke of Argyll, and his brother, Archibald, who succeeded him but is always referred to by his former title, 'Islay', presided for decades over an 'Argathelian' system which now seems monstrously corrupt, but which suited many Scots very well, in particular those who profited from a disproportionate siphoning of opportunities in the East India Company to avid aspirants north of the Tweed.

There were plenty of Scots on hand to join in Baron Robert Clive of India's zestful Rape of Bengal after his victory at Plassey in 1757, and to do very well from the extension thereafter of British rule through India. From the 1770s, Scottish patronage was ordered by a lairdly lawyer, Henry Dundas, 'King Harry the Ninth', who became the most powerful man in British politics – not excluding his protégé prime minister, William Pitt the younger – through his near-absolute control of Scotland's few thousand parliamentary voters.

Dundas, who never set foot outside Britain, did everything he could to repair and extend Britain's intercontinental trade and imperial power after the loss of the Thirteen Colonies.

No Scot had the least quarrel with such a project. Since the Union, Scots had thriven mightily within the British, formerly English, Empire. Glasgow had won virtual monopoly over the rich trade in Virginia tobacco, which set it on its way to becoming a great city. It was said that a third of the planters on Jamaica, the wealthiest sugar-producing island in the British West Indies, were Scots. After Canada fell to Britain in 1759, Highland Scots came to dominate the North American fur trade.

Fortunes earned, or pillaged, overseas were brought back to Scotland and applied to the startling 'improvement' of Scottish agriculture and the rapid rise of Scottish industry. Scots followed close on England's heels into the so-called commercial revolution and, if anything, outstripped their southern neighbours in the industrial revolution which followed. In Adam Smith, Scotland provided the prophet of a new world order, and the rapidly expanding middle class of his homeland throbbed with the pulse of prosperity. After Dundas' death, with final victory over Napoleon, Britain realized the old rogue's vision – a virtual monopoly of overseas colonies, advanced engineering technology, complete naval dominance in all oceans and pole position in the new era of mass production in factories using steam power.

It was extremely easy for Sir Walter Scott to be both a devout Scottish patriot and a convinced believer in the Union with England, from which such benefits seemed to have flowed, along with a gratifying share in military and naval glory.

But Scott was at odds with the Whigs grouped around the *Edinburgh Review* who took the dismal science of political economy to the point where historic differences between Scotland and England seemed irrelevant in the new era of free trade and utilitarian social policies. It was after such men had triumphed with parliamentary reform in 1832 and the *ancien régime* of Dundas, which his son had maintained, was finally scuppered, that Scottish self-command was jeopardized.

The disruption in the Kirk which produced the breakaway Free Church in 1843 represented and created unease, at a time when heavy Catholic immigration from Ireland was changing the character of Scotland's population. The new railways cut travel time to southern England so sharply that Queen Victoria could make Balmoral her second home, and Englishmen could comfortably sit as MPs in Scottish constituencies for the Liberal Party, which Scottish burghs now overwhelmingly favoured.

Rich Scots sent their sons to English boarding schools, and the sporting estates of the Highlands became a favourite playground of their friends in the imperial ruling class and their foreign cronies.

Edinburgh lost its position as a great independent capital of enlightened thought, and its university gravitated towards English norms. Many of the best Scottish talents – Carlyle, Stevenson, Buchan, Barrie, the painter Orchardson, the composers Mackenzie, Wallace, McCunn and McEwan – would seek and find fame south of the Border.

Yet, paradoxically, the disproportionate Scottish stake in the overseas Empire helped to maintain a strong sense of national distinctiveness. The local politicians who brought off Canadian federation in 1867 were Scottish almost to a man. If Moffat, Philip and Livingstone worked in southern Africa under the aegis of the London Missionary Society, Scottish missions and schools in India, Kenya, Malawi and elsewhere had a sharp and peculiar impact.

Scottish merchants flourished mightily in trade with the East, where Dundee, through jute, was in virtual symbiosis with Bengal, and the importation of tea became almost as fully a Scottish preserve as that of tobacco had once been.

Above all, Glasgow, by 1900, revelled boastfully in its status as Second City of the Empire. Its shipyards sinewed the Empire's commerce and navy. With its unique array of free and cheap municipal services, its wonderful art collections and its remarkable architecture, there was plenty to help its people transcend the appalling standards of housing, far behind those of England.

In 1914, Scots were by and large complacent about their status in the world. Since Gladstone had put home rule on the agenda in the 1880s, on the grounds that if Ireland got it, Scotland should, there had been pressure, mostly from Liberals, towards it. But within the mighty British Empire Scots believed, not without reason, that they provided the most enterprising businessmen, the most visionary industrialists, the most dynamic missionaries, the most skilful administrators, the most devoted and trustworthy professional men, and the best farmers. They had the most fish and a superabundance of coal. They had developed the great tradition of working-class self-help which informed the highly successful Co-operative Wholesale Societies, and which had inspired the creation of a Labour Party in Scotland ahead of England. Scotland had huge social problems, but Scots believed that Scots could tackle them. Onwards, as Ramsay MacDonald would put it, and upwards.

But by the time the confusedly idealistic MacDonald became Britain's first Labour prime minister, Scotland had been traumatized. It was not so much that the country had paid the price for disproportionate volunteering zeal with disproportionate casualties in the Great War. France, Germany and Russia had lost many more, and the Scottish population actually rose between 1911 and 1921. Very suddenly, Empire ceased to be a good deal. Scotland had depended on heavy industries and overseas markets. The post-war slump hit these especially hard, along with coal-mining, and the country was not well placed to acquire and build up the new light engineering, automobile and aircraft industries which brought prosperity to large parts of England.

As unemployment soared – to two-thirds at one point in Greenock – people drained away. Skilled and enterprising emigrants left despair behind them. Scots now had a grudge against history. This, not 1707, was the decisive watershed in Scottish attitudes. Boast gave way to whinge.

Though spite against Catholic immigrants persisted, and sectarian Protestant parties briefly did very well in local elections in Glasgow and Edinburgh in the 1930s, the old religious spirit which had animated Scots and kept some of them sober was in decline. For many, socialism became a substitute. The legend of the Red Clyde linked several discrete phenomena – the successful 1915 rent strike led by women which forced the Government to legislate against grasping landlords, the impalpable effects of John Maclean's adult education courses in Marxist economics, and the more tangible public response to his martyred imprisonment for his anti-war views, the agitation of shop stewards against de-skilling of jobs in engineering under war conditions, and the sudden rise of Labour to dominance in the representation of the west of Scotland some time after the war, which reflected John Wheatley's success in switching the Catholic vote leftwards. Red Clyde MPs thereafter formed a truculent element at Westminster, and more than incidentally tried to push through bills for Scottish home rule within the Empire.

The rupture of the Independent Labour Party from the Labour Party in 1932, after Ramsay MacDonald had 'betrayed' the movement at the moment when Britain's economy felt the impact of the Great Depression, left Glasgow for a couple of decades with the only ILP representatives at Westminster, but otherwise under the control of Labour machine politics, not very Red, but electorally dominant, from Paddy Dollan to Pat Lally, for the rest of the twentieth century.

The tradition of self-help was travestied by a new politics of patronage, which eventually replaced bad old housing with disastrous new housing, and provided Labour with a stream of machine-made nonentities safely elected to seats at Westminster.

The thirties, forties and fifties saw the climax of the Union with England. The administration of Scotland was devolved to Edinburgh's rather spectacular new Scottish Office, where Walter Eliott, wettest of Tories, made a start on the quangification of Scotland. Churchill selected Tom Johnston, erstwhile Red Clydesider, as secretary of state in his coalition government. Partly by invoking the bogey of nationalism, lurking ready to undermine the imperial war effort, Johnston was able to set up more quangos. These did useful work, and reinforced the welfare state which Labour brought in to popular acclaim after the war, in which Scots had fought and suffered alongside the English to win total victory over Nazism, heavy industry had recovered, and the country stood poised to accept gratefully Labour and Tory support for regional economies in the new era of full employment.

In the 1950s, the great tradition of Scottish Liberalism finally collapsed. Conservatives won more than half the vote in a general election, Labour abandoned its seventy-year-old commitment to home rule, and English television magnetized every Scottish home. In short, Scottish political culture had plunged weightlessly into a Unionist vacuum.

So why do we have a new parliament this week, elected on novel principles of proportional representation, certain to contain many representatives of the Scottish National Party and likely to have four women for every ten members?

There are three possible reasons. One is the revival of Scottish culture from the 1950s, spearheaded by the folksong movement led by Hamish Henderson and Norman Buchan and vitalizing the so-called Scottish renaissance in the arts proclaimed by Hugh MacDiarmid three decades before but hitherto chiefly represented by his own lone efforts. Before long Scotland proved to have a half a dozen or more leading poets, brilliant painters revived the great Scottish figurative tradition and that snark, the Great Glasgow Novel, was captured at last and proved not to be a boojum.

Secondly, the final breakdown of the Empire in the 1960s coincided with the achievement of independence by many poor countries, some less populous than Scotland, the marching politics of CND, Black Power self-assertion in the United States and minority nationalist movements in several parts of Europe.

Bright young men who might previously have looked to safe and lucrative employ in colonial administration, banking or commerce now sought to realize their ambitions at home.

The Labour machine had no grip on urbanites decanted into new towns. The Scottish National Party found a motley constituency, and its sudden rush of electoral success pushed Labour into schemes for devolution. But granted a century-long history of failure by caucuses and conventions working to achieve home rule, after the débâcle of the 1979 referendum the issue might just have gone away.

What made a new parliament certain in the end was the way Margaret Thatcher rubbed our faces in the democratic deficit, and rallied up to three-quarters of Scots behind the idea of home rule; sufficient to prevent any future government from thus imposing abhorrent policies by overruling the people's wishes.

Edward I's arrogance forced Scotland into precocious nationalism; now Thatcher has ensured that we vote in the first ever democratic election for a Scottish parliament.

5 May 1999

The tree of liberty:
Home Rule Handbook Part 1 – Democracy

ANGUS CALDER, ALASDAIR GRAY

Alasdair Gray's preface

Imagine an old tree with the trunk broken or sawn off just above the roots. This stump is not dead. A leafy branch sprouts from it which could grow into a new trunk giving protective shade to the ground below. If the tree is a Scotch pine, that branch might be an emblem of the first Scottish parliament elected in 1999. It will be a very green, frail thing at first – what Billy Connolly calls a 'pretendy parliament' – for two reasons.

Firstly, the leaders of the present Labour Cabinet (mostly Scots) are allowing it very few powers a government possesses. They intend it to be a huge sub-committee or quango of local loud-mouths arguing over Scottish differences, thus making it easier for the Westminster Assembly to manage all Britain in ways the New Labour Party have inherited from Thatcher and Major. This is making more and more traditional Labour Party supporters vote SNP. But if a majority of the new Holyrood assembly want to govern Scottish affairs they will find a second difficulty. Scottish affairs have been so dominated by those of England that most Scots hardly know how their affairs stand.

A cynic may say that voters and politicians in most countries are equally ignorant. I disagree. People in many European democracies get early schooling in the history, culture and government of their nation, so share a store of useful information that later experience enlarges or corrects. Expensive English private schools such as Harrow, Eton and Rugby also give children such educations. But when the last Scottish parliament became a fraction of England's in 1707 it became impossible for Scots to manage their own most important affairs without seeing them from an English viewpoint. That is why wealthy Scots send their sons to English private schools such as Eton and Rugby or to private Scottish schools emulating them. So Scotland is governed by a system most people do not understand because it is kept private.

Charles McKean, graduate of Fettes College, architect, arts administrator and journalist, recently described the system in one sentence. When telling a newspaper of negotiations leading to the new Scottish national museum, he said: 'We are a small country run largely by unelected and unaccountable people, based on a system of mutual favours.' He was not attacking the system. He thought it worked well and, like all political systems, this one does work well when the minority within serve the majority outside. In the forties, for instance, the Scottish secretary of state Tom Johnston used it to strengthen and create important public services (one of them was Scottish Hydro Electricity) which have since been weakened or privatized. But a nation run by unelected and unaccountable people is not a democracy, and the first parliament elected by the Scottish people in May this year will do no good if it does not get those who run the land to identify and justify their doings. It should also, after sufficient public debate, start improving it in new, accountable ways.

I am an artist and fiction writer, so as ignorant of Scottish politics as any farmer, policeman, coalminer (we still have miners) or nurse. In other words, I know how politics influence my own work but have a very blurred picture of politics as a whole – the politics of big property owners, bankers and administrators, of the Marquis of Bute and the immovable leader of Glasgow District Council. So when I heard we were to get our own parliament I felt in need of a handy book to teach me both how Scotland is run and how it might be run better. I could imagine that book very clearly.

It would give factual information about the bodies owning and managing Scotland, and their powers to influence or change it, for without such shared knowledge political debates are mere noisy exchanges of prejudice, and nothing a majority votes for can be made to work. The book would use the reports of publicists and truth-doctors employed by private and public organizations to say how good they are but also reports by more lowly workers: labourers, teachers, shop assistants, legal-aid lawyers, who would tell why their jobs are difficult nowadays and what they need to serve the public better. Each entry on a trade or profession would give a brief sketch of its history to show how it had improved or deteriorated, with news about how things are organized in other nations, for nowadays all political parties are willing to learn from other lands. Margaret Thatcher applied, for instance, and Tony Blair applies American business methods to the running of Britain.

This was the book I needed and thought Scotland needed, but I could not write it. My imagination starts with facts but has an inbuilt habit of swerving into fiction. I could suggest the plan of this book and design it but the main author would have to be a social historian who knew more than me about modern Scotland, one who wanted the Scots parliament to work yet had an international view of it. The only writer of the sort I knew well enough to approach was Angus Calder. He liked the idea. Together we drew up an alphabetical list of entries starting with Aberdeen, Advertising, Aristocracy and Armed Forces and ending with Unemployment, Universities, Wages and Workers' Educational Association. We meant each entry to be short but wonderfully informative.

Unluckily Angus, like me, had first to finish another book. He also lacked the research assistant and secretary needed to complete such a Home-Rule Handbook before the new parliament met. The first edition of this work will therefore be a lot slimmer than the pocket encyclopaedia of Scottish affairs we had planned.

Angus Calder proceeds . . .

The articles coming up represent one element in our scheme – the provision, beside our factual information, of suggestions about what to do to change the circumstances represented by bad facts and gloomy statistics. We planned that a wide range of voices should be heard, some of them representing viewpoints which we ourselves don't go along with at all.

My own postgraduate degree comes from a thesis about politics involving quite heavy use of statistics. While I was working on it, I came across an invaluable little book by Darrell Huff called *How to Lie with Statistics*. Something like this should be put into the hands of every parliamentarian and schoolteacher. Recently there has been a sterile and dismaying set of exchanges between Labour spokespeople arguing that Scots profit from the Union and are subsidized by it, and SNP nominees who counter that, on the contrary, Scotland has subsidized Westminster. It is likely that both sides are using quite accurate figures. It is difficult, though needful, to detach statistics about Scotland from the UK series in which they are embedded. It is also needful to bring a sensible perspective to bear on them and to keep in mind that they are often partly or wholly fictional in character. Adam Smith, mindful of the widespread and successful operations of smugglers, dismissed the trade statistics of his day as 'those public registers of which the records are sometimes published with so much parade, and from which our merchants and manufacturers would often vainly pretend to announce the prosperity or declension of the great empires'.

It is extraordinarily difficult in many cases to discover how much money is spent in and from Scotland on what. Important facts known to, or inferred by, actual health workers or police officers or schoolteachers or trade union activists can escape statistical trawls. (How much time, for instance, is wasted on form-filling to do with 'quality assessment' of public servants who are visibly doing a good job? What part does the unofficial 'black economy' play in the lives of poor people? How many racist abuses go unreported?) From the criminologist who shows by statistics success for 'community policing' in Glasgow one has a right to ask why crime, dysfunction and violence related to traffic in illegal drugs dominate large tracts of the city. It is also fair to ask those who promote 'tourism' to explain why attendance by local Scottish people at exhibitions in famous galleries and museums created by the civic pride and zeal for enlightenment of our forebears over the last couple of centuries should be amassed in their self-applauding statistics with visits to those same places by Germans and Londoners here on business.

Whatever statistics and other information may tell us, our parliament, whether devolved or independent, will have only such-and-such money to spend.

We need to establish priorities by which to use it. To adapt a saying of Aneurin Bevan, who established the National Health Service, the language of priorities is the religion of democracy. If our priority is a better health service, we should be prepared, through our taxes, to pay for it.

Before 1707, Scotland was governed by landowners large and small, burgesses and clerics. Revolts, mobs and rabbles were the ways in which ordinary folk expressed their opinions, sometimes to effect. Since the Union, Scots leaders, like Tom Johnston, have found in London power over the public purse and the creation of new institutions. They have used this power through, and often on behalf of, cronies, landowners, and, latterly, businessmen, bureaucrats and preferred experts. The mob has now been appeased, it seems, by social security benefits, twenty-four-hour television and intermittent elections. Most people vote in general elections. Only minorities vote in elections for local councils and the European Parliament.

The Holyrood parliament gives us a chance to create democracy in Scotland. If it made democracy a priority, it could pass measures enhancing it which need not cost money. Indeed, abolishing all quangos would surely save money, in salaries and fees generously allotted to favoured but unelected persons. Elected

MSPs will be paid to govern the country. Why should committees of MSPs not be mandated to take decisions now made within quangos? If there are good reasons, these should be exposed to public view at once.

How can MSPs be truly representative of all of us, the modern rabble? Proponents of proportional representation often talk evangelistically as if that will guarantee that every vote counts, and counts equally. This is by no means clear. One of the first things our parliament might do is set up a standing committee to review the operation of the PR system under which it is elected and to consider and suggest alternatives. 'First past the post', as in Westminster elections, is the bizarre system in which someone gaining, say, 26 percent of the vote in a four-cornered contest could be elected, 'disenfranchizing' three-quarters of the voters. Various PR systems have produced results equally unacceptable in principle or in practice. Where parties have to negotiate to form coalitions – and every commentator assumes that this will be a normal process at Holyrood – one of those out of power may actually regain power (ministerial office) after an election in which it loses votes and seats. There are fearsome examples of unattractive parties with just a few seats – fundamentalists, neo-fascists – exercising wholly disproportionate influence through 'proportional' representation.

Deep into the nineteenth century, 'democracy' was a boo-word for quite thoughtful and humane people who believed that the rule of the mob and the rabble would involve tyranny. The philistine mass, overthrowing hierarchy, would also obliterate quality and true freedom. In so far as democracy became linked with the aspirations of ethnic groups to create their own 'racially homogeneous' states, one must concede that sometimes these fears have been realized. Hitler arrived in power initially through democratic processes. Events in the former Yugoslavia suggest that such processes may sustain extreme, and widely lethal, contempt for difference. A majority is not always just. If opinion polls show that the majority of Scots want to bring back hanging for murder, will our new parliament agree to this, and if not, why not?

So far as we have got in Scotland the answer would be: 'Because our political parties, with all their imperfections and limitations, will usually select people as candidates who are attuned to the rational arguments against the death penalty.' Implicit in the ideal of democratic representation is the hope that those elected will be, however marginally, better informed and more sensible about important issues than most of those who have elected them, because their political activity has involved them in study and serious thought. Our proposed handbook might help more non-politicians reach a similar level of awareness.

By being different from each other in regional origin, in religion, in gender, in age and sometimes, we must hope, in skin pigmentation, MSPs themselves will represent difference. Their very embodiment should imply that Scottish society is not and should not be exclusive. It is tempting to suggest that Holyrood should enshrine respect for difference in tight new laws, imposing stronger penalties for anti-English sneers and insults directed at folk from the Indian sub-continent. But pious new laws might count for far less than action taken in other areas which would represent a contempt for exclusiveness. Parliament must clarify the right to voting citizenship here of anyone from whatever place who genuinely wishes to live here rather than somewhere else. It can seek to mitigate the problems faced by those seeking asylum from tyrannous regimes. It will be left, whatever it does, with awkward, perhaps insoluble problems arising from difference – most seriously, perhaps, the demand of religious denominations, Catholic and Islamic, to control their own schools; less gravely the rumbling dispute over the status of the Scots language, and Gaelic, in Scottish schools in general.

Democracy is not a beast which we have hunted and captured. It is a just-born child whom we must teach to talk and walk as we think best.

12 February 1999

Law and Disorder:
Home Rule Handbook Part 2 – Justice

ANGUS CALDER, ALASDAIR GRAY

In Scotland we have rejoiced that under the Treaty of Union, 1707, our country retained its separate legal system. Sophisticated thinkers have further chortled over the fact that Scots law retains a basis in Roman law, like that of other European countries, while the silly English long ago diverged from that. But, in fact, Napoleon's onslaught on Europe in general resulted in countries there starting off from new legal baselines. Equivalents of the French Code Napoleon were produced. Scotland meanwhile continued in ever-closer relationship with English law. After 1707, commercial law flowered, shared by both countries. Though Scottish lawyers continued to seek principles in Roman law and in the works of our own Stair and Erskine, Scots law was not codified. But the learned judge who made these points to us went on to specify ways in which Scottish practice remains, valuably, different.

English procedure in criminal cases is such that the prosecuting counsel at the outset puts the whole of the Crown case to the jury, anticipating what witnesses will reveal. ('You will hear this ... you will further hear that ...') In Scotland, this does not happen. The jury merely develops its sense of the case from what witnesses, called in order, say. This may not in practice be much fairer to the accused, but it surely tends in that direction. The English verdict 'not guilty' is decisive. The Scottish verdict 'not proven' states as a fact that there was no corroborative evidence to satisfy the jury as to guilt. It seems to us that the first charge upon any system of justice is that it should not convict people unjustly. It is better that a criminal, even a murderer, should walk free than that someone's life should be ruined by conviction for a crime which that person did not commit. Every second television detective drama will remind us of the pressure on the police to secure convictions when crimes particularly outrage public opinion. Surely, in the case of that psychologically disturbed man who was recently judged 'guilty' in Kent of the terrible murder of a woman and her daughter walking in the countryside – especially hard on our feelings because a second daughter was left for dead, yet survived – the safe verdict would have been 'not proven', since the only evidence against the accused was an alleged confession to a fellow convict in prison? (Meanwhile, the real murderer might still be at large.)

Pressure on the police was at its most extreme when IRA outrages killed many people on the British mainland. According to formerly settled conventions of British justice, the police were restrained from breaking into our houses without warrant, from arresting people without charging them with crimes and from quoting their version of what an arrested person said to them if that person denied it and no independent witness corroborated it. Reading about the trials, convictions and sometimes releases of Irish Fenian rebels in mid Victorian Britain, we may be touched to notice how much scrupulous consideration was then given to the rights of individuals who were actually, or very likely, guilty as charged. In 1982 the British Government abolished safeguards which had sustained rights and liberty. The IRA was getting away with murder. In effect the Government told the police: 'Fight the dirty bastards as dirtily as you like. Arrest people on suspicion and get the evidence afterwards. Up and at them!' Since our police now had some of the freedom enjoyed by Stalinist police, they got the quick results desired. The Ukanian government, press and people were sombrely glad when the Guildford Four and Birmingham Six were jailed. The police were relieved. Had they worked carefully to secure evidence, without using torture and perjury to back their suspicions, innocent Irish would have walked free, but the guilty might not have been caught and the Government would have looked impotent. Recent governments have willingly declared their impotence when confronted by unemployment and wage reductions (their strongest supporters are enriched by these) but when confronted by violence they have preferred injustice to looking impotent. It was good, recently, to see the present head of the Royal Ulster Constabulary politely resisting pressure from a television interviewer to say that he would soon be charging people for the horrific bombing of Omagh town centre in the summer of 1998. This time, his words seemed to imply we must be quite sure we are charging the real villains.

To pursue this point about 'impotence': governments of Ukania latterly have not really attempted to do much about the underlying causes of crime, which are often found in the despairing lives of people who cannot get worthwhile jobs, find it hard to feed their children and live in disgusting environments which generate resentment and cynicism. Rather than seem useless, governments like to appear to be taking decisive action. Our current one has appointed a so-called 'drugs tsar'. Some of the tsars of Russia were not outright sadists and possessed this, that or the other personal virtue. But the system which they presided over censored even mathematics textbooks and executed or exiled to Siberia mildly dissident students and harmless religious eccentrics. It was a very devisive and extremely unjust system. It was also, as the country's great writers showed, characterized by ludicrous stupidity on the part of bureaucrats and time-serving hypocrisy among officials.

Both stupidity and hypocrisy characterize the attitude of the Ukanian state towards drugs. One extremely potent and frequently lethal substance is freely advertised on huge hoardings and on prime-time television. Its bad effects are well known to all doctors and policemen. It destroys homes, ruins careers, provokes criminal assault and homicidal carelessness, aggravates physical and mental sickness and leaves vomit and broken glass on our pavements every weekend. Yet we may feed it to our children without illegality and, in its more expensive packages, it attracts the attention of distinguished connoisseurs including prominent lawyers and politicians.

For nearly fourteen years, between 1920 and 1933, the manufacture, sale and transportation of alcoholic beverages was prohibited throughout the United States of America. Folk who wished to get drunk found ample illegal ways of continuing to do so and there were so many such folk that highly organized crime flourished in a spectacular way, which generated many effective, if disturbing, gangster movies and a great deal of fear and misery. No Western government, one might imagine, would be likely to repeat the disastrous experiment of Prohibition.

Yet, in effect, that is what most have done in respect of various widely used drugs rendered illegal by law. 'Psychoactive' substances which affect mood and mind are legion. Their use among humankind goes back to the Stone Age. Coffee and chocolate are two of them. Nicotine is a third – tobacco is frowned on by the righteous, but not Prohibited. Heroin and cocaine are Prohibited. So, quite weirdly, is marijuana. Let that remarkable Glaswegian writer Alexander Trocchi take the argument further. In *Cain's Book* (1961), the narrator Joe's friend Tom is repenting his own addiction to heroin. Joe, a Scottish junkie living in New York, tells him that the Americans are an alcoholic people who find it convenient to demonize 'drugs'. It gives them, he says, 'a nice tangible cause for juvenile delinquency ... There's an available pool of wasted-looking bastards to stand trial as the corrupters of their children. It provides the police with something to do, and as junkies and potheads are relatively easy to apprehend because they have to take so many chances to get hold of their drugs, heroic police can make spectacular arrests, lawyers can do a brisk business, judges can make speeches, the big pedlars can make a fortune, the tabloids can sell millions of copies. John Citizen can sit back feeling exonerated and watch evil gets its deserts.'

Marijuana seems to be a vastly less problematic substance than alcohol. It relaxes you and makes you too woozy to drive safely.

Peaceable Rastafarians dote on it. Many other sane people find it pleasant. The present government inquiry into its 'effects' pending legalization is farcical almost beyond the imagination of Nikolai Gogol, that painfully hilarious satirist of Tsarist officialdom. Just as humanity has always had reason to believe that eating too little food starves you to death, so in numerous cultures over many thousands of years the effects of cannabis have been generally known. It would be more pertinent to set up an inquiry into the alleged medicinal benefits of drinking red wine, with a view to introducing claret on prescription. Heroin on prescription would be no problem. People who grow poppies in Pakistan could be paid more for their crop by official NHS agents than evil men now give them. Wholly pure heroin would be guaranteed, so addicts would not die from 'spiked' drugs. Similar arguments apply to cocaine, favoured fun-drug of rich people, and that more plebeian substance, Ecstasy, which may be at least as dangerous as eating double cream or too much salt. These could be sold in chemists'. We buy paracetamol freely at our own risk and it actually kills a lot of people, more than adventurous rock climbing, more than hillwalking in bad weather. The chief problem arising from all-round legalization of drugs would be that young people in revolt against their parents and society would surely work out some other way of expressing their badness and their disgust at the rotten world their elders have created.

As in Al Capone's America, Prohibition generates crime among us. We suffer from the activities of criminal syndicates operating worldwide with a turnover of billions. Apart from the crimes of selling and possessing drugs, much theft is by addicts seeking cash to feed their habits. Lothian police surveys suggest that while almost all crimes of violence are related to alcohol, perhaps four-fifths of crimes of dishonesty – housebreaking, shoplifting, credit card fraud and so on – involve drug users or people connected with drugs. Only about 30 per cent of police effort in the area goes into crime. But legalization of drugs could clearly release much of that effort into other spheres, such as eliminating drunk driving and coping with the epidemic of badness among males aged sixteen to twenty-one, who account for most petty crime before they settle down and stop behaving like assertive young chimpanzees. In Glasgow, incidentally, with its culture of gangs and turf wars, drugs are strongly correlated with crimes of violence.

Would undesirables from many quarters flock here if we legalized drugs, so that they could get high, exploit our social services and maybe go in for a spot of crime? From Holland, with its liberal drugs policies and exceptionally porous frontiers, lawyers report no grave related problems.

However it proceeds, legislation on drugs by our new Scottish parliament should be as simple as possible. As one wise lawyer has explained to us, Westminster statutes are formulated on the assumption that you must provide specifically for every contingency. As he puts it, this produces a 'net' effect – 'the more lines you draw, the more holes you are creating'. If our Holyrood statutes set out principles and make rules which clearly cover the core majority of cases, our able judges can cope with the exceptions by referring back to these principles. At Holyrood we have a chance to escape at last from English obsession with unnecessary detail. MSPs could also terminate here the wicked practices by which the Ukanian state has attempted to prevent justice prevailing in cases where its own agents break the law or violate its spirit – otherwise known as 'cover-ups'. We might complacently define 'official secrecy' as another English mania of which our new Scotland can easily be rid, were it not for at least one recent case within our very own system of crime and punishment. A doctor in a famous Scottish prison saw what he thought was brutality exercised by warders upon prisoners. (We fear that no one who talks, as we do, to former inmates of our jails, will be altogether surprised to hear rumours of such happenings. Warders, it is fair to say, are also imperilled.) The doctor was suspended for many months while the matter he had raised was investigated. It was decided that there was no evidence that warders had misbehaved. A few months later a law was passed making it a criminal offence for employees under the Ukanian Crown to give information about misconduct within their departments to people outside. Tsarism rules, OK? Why should the operations of prisons, which are supposed to be there to protect all of us from dangerous people, be kept secret from the public which votes for the parliamentary representatives whose consent to their funding sustains such operations?

When the Foreign Office archives for 1938 were thrown open, it was found that the so-called 'Munich Agreement' between Chamberlain and Hitler had disappeared. The broad nature and the effects of that shameful agreement had always been 'in the public domain', but of course officials involved in bad deeds will normally be able to destroy, or fabricate, evidence. Such delinquents would be compelled to be more expeditious and ingenious if all the operations of government in Scotland were always open to public inspection so that researchers and journalists had automatic access to current official papers and were only subject to punishment if they abused this right and, with malice, reported incorrectly. If any evidence were found to have been withheld or destroyed, the officials concerned should themselves be exposed to the rigours of the law. Why not? Upstairs or downstairs, 'public servants' should surely be our 'servants'.

Which brings us back to the 'services' provided by those directly responsible for law enforcement and justice. In our experience, most policemen are polite and helpful. Socially, they can be very pleasant. We believe that certain goings-on depicted by Ian Rankin in his Inspector Rebus novels and by Irvine Welsh in *Filth*, which have given Lothian and Borders Police an interesting reputation throughout the English-speaking world, should not be taken to be representative of the general behaviour of our bobbies, who are actually no more sexist, racist, corrupt and drunken than the rest of us. This means that it is a pity that so many young people and folk with darkly pigmented skins feel that they cannot be trusted at all. There are now districts in Scotland where the police are expected to arrest all schoolchildren using the streets after a certain time of night. (Note our point above – it is young males who have left school who are the major problem.) This is unlikely to generate cordial relations between the police and children whom they have harassed when the latter grow large enough to cause GBH efficiently. Curfews are kneejerk reactions to problems. Holyrood should apply mindjerks to them.

A poor person seeking justice will always be at a disadvantage compared with a rich one. But this sad circumstance can be mitigated. At the moment, legal aid in Britain has its Gogolian aspects. Rich men avail themselves of it. Poor people don't get enough of it. It is presented to us not as a right but as a costly favour accorded to us by the benevolent state and kindly, self-sacrificing lawyers. The first condition of justice in Scotland is that enough lawyers should be paid from public funds at a sufficiently high rate to guarantee free, first-class representation to anyone below a certain income level; and service to others according to their means.

Roman law or no Roman law, that surely should be Holyrood's prime policy. Our Scotland. Our parliament. Our rights.

13 February 1999

A leviathan awakes?:
Home Rule Handbook Part 3
– Land Ownership

ANGUS CALDER, ALASDAIR GRAY

ALASDAIR GRAY: The Scottish people grow particularly warm
in argument concerning the land and its ownership. We understand from the Secretary of State that eighty-five organizations
and individuals submitted responses to one document produced by the Land Policy Research Group, which made its
recommendations at the start of this year.

ANGUS CALDER: Perhaps we should be concerned that the
number of responses was so small, since we all live on the land
(now that lighthouses have been fully automated) and a large
proportion of us own properties on it, subject to keeping our
mortgage payments up to date. However, 'land' as a term in
political debate usually seems to mean 'rural land, especially
in the Highlands'. Only a small proportion of Scots live in the
Highlands but we tend to believe that our true identity as Scots
derives from those windy, wet, remote, infertile but, to many,
perversely attractive landscapes. There is a widespread belief
that Highland chiefs in the eighteenth and nineteenth centuries
effectually stole land which properly belonged to all the folk
who dwelt on it, the whole clan. They then extruded people
and in their place introduced sheep for profit and deer for
sport. Finally, their inheritors sold out to Englishpersons or
Europeans who compounded the original theft by controlling

the land as absentees. Just as wildlife protection groups take no interest in those resourceful and successful creatures, urban seagulls and pigeons and urban rats and foxes, so land ownership is rarely discussed as an issue affecting the urban areas where the great majority of Scots live.

AG: I observe that you are set upon provocation. Was it not admirable that, in 1993 and 1997 respectively, the crofters of Assynt and the islanders of Eigg, with heartfelt support from many Scots elsewhere, were able to purchase the estates on which they live?

AC: Yes, but they are not clanspersons of the clans from which the land is supposed to have been stolen. The principle involved is not like that involved in the transfer of lands back to people of Maori descent in New Zealand. It does not invoke aboriginal rights to the soil. It is the conception – perhaps sound, and universally valid – that estates should be controlled and developed by *ad hoc* co-operatives of actual residents. It might be applied to housing estates, or 'schemes' as we call them here. However, such groups, as things stand, do not have ultimate ownership of the land.

AG: But surely, in the worldview prevalent in the West since the seventeenth century, property is deemed to be sacrosanct. Those who have paid for the island of Eigg, own it. If they don't who does? . . .

AC: We all do.

AG: Sir, I perceive that you are intoxicated.

AC: Nothing stronger than mango juice has passed my lips this day. What I say is true. Just one mortifying shadow falls over my glee at this discovery. The English, the Welsh and the Northern (although not the Southern) Irish also own the whole of Scotland.

AG: Pursue this point if you must, but I fear that you will confound yourself.

AC: You are aware, of course, that alone in Europe Scotland still has a feudal system of landownership?

AG: Yes, and lawyers and civil servants have been struggling for several decades to invent a sound scheme for getting rid of it. We understand that a major obstacle has been that Scottish land law is so intricate and outlandish (please forgive my childish wordplay) that the Westminster parliament could never have found time to discuss it properly. Thus, though Mr Dewar's group has worked out how to do away with it, and his party will probably command a large number of seats in our own new parliament, where he promises that land will be a topic for early discussion, feudalism, for the moment, survives.

AC: Perhaps we should retain it.

AG: If I ever ingest mango juice, it will be with extreme caution. Why should we propitiate the evil ghosts of rapacious noblemen who oppressed poor men and, to boot, ravished their wives, while they persisted in betraying Scotland to the English?

AC: Because we ourselves possess feudal sovereignty.

AG: I think that you should hasten to report that to the marines.

AC: Nay, hearken ... The Queen, you will agree, is nominal sovereign of the United Kingdom of Great Britain and Northern Ireland ...

AG: 'Ukania', as Tom Nairn has called it, yes ...

AC: But since the eighteenth century it has been understood that Ukania is governed by the monarch-in-parliament. Effectively, this meant at the outset that the monarch's ministers, led by the prime one, and commanding as a rule a majority of votes in the House of Commons, shared out among their friends and other persons who might be useful to them, including Members of Parliament, moneys acquired by direct and indirect taxation of the gentry and populace. To justify this

larceny they maintained armies and navies which could sally
forth and loot the rest of the world, while extending scope for
Ukanian merchants and manufacturers and so, as they could
argue, increasing the nation's general wealth. During the nineteenth century, the fraudulence involved in all this was made
less blatant. A civil service emerged which was presumed to be
wholly incorruptible. The army and navy were only allowed
to steal the property of non-white peoples. Some governments
in the twentieth century have actually used the tribute rendered
by taxpayers to improve the comfort and prospects of the
generality as, for instance, in the creation of a National Health
Service . . .

AG: You wander off your point . . .

AC: Not so. My point is that in our own times the notion that
we, folk at large, have our interests genuinely represented by
a parliament which is in effect sovereign throughout Ukania
has, intermittently at least, ceased to be fictional. In a democracy, the interests of the people are expressed through representatives who govern on their behalf. Do you deny that we live
in a democracy?

AG: That is debatable, but most folk seem to think so. Pursue
your point.

AC: It follows that under Scottish feudal land law the Ukanian
electorate have ultimate sovereignty over all the straths, braes,
landfill sites, council schemes, football stadia and back greens,
et cetera, of our bonny country. Whether tenure is by feuing
or allodial, whether land is held by 'box tenure' as in Paisley
or by a 'kindly tenant' in Lochmaben or under old Norse 'udal'
custom as in the Northern Isles, all of us, voting adults, possess
the regalia – the Crown's sovereign and inalienable rights.

AG: But if we were to create a Scottish republic . . . ?

AC: That 'state', if we must use a term which many, not without

reason, find sinister, would take over sovereign feudal ownership of the whole of Scotland.

AG: Are you suggesting that our new parliament – assuming, as
Mr Dewar clearly does, that sovereignty in this sphere of interest is devolved from Westminster – might assert its feudal
superiority over tenement flats in Partick and modest villas in
Broughty Ferry? Might it, for instance, compel all tenants to
acquire digital TV at once, on pain of eviction?

AC: No – that would clearly be tyrannous, though such a consideration would not necessarily deter the present Ukanian prime
minister's very good friend, Mr Rupert Murdoch. Sovereign
though we are, we must legislate when needful to restrain the
exercise of our own power. Law needs must safeguard honest
tenants against cruel and arbitrary treatment by our sub-
landlords, just as it might prevent the inhabitants of Knoydart,
were they to wrest immediate control of their 17,000 acres from
an English businessman currently under investigation by the
Serious Fraud Office, from turning the whole area into a Highland theme park or using every tract of water for insanitary
fish farming.

AG: Mr Dewar himself clearly believes that our parliament will
be within its rights to dispossess absentee and otherwise delin-
quent landlords.

AC: Yes. A very wise man once pointed out to me that if one
had an idea which was wholly original it would certainly be
wrong. So I am happy to think that Mr Dewar might agree,
in effect, that the principle of common sovereignty over land,
if we can preserve it from the devastation of the rest of our
feudal system, would permit our parliament to act decisively,
without particular legislation, overriding unsatisfactory landlords. 'According to our power as sovereign, yew are oot,
Jimmy' . . . – a formula as brief as that might suffice.

AG: But is that not the language of Thomas Hobbes's *Leviathan*, erstwhile assimilated by some sincere Christian folk with the voice of Antichrist himself?

AC: Up to a point one must go along with Hobbes. Consider these facts. Half of Scotland's 19 million acres are held by 608 landowners, three acres out of ten by 135, one-fifth by 58, and a tenth by just 18. If one takes out of account the 12 per cent of Scotland which is owned by public bodies such as the Forestry Commission and the 3 per cent covered by our major cities, one half of the privately owned rural land in Scotland is controlled by less than 350 owners, and over a third by less than 125 owners, each with more than 20,000 acres. Mr Robin Callender, from whose book *How Scotland Is Owned* (Canongate, 1998), I have plagiarized these statistics, notes that at the end of Victoria's reign, in that classic era of English country house culture, less than 7 percent of England was held in estates of more than 20,000 acres. 'It appears that no other country in the world can match the concentrated land ownership in Scotland.' Good old Hobbes would surely have pointed out that it takes some brute of a leviathan to sort our six-score monsters out.

AG: You do not consider the suggestion, long advanced by the Old Labour Party, that all land should be nationalized.

AC: Of course I don't. You obstinately ignore my point. We, as voters of the nation-state of Ukania, own all of Scotland already, jointly with most of the other occupants of the North-West European Archipelago.

AG: So a large question might be this – can we restrict sovereignty over Scotland to the people who live and vote here?

AC: Subject to European Union law, if we secured a sufficient measure of independence within or outwith Ukania, yes, presumably we could do that.

AG: But might not our continental partners take it amiss if we exercised our sovereign authority to dispossess absentee Teutons and distasteful Iberians?

AC: This is a particular instance of a general problem facing our parliament. Scotland's membership, through Ukania, of the European Union will necessarily constrain any sovereignty devolved to us. I am pretty clear that we have the right to put desolate housing schemes under the immediate ownership of their inhabitants and assist them with resources, such as dynamite, which will enable them to develop their land as they themselves wish. But in other areas, policies will change in ways that we ourselves, alone, Sinn Fein, cannot control. For instance, the Common Agricultural Policy, a racket operated on behalf of the numerous peasant voters of certain European countries, is likely to change because if the Community is widened, as it is hoped, to include countries formerly in the Eastern bloc, inconveniently large numbers of genuinely indigent peasants would join our union, costing well-to-do city dwellers far too much. I am not clear whether we might or might not be prevented or inhibited from imitating an excellent idea of the Movimento Sem Terra of Brazil, as reported recently by Mr Richard Ross, formerly a singer with a musical ensemble called Deacon Blue, who went there at the request of Christian Aid Scotland . . .

AG: You intrigue me. Most people in the wealthy north assume that only pale-skinned persons have good ideas.

AC: Briefly, the MST, in the teeth of opposition from powerful landowners, has taken over underdeveloped land and resettled over 150,000 landless families in the last fourteen years or so. These people enjoy a large measure of self-sufficiency in food. By 2002, the MST plans that all its farms will be completely 'organic'. I should like to suggest to MSPs that we should legislate to ban non-organic farming in Scotland, phasing it out as swiftly as possible. The Wisdom of the Serpent tells me that if we maximize production of organically grown crops, we should be able to export them advantageously, as many customers in the so-called advanced countries are weary of being poisoned by what they eat and fearful about the pollution of farmlands. Of course, with our sovereignty at their disposal, our representatives might simply order all our tenants to comply forthwith . . .

AG: I think, too, that local authorities should supply allotments where folk, in or out of built-up areas, could grow their own vegetables. In most large German cities – Berlin included – there are great areas of allotments, each with a small summerhouse and toolshed. In Britain, the allotment movement has only been actively sponsored by government during the two world wars. Our education system could teach everyone land use as a recreation as well as a necessity.

AC: Yes, and digging and tending our allotments, we would express our actual possession of our own land.

15 February 1999

The bucks must not stop here:
Home Rule Handbook Part 4 – The Arts

ANGUS CALDER, ALASDAIR GRAY

The very learned William H. McNeill, Professor of History at the University of Chicago, has argued that what we might perceive to be specifically human about us – our capacities for speech and for complex social co-ordination – originated many millennia past in the propensity of *Homo sapiens* to dance.

Be that as it may, dance, music and poetry are certainly primeval. Play-acting is something which children enjoy. If there were no books, films or TV, folk would still tell stories. So when well-meaning persons imply that without greater public support the arts must perish, they are being rather silly. The arts are indestructible.

In Iceland, a country with a population which is roughly the same as that of Aberdeen, one may find a large bookshop selling works old and new in Icelandic, Danish and English. Reykjavik has three sizeable theatres where productions, one has experienced, sell out completely, and also an internationally respected orchestra. Talented sculptors and painters have flourished. This is not because large sums of public money are, or could be, devoted to the arts by the parliamentarians in the Althing, a building no larger than a modest town house. It is because an energetic and imaginative people, proud of their own language and culture, provide the enthusiasm to sustain an astonishing level of artistic activity. The aim is not to be world-famous. It is to enjoy artistic production and share pleasure with others.

There are other enjoyable activities which variously enhance the lives of individuals and bring folk together. These include walking or cycling in such attractive hilly country as abounds in Scotland, bird-watching, swimming off clean beaches or in attractive public indoor pools and, of course, participating in sports.

Scots probably invented two sports of international significance. Golf depends on well-kept greens, curling on ice rinks open to the public. It is more unusual to suggest that Scots effectively invented association football, but this can be rationally argued. By the 1870s, when the English still had a charging, primitive, headlong notion of the game, Scots had devised a deft, passing game which became one basis of the sport now played almost everywhere. Another basis of football is publicly provided pitches.

For local government purposes, 'arts and recreation' go together. This makes sense. What they have in common is that while some of the activities thus denominated may make money, sometimes very large sums, for individuals, either directly or indirectly, they normally stand outside the diurnal processes of receiving and spending. As with much TV, major films depend on artistic creativity, but are so expensive to make that only great capital investment can sustain their production. Though big films can lose large sums of money, to create laws and institutions which encourage large-scale film production in Scotland would seem to be hard-headed policy for the Scottish parliament, because the return would be enormous. TV and radio, meanwhile, have such a level of unflagging support from politicians, commerce and the general public that their preservation is not problematic – though Holyrood should probably agonize over what, if anything, can be done to preserve the virtues and prestige of public service broadcasting in a new era of multiple digital commercial channels.

However, almost everyone actively concerned with certain creative arts in Scotland is gloomy about their current state and future prospects. We doubt if rock musicians and soap stars are always despondent. The National Lottery has brought some relief to some hard-pressed arts organizations. Yet there is a general belief that the arts are in a parlous state. Contrary to bourgeois mythology, there is no evidence that those who 'suffer for their art' produce better, or even good, work as a result. They will probably turn to hackwork to pay their fuel bills.

Few painters are prosperous in proportion to their talents (and the lucrative end of the 'art market' often seems to be a sinister mechanism for coining money out of fashionable items of very dubious value – for making, so to speak, silk purses out of the ears of dead sows preserved in formaldehyde).

As writers, we are tearfully aware that Scottish publishing is underfunded. Very good, established writers struggle on incomes which, as Catherine Lockerbie, the literary editor of the *Scotsman*, has put it, barely reach those of junior bank clerks. We are often told that there has been a mighty flowering of Scottish literature in the last couple of decades. However, most of the more talented writers have to find publishers in London to get their work out on time, to get it usefully reviewed and to make a living.

Perhaps there is a geographical imperative at work. We share one of our three (or more) languages with England, where the market for books must be ten times as large as ours. A Canadian novelist published in New York should not be seen as a traitor to her country. But while we may purchase without patriotic qualms a book by one of our authors published in London, we cannot whizz up and down the M6 every week to hear concerts in Birmingham or watch plays in the 'National' (sic) Theatre. We need live music and drama here. How are they to be funded?

Should they be publicly funded at all? Much of the best drama in Scotland is performed in small venues by dedicated actors paid at near-starvation rates to perambulate with touring companies. Folk music can proceed without outside funding. Four classical musicians and a singer could put on a delightful concert at no great expense, and maybe even recoup on ticket sales. Does it matter if Scotland's largest theatres are always short of cash? Would it matter if they closed down altogether, if Scottish Opera and Ballet went under completely in their next financial crises, if the RSNO and SCO disappeared, leaving only their many recordings behind them?

There is even an argument from equity and justice that state funding for the arts, which has favoured art forms enjoyed mostly by better-off people, should be abolished altogether. Should not opera be left to survive, if it can, with the help of its rich patrons? Why not let theatres struggle for existence by putting on plays and other entertainments which will attract full houses? Couldn't the public money thus saved be devoted to rather expensive recreational necessities? Libraries are cutting their opening hours. Swimming pools have closed down. Beaches need cleaning . . .

Yes, but do we need a Scottish national football team? If we answer that question in the affirmative, and most people would do so, even if they don't care for football much, then the case for subsidized arts begins to look stronger. Small to medium-sized countries like Scotland have pride at stake in showing that they can enter prestigious spheres of international competition. Even Iceland has its National Theatre. Finland's achievements in music, notably in opera, with a population like ours, are quite remarkable. Most thinking people, even if they prefer other sorts of music, will be pleased by the international reputation won for us all by the Scottish Chamber Orchestra. Many will perhaps further incline to feel that a well-funded Scottish National Theatre Organization, dedicated to helping our actors become more skilful, versatile and prosperous and to giving our directors the chance to stage full-scale productions of great plays, might be a reasonable priority for our new parliament.

'Flagship' arts organizations – what one might call 'national amenities' – are intrinsically costly. You cannot stage a Verdi opera without a chorus. Shakespeare and Chekhov are usually much more inspiring if enough actors are retained to play all the parts. Festivals, whether huge like Edinburgh's or small but perfectly formed like Orkney's, also require large injections of money. One function of money put into prestige arts events is to help keep prices for the public down so that more people can afford to buy tickets. Parliament, as it considers the arts, will be thinking about four alternative or overlapping sources of funds:

- Sponsorship: This can of course be invaluable, but is intrinsically unreliable. Talented people working in arts organizations can waste immense tracts of time courting and pursuing sponsors instead of actually creating something. Then the potential sponsors in question decide to go on backing golf or marathon running.

- The National Lottery: Unlike taxation of income, which preserves some vestigial attachment to a principle of fair contributions into and out of a pool of money for the common good, this is a sneaky way, when profits are applied to the arts, of seducing ordinary folk into paying for things they may not want and probably won't hear or see. The counter to this profound ethical objection is that such folk would probably gamble the cash anyway, and the profits accruing from this widespread weakness are better applied to theatre and music than to villas in Andalucia for individuals.

- Parliament: National public funding for the arts is currently administered by the Scottish Arts Council, a well-meaning but secretive and unaccountable quango. Suppose that instead a standing committee, or committees, of the new parliament, assisted by expert advice and besieged, no doubt, by anguished appeals, deliberated on the level of funding needed by the 'flagship' organizations: festivals, opera, ballet, the major orchestras, the yet-to-be-founded National Theatre. A committee of elected representatives could then submit to the whole House its opinion that Scottish Opera, for example, needed X amount of euros per year for the next three years, while National Theatre required Y amount of euros. This could be voted on. At regular intervals the priorities involved and the aims of this funding would be publicly debated and reported. People who thought major libraries and museums to be equally, or more, important could have their say.

But MSPs would surely not wish to debate the merits of publicly funding belly-dancing in Braco, writers' workshops in Wick, or folksong in Fochabers ... so ...

- Local authorities: Assuming that local authorities still exist in the format in which they do now, they could be obliged by legislation to devote a proportion of their total annual budgets to arts and recreation. Councils could debate, at their own level, the rival merits of extending library hours, improving sporting amenities, encouraging art galleries, or sponsoring touring theatre.

Finally, the London press has recently exposed, in relation to lottery funding of the arts, a particular example of a vice now generally rife in our public institutions. It might be called Administrative Self-Engorgement (or Extremely Well-Paid Masturbation). Just as administrators of universities, schools and health services delight in introducing bureaucratic procedures, often decorated with the devalued word 'quality' and frequently introducing the sinister term 'assessment', thus making themselves more conspicuous and more important and justifying large increases of salary, so, it seems, lottery funding for the arts in England has been set up as a trough in which bureaucrats and their preferred agents can place their comely snouts. Arts organizations applying for help have been told that their ideas are excellent, but the handing over of lucre will depend on satisfying some dozens of criteria. Many of these are financial. Theatres, for instance, are asked to estimate their audiences and how much they will pay at the box-office, and to explain the 'marketing' devices which they propose to employ to achieve them. (That is, they are invited to offer suitable samples of the solid excrement of male cattle.) A gifted artistic director or administrator will spend weeks or months preparing plans and budgets and then be told that consultants must be employed to assess them. In the case of one unfortunate theatre in the north of England, the consultancy cost so much that the place had to close. The Scottish parliament should consider how to ensure that bids for public money are subject to reasonable scrutiny, while at the same time ensuring that funds set aside for arts and recreation are not engrossed by accountants, consultants and persons with dodgy degrees in business studies who earn much more than the actors, the musicians, even the gallery directors whose plans they thus 'assess', much as crocodiles assess fish.

16 February 1999

Past caring: a history lesson for our schools: Home Rule Handbook Part 5 – Education

ANGUS CALDER, ALASDAIR GRAY

Many Scots care a lot about education. Many also care a great deal about football. It may be that our performance in neither case measures up to our avid caring. But the fact that Scots care so much about education is something with which our new parliament will have to contend.

Our care for education, centuries old, has spawned myths. Here is a version of one of them.

In the obscure village of Strathclarty, the old dominie Cleishbotham presides over the small school. His temper is uncertain, especially with children who cannot recite the prophet Micah with perfect exactitude from memory. However, behind his wizened exterior beats the warm pulse of a good man. In the corner of his class sits Hugh, or Shuggie, a child, or 'bairn', of the helot class. He is redolent of the byre in which he is said to sleep, stains from which disgrace his exiguous vestments. But he knows his epistles from his apostles and when Cleishbotham overcomes his nausea sufficiently to approach him closely, his old heart cleaves to a lad whose immediate aspiration is to read the whole of Homer in Greek. He offers free private tuition. The youth proves apt. Ere long the moment comes when the dominie declares: 'You must go to the varsity – but first acquire a sack of oats.'

The benevolent Laird of Strathclarty sees the lad off with a few silver coins. Arriving in Edinburgh, Hugh seeks out the cheapest clean lodgings (by now his personal hygiene has greatly improved) and empties his oats into a drawer. With water these form abundant porridge and on this, scoop by scoop, he lives till scholarships and prizes begin to take him to dizzy academic heights whence he will propel himself to be Professor of Divinity in a distinguished colonial university, to create the *Oxford English Dictionary* (or suchlike) or, in the twentieth century, to invent a war-winning device for guiding Lancaster bombers over Berlin and a particularly successful gadget for waking folk up to a nice hot cup of tea. He will prove himself, in short, to be a 'lad o' pairts'.

The basis of the myth that in Scotland the way to the peaks of education was always freely open to clever lads of lowly origin is that a few such did achieve great things. But the ascent to fame of Burns, Thomas Telford and Livingstone, in different ways learned men, owed much less to formal education than to the passion for self-instruction, then widespread in lowland Scotland. Piety required that every home, however poor, should have its Bible, translated into remarkably good English. To this, beside grim tracts, a surprising number added such items as the poems of Lindsay and Montgomerie and, later, Burns. Workman geologists and zoologists contributed significantly to our store of knowledge of the wonders, as they perceived such matters, of God's creation.

In any case, the international prestige which Scottish education acquired in the eighteenth-century age of 'Enlightenment' was based not on academic pre-eminence as such (for all the brilliance of our philosophers) but abundant tuition in practical subjects needed for success in the professions, commerce and industry. Scottish universities taught science for the sake of producing doctors of medicine at a time when Oxford and Cambridge were still submerged under the ancient classics. Parents (like Burns's) sought private tuition for their children to enhance their prospects in life. Professors and dominies employed in the forerunner of our 'state system' augmented their earnings by teaching for private fees what folk wanted to learn, or wanted their children to learn, not what was thought by others to be good for them.

If lowland Scots were almost universally literate well before most other European peoples, this was because, for both godly and secular reasons, they made it their own business to be so.

A lesson our new parliament might draw from this is that encouraging demand might improve our education more than tinkering with supply. We need to overcome the twentieth century attitude represented by the brother of James Boyle who wrote to him when he was learning things in Barlinnie Special Unit: 'We're not meant to be educated. All these books you're reading, all this art stuff – this is not our world. Stop this.'

However, we are encumbered with numerous existing educational institutions, many of which young people have no great desire to attend. Formal education in these places is on the agenda of the new parliament. What should it do to change what happens in them?

Readers of *The Prime of Miss Jean Brodie* will be aware that 'education' is an extremely duplicitous word. On the one hand, as she knows, it may imply 'drawing out' – as in the meaning of its Latin root *educere*, 'to lead forth' – the special gifts of each particular child. On the other, it may suggest a tyrant hectoring a congregation of small people as Il Duce, Mussolini, Miss Jean's hero, harangued the Italian masses: (Latin root: *Dux* equals 'leader').

The Scottish educational tradition is duplicitous in exactly the same way. We have the prevalent notion – mythical – that Knox started it by decreeing that there should be a school in every parish. (There were a lot of schools in Scotland before Knox's Reformation, and the decree that there should be one in every parish came in an act of 1696, more than a century after his death.)

The stereotype of the grim, tawse-wielding, sneering dominie relates closely to our mythical view of Knox as the unbending opponent of all fun and games. The schoolmaster stands for unwelcome discipline and severity, as in one ditty directed in the northern lowlands against a certain headmaster: 'Mr X is a very good man, he goes to church on Sunday, to pray to God to give him strength, to beat the boys on Monday.'

Yet the most important Scottish educationalist of the twentieth century was, surely, A. S. Neill (1883–1973) who, after experience in orthodox schools, set up his own co-educational progressive school, Summerhill, in Suffolk in 1927. This difficult but sincere and humorous man believed that the pupils entrusted to him should express themselves with complete freedom. 'That dreadful school,' as opponents called Summerhill, associating it with premature, and even practical, sex education, was aimed to 'draw out' their personalities and attainments, not mould or crush them.

'Progressive' ideas such as Neill's spread widely in the purportedly 'permissive' sixties (when the purchase of a condom, in fact, still caused acute embarrassment to chemist and customer alike). 'Child-centred education' was blamed for all the ills of society in the eighties and nineties, though those denouncing it seemed often to revel in newspapers intruding grossly into private sexual behaviour and to connive in advertising techniques which would link any product – from vodka to dog food – with images of sexual 'freedom'.

In particular, 'progressive' ideas have been blamed for innumeracy and illiteracy. Back to the three Rs, taught by system, has been the cry. Yet once the basic 'cat sat on the mat' knack of reading has been instilled, a child can extend its use for itself, ranging through Dennis the Menace and the Simpsons on towards Catherine Cookson and maybe Homer. Why do we have this shibboleth about the key significance of maths teaching? The higher mathematical skills are useful for cracking Nazi codes or extending concepts in physics. For most of the rest of life, we now have pocket calculators. The necessary basic skills of arithmetic can be experientially extended by shopping for toys or adding up scores in games. (Perhaps every classroom should have a dart board.)

If basic skills can be self-taught, what are our schools for? Why was formal education made compulsory in 1872? Partly because of the charitable if sometimes oppressive idea that all children should be instructed in the principles and practices of one brand of Christianity or other, but more broadly because schools were perceived as instruments for disciplining and socializing the poorer classes and making them less dangerous and more useful to the rich.

They made it possible to inculcate in all a notion of the unmatched glory of the British Empire, as nowadays they may feel obliged to instil a sense of the virtues of private enterprise in the free market. If state schools today are happy, lively places it is in spite of the purposes behind their foundation, not because of them.

Of course, teachers in general are decent, dedicated people, underestimated and underpaid like most such. In good schools, children can play games with friends, enjoy trips and activities, learn to draw and paint, act in plays and make music together. They can take delight in interesting thoughts put into their heads by intelligent teachers. Schools can give a buzz to whole adult communities. Providing good schools free to all should surely be an unshakeable objective of the Scottish parliament. (And making university education free again might be a further one.)

However, interesting teachers and responsive charges are likely to have their pleasures spoiled by children who hate school. When they are not playing truant, these children disrupt lessons and create disciplinary problems which can reduce teachers to nervous wrecks. MSPs might ask themselves if it might not be better if education were not compulsory. Why should teachers have to behave like policemen or psychiatrists and spend so much time on children who literally do not want to know them? Might not many of these be better employed as errand boys and shop tenders, or assisting their fathers and mothers at their work, which was once a very common practice?

Most teachers in what is called 'higher education' have met students (sometimes colleagues) who hated school, received bad marks, did evil things, but eventually discovered a desire to learn. An unhappy child reacting against school may well develop into a successful adult. The trait of rebellion may itself be a sign of promise.

So long as information is freely available where people so

motivated can find it, drop-outs and late developers can go most
of the way towards instructing themselves. This is one reason why
we believe that the new parliament should give priority to the
rescue and enhancement of the public library service, with more
funds to permit the acquisition of more books and longer opening
hours. It is bizarre that such places are closed at weekends, when
most folk are freer to use them, though if this were redressed our
underpaid librarians would need to be recompensed for working
even more unsocial hours.

For our generation, free public libraries were keys to the world.
Through them one might indulge a juvenile passion for aero-
planes, learn about the French Revolution or survey the masterpieces of Western drama. One could travel Arabia with T. E.
Lawrence and go to the moon with H. G. Wells. The Internet
undoubtedly has, as they say, 'potential'. CD-Rom offers exciting
possibilities. These, and any successor systems and devices, should
be freely available everywhere in libraries. However, we think there
are still advantages in those rectangular containers of pleasure and
learning which one can devour on a bus ride to the beach, pass
to a girlfriend or keep in a case on the wall. As writers of books
ourselves, we could hardly think otherwise.

Back to the business of the three Rs, systematic teaching of . . .
Despite 'making the trains run on time', Mussolini led Italy to
catastrophe and defeat, not only because his ideas were bad, but
because his weaponry was obsolescent. Much was made not so
long ago of the prowess of Far Eastern children in the three Rs
compared to our own undisciplined brats, corrupted by child-
centred education. We hear less about this now that mathematical
skills have failed to save the tiger economies from serious problems and impending ruin.

Of course it is important that children should be helped to
read and write and acquire technical skills with a mathematical
basis. But when steam came in, folk expert in the arts of navigation
by sail had to adapt to it. Ten-year-olds nowadays who can flip
on videos, play computer games and trawl the Internet often
have, in quite advanced form, skills which their parents and

teachers lack and may find it hard to acquire. History teaches us that there is in fact much less relationship between schools and skills (and prosperous ways of manufacturing objects and making use of them) than much present-day argument assumes. Schools will surely serve Scotland best if they turn out adaptable young people with lively and imaginative minds, even if they misspell certain words and occasionally get their sums wrong.

If our parliament wants to make schools more useful – that is, livelier – they should give urgent attention to the pay of teachers. Granted that we produce too few scientists and technologists, may this not partly or chiefly be due to the fact that lively graduates in the relevant disciplines can earn so much more in business and industry that they would be foolish to take up teaching?

It would be good, too, if our MSPs could transcend the tunnel mindsets which suggest that in times of cramped funding, obviously enjoyable goings-on should be the first target for cuts. If we want a healthier Scotland, why have sporting activities in schools been permitted to decline steeply? Should music classes, of all things, be axed when our airwaves are choked with the noises of people gainfully employed in music through television and radio?

'Those who can, do. Those who can't, teach.' Those incapable of teaching, it seems, become educational bureaucrats grimly determined to deny others such liberties as their own mole-like faculties do not permit them to enjoy themselves.

17 February 1999

Counsel of hope:
Home Rule Handbook Part 6
– Local Government

ANGUS CALDER, ALASDAIR GRAY

Our new Parliament will be relatively 'local' for all of us, compared to Whitehall. Our population of just over five million is less than a third of that of New York, not much more than half that of Paris, and almost exactly the same as that of St Petersburg. If we agree that London, with over seven million people, needs the unified local authority of which it was deprived by the Thatcher administration, doesn't it seem to follow that we could make do with a single representative body controlling all affairs in Scotland? In this era of instantaneous electronic communication, could not Holyrood be directly responsible for fire-brigades in Fife and roads in Lewis?

Heavily publicized scandals have given local government in parts of Scotland a very unsavoury reputation. For years opponents of a devolved parliament invoked the spectre of 'Strathclyde councillors' and their Lowland like dominating the new assembly to the disadvantage of honest fisherfolk in Buchan and decent hoteliers in Highland Region. Might not the tables be neatly turned if representatives from Shetland helped to control Glasgow's linked housing and crime problems and Edinburgh's obsession with attracting visitors were weighed alongside the desire of Aberdonians to get a bigger slice of the tourist trade?

An answer might be that while some of the tasks now allotted to local councils might be more efficiently and imaginatively handled by the Holyrood parliament (and dealing with bad city housing schemes could be one of these), others should stay with our thirty-two local councils or perhaps be devolved further to elected bodies which parliament might create.

We should delight, surely, in the differences which exist between regions in our country. The great opponent of the 1707 Union, Andrew Fletcher, had a vision of a Europe of city states in which Inverness would rank equally with Edinburgh. Shetlanders have long been prone to see no great advantage in being governed from Edinburgh rather than Westminster. The Western Isles council building in Stornoway, with its facilities for simultaneous translation between Gaelic and English, already rather resembles the parliament houses of certain small independent nations. The development of a new Highland Party suggests that Holyrood will always be confronted by devolutionist demands.

In our new Scotland, we should consider daily what we can learn from examples set in other countries. Perhaps the most relevant comparisons will always be with our prosperous and enlightened Scandinavian neighbours. Denmark and Finland have almost exactly the same population as Scotland, Norway has less than a million fewer people. Sweden, at nearly nine million, is in a bigger league, along with Portugal, but still fails to match the population of Paris.

Clearly, land area matters when we are discussing how much local government is needed where. It would seem rather grotesque if Norway and Finland, both with three times Scotland's area, were governed entirely from their respective capitals. Denmark, however, has less than 17,000 square miles compared to Scotland's 30,000-plus. How is local government structured there?

Copenhagen, with over one and a quarter million people, is a district on its own. It has a city council of 55 members with an executive of one chief burgomaster and six other burgomasters appointed by council for four years. The rest of the country has 14 counties, each with an elected mayor. So far, that looks like a ratio of elective local government to population much lower than what we have in Scotland – 15 councils to our 32. However, there are also 275 communes with district councils ranging between 7 and 31 members each, all under elected mayors . . . If we take out Copenhagen, that gives an average of one mayor for less than 15,000 people. If one further throws in 2,100 elected parish councils, it seems that the Danes have a commitment to local democracy far more intense than we can readily imagine in our present Scotland, where the Ukanian state has steadily beaten down a once-proud tradition of local initiative.

The Finnish system seems to derive distantly from the top-down traditions of the Tsarist Russian Empire of which the country was for some time part. The national president appoints governors for six provinces. Each governor directs a provincial office and many local districts. But there are also 452 municipalities. With an average population base even lower than Denmark's communes, these raise taxes for the same types of purposes as Scottish councils. They form associations to fund such major services as hospitals. Alan Grant of University of Dundee Library Information Services, who dug out this information, and much else, for us, could not forbear to remark at this point: 'Lord save us, a democratically run health service!'

Obviously, we need to know more about how Scandinavian systems operate in practice Do the 435 municipalities of Norway – average population 10,000 – actually cut much mustard, and if so how? But it seems that Scandinavians must have some of the passion for local self-government which once inspired the citizens of Glasgow in days when that city was a world leader in municipal reform.

The great phase of Scottish municipal initiative began in 1855 with the astounding plan, empowered by the Glasgow Corporation Water Works Act of Parliament, to tap Loch Katrine as a source of clean water for a growing city. The £1.5 million which this cost would translate into a sum of NASA proportions today. By 1859, 50 million gallons of water a day were speeding along a 35-mile route which included 13 miles of tunnelling and 25 important aqueducts. So Glasgow got off lightly in the cholera epidemic of 1865–6, and other Scottish towns copied its example.

The thriving middle class of Glasgow, generally contemptuous of the aristocrats who ran Scotland's countryside in their own casual fashion, created the most advanced municipality in Britain. A writer commented in 1903 that in Glasgow a citizen 'may live in a municipal house . . . ride on the municipal tramcar and watch the municipal dust cart collecting the refuse which is to be used to fertilise the municipal farm. Then he may turn into the municipal market, buy a steak from an animal killed in the municipal slaugh- terhouse, and cook it by the municipal gas stove. For his recreation he can choose among municipal libraries, municipal art galleries and municipal music in municipal parks. Should he fall ill, he can ring up his doctor on the municipal telephone, or he may be taken to the municipal hospital in the municipal ambulance by a municipal policeman . . .'

Since Glasgow and other Scottish cities did not, unlike their counterparts south of the Border, expect to make a profit or subsidize the rates from such municipal initiatives, they antici- pated what we have long come to take for granted – the provision of free or cheap public services open to everyone as of right. Tony Roper's popular play *The Steamie* is fuelled by nostalgia for days when ample public amenities compensated for the admittedly dreadful housing in which so many urban Scots lived. When the Glasgow Corporation made all elementary, and some secondary, education free to all in 1892, and threw in bursaries to enable poorer children to attend fee-paying schools, it expressed a Scot- tish sense of community which extended from the rich men who rewarded the cities in which their workforces lived with magnifi- cent public buildings, to the ordinary folk who kept clean in municipal baths where there prevailed what George Orwell would call 'the naked democracy of the swimming pool'.

However, the Ukanian state, with its inordinate centralizing tendencies, has made sure that such things couldn't happen now. It performed a useful service, moving in by 1900 to reorganize and regularize the smaller Scottish local authorities which had lagged behind English counterparts in such fields as public health. On the other hand, its abolition of parish councils in 1929 did away with a tier still significant in Scandinavia, and arguably helped to promote the apathy about local government characteristic of Scotland today, when turnouts in elections are obscenely low. According to evasive statistics available from the Scottish Office website, 'general government expenditure in Scotland' in 1996/7 amounted to £4,748 million – just over a tenth of the UK total. (Since defence expenditure is not included, this cannot be the complete picture.) Scotland's local councils between them budgeted for net expenditure in 1998/9 of £6,675,997,000. But of course the disproportion between central and local spending is far greater than these figures appear to suggest, since six-sevenths of moneys disbursed locally are supplied by the Government.

Government also lays down absolute obligations on local government. Class sizes in schools, for instance, must not rise beyond a certain point, and with teachers' pay regulated nationally, that immediately entails such and such a council spending more or less exactly such and such. Aggregating all local budgets we find that education, at 36.5 percent, and social work, at 16.6 percent, between them account for over half the total. Police, at 10.2 percent, might seem curiously scant, though the proportion is significantly higher in Glasgow and Edinburgh, lower in Hamish McBeth country. Environmental health (a mere 0.8 percent) is one area where councils have wide scope to express their own priorities. Glasgow, with a budget of 1,005 million, elected to spend £5689 million on this, Edinburgh, from a total of £557,679 million, a not very discrepant £3303 million. It is interesting that South Lanarkshire, from a total budget of only £363 million, sets aside only a few thousand less than Edinburgh for environmental health. Highland puts in well over 1 per cent of its total, and with not much more than half Edinburgh's budget devotes several thousand more pounds to this purpose. Perth and Kinross and Stirling are other authorities which spend over 1 per cent on it.

Herein we may find an instructive tale. We produce, in town and country alike, immense quantities of refuse, ranging from sweetie-papers and fag ends to fridges and wrecked sofas. Perth and Kinross provide twenty civic skip sites, of which eight are 'transfer stations', where bin lorries offload into refuse freighters. These latter, with their special skips for bottles and paper, are denominated 'civic amenity sites' and by law all local authorities must provide them. But Ukanian law does not specify how many. Stirling, stretching from fair Killin in the north to Bannockburn, from Dunblane to Loch Lomond, provides just one civic amenity site. It is in such spheres of life as this that the representatives whom a minority of us bother to elect express freely what they take to be the Will of the People.

Landfill sites, where our detritus largely wends, are not necessarily ecological abominations and are a valuable source of methane gas. However, from April 1999 there is a 'landfill tax' of £10 a ton. What, ideally, should we do with our waste? The Swedes came up with a stunningly simple answer. Forget about recycling. You can burn the lot – sofas, bottles and all – and cost-effectively, fumelessly, generate electricity. The Swedish example has been successfully followed in Nottingham. The only snag is the heavy capital investment required.

The slogan of the revolution which produced the USA – 'No Taxation Without Representation' – can be turned round, thus. 'No Representation Without Taxation'. In Germany, local authorities are given power of general competence and can raise their own taxes. (One does not hear of capitalists terrified of taxation fleeing that prosperous country *en masse*.) In Britain, the pathological fear of democracy which infests Westminster ensures that local government basically exists to apply, with greater or lesser discretion, national statutes, using funds mostly doled out by the grudging Ukanian state. It would be interesting to inspect the budgets of the Glasgow Corporation in its Victorian heyday. The pathetic proportion of total expenditure represented by a mere £110,000 budgeted in 1998/9 by local authorities for museums, galleries and libraries would surely have been exceeded – yet not at the expense of waterworks and tramlines and underground railways. A soupçon of tax-raising discretion has been devolved to the Holyrood parliament – the notorious 3 per cent up or down on income tax. But could not Holyrood itself enable local authorities to put ambitious plans before the people and ask them, according to their means, to pay for them? We are sure that interest in local government elections would revive mightily if issues involving local taxation were vigorously presented to the populace. And why not create, on the Finnish model, a tier of government at very local level, with power to act decisively and to spend money? Not all Scandinavian precedents are favourable. In Ibsen's great play *An Enemy of the People*, good Dr Stockmann is hounded out of a small Norwegian town when he exposes the pollution from a tannery which affects the spa waters on which its tourist trade depends. We are told that in one rather prominent Scottish burgh there was a time when a local bylaw prohibited Catholics from playing sports in public parks. National statutes are necessary to protect individuals and all of us against narrow parochial prejudice and self-interest. But Holyrood might attempt to reinvigorate Scottish democracy by striking the right balances of power between centre and locality in all areas of public spending.

18 February 1999

Scottish secretary may find it tough toeing

TIM LUCKHURST

At the Scottish Labour Conference a senior and well-connected party activist approached the secretary of state's special adviser, Wendy Alexander. The activist was concerned about the tone of speeches made by Donald Dewar and his Cabinet colleague, the Defence Secretary, George Robertson. Alexander offered a succinct explanation. 'That's the line,' she said.

As all good Blairites know, 'the line' is sacred. It is centrally decided with the approval of the prime minister himself. Those who deviate from it are deemed heretics and banished from the corridors of power and privilege. Once the line has been chosen all good New Labour apparatchiks know what they must do next. They must stay 'on message'.

That message is clear. The SNP is now public enemy No. 1 and must be attacked relentlessly. Another conference delegate was shocked by the level of venom directed its way.

He added: 'The government has just achieved a significant triumph in the Gulf by threatening the use of British force. I thought the Defence Secretary might want to talk about that. He was personally involved. Instead George Robertson conveyed the impression that Alex Salmond is more dangerous than Saddam Hussein.'

Why has Labour decided on such a dangerous tactic? There is a powerful argument that by focusing so much fire on the Nationalists the Government simply hands the SNP a profile it does not deserve.

Several Scottish Labour back-benchers take that view. One summarizes it like this: 'It is quite appalling that Donald Dewar used the SNP against the Tam Dalyells of this world throughout the referendum campaign and then began to be nastier about them than anyone else. It leaves a nasty taste. The party is going sour on Donald.'

Another argues: 'Donald's self-esteem has never been higher than when he was able to play the father of the nation role in the immediate aftermath of the referendum. He seemed much happier doing that.

'He should remember that without Alex Salmond he would never have delivered such a convincing result.'

Critical back-bench opinion is that Mr Dewar has been ordered to go on the offensive after losing influence in the Cabinet to his arch-enemy, Derry Irvine, and other devolution sceptics like the Home Secretary, Jack Straw. That case is unprovable but it is not implausible.

To understand the scale of Mr Dewar's problem it is necessary to return to the summer of 1996 and Mr Blair's shock decision that Labour's devolution commitment would, after all, be subjected to the double-lock of a binding two-question referendum.

It was immediately clear that Mr Blair was not wholeheartedly in favour of a Scottish parliament with tax-raising powers. The conventional wisdom at the time was that Mr Blair had insisted on the referendum and the shadow Scottish team, then led by George Robertson, had buckled under intolerable pressure.

An alternative explanation is now current. It is that Mr Blair was keen to ditch the tax-raising element of the devolution package altogether. The referendum idea was a last-ditch bid to save it, proposed by the party in Scotland and backed by pro-devolutionists in the shadow cabinet as the only way of keeping the constitutional convention plans intact.

This explanation contends that Mr Blair accepted the dual-question referendum first because he thought the electorate would vote against tax-raising powers and second because he knew that a referendum could be presented in a positive light whatever the result on the second question. When Labour won the general election, Mr Dewar fought a highly successful campaign in Cabinet. He persuaded his colleagues, not least the prime minister, that a grown-up Scottish parliament would consolidate the United Kingdom. The problem with Dewar's argument is that he is one of very few senior politicians who really believes it. One London-based academic and Labour insider says, 'Donald underestimated the fluidity of the situation. Traditionally, Labour existed to operate for one social class within a unitary British state. Devolution changes the game. Blair was right to be dubious. After all, if you, give a nationalist most of what he wants why on earth should he go away?' Another critic of the Labour leadership says, 'Labour is simply giving people two reasons to vote for the SNP: first because it can now form a government and second because it is clearly more in tune with classic Scottish welfarism than Blair is.' Mr Dewar is a profoundly sincere man. There is no doubt he does believe his own case. But even his admirers are beginning to ask whether he might be spectacularly wrong.

11 March 1998

Rule of flaw

IAN BELL

Britain diminishes, nationalism grows: it is the defining assumption in these islands at the century's end. More than that, there is the assumption within the assumption, the belief that one fact flows from the other, that the withering of British identity has bred nationalism, or that nationalism has weakened the bonds of Britishness. Goodbye to all that. So people who write on the condition of Scotland invariably wind up considering whether, and to what extent, it is possible both to be Scottish and British.

Even while conceding through clenched teeth that loyalty to the idea of Britain is much reduced, Unionists still insist a dual identity is both possible and desirable. Nationalists assert the opposite. Hence the brawling. Yet both camps share a diagnosis, each pointing to the retreat from empire, the rise of the European idea and the resurgence of a Scottish identity displacing the sense of Britishness. All this has happened. But are these events causes or coincidences?

Nationalism may be filling a void left by a decay in the belief in Britain. Did nationalism, the politics of identity, really cause the decay? In the constitutional debate, this matters and matters most to those who would keep Britain intact. It falls to them to prove the worth of the Union and the meaning of the British idea. If it still lives, any nationalist competition will be defeated. If it is dead or dying, the story is over. Discovering which is the case will matter more, in the end, than arguments over block grants.

Historians such as Linda Colley tell us British patriotism was always something of a fabrication, a kind of propaganda exercise meant to justify the political and economic drive for Union and assimilation. That being so, it is not enough for Unionists to say simply that Scotland and England are better off together than they would be apart. There is no basis for comparison, no alternative experience with which to test the claim. Britain has to stand on its merits, on its intrinsic worth as something more than a refuge from the supposed horrors of Scottish independence. And Britain stands, if it stands, as a constitutional settlement.

So how would things be if the decline in the British identity had less to do with post-imperialism, Europe or new nationalisms than with its own nature? What if the problem is within Britain, perplexing as that may seem to those who fantasize that something called Britain has been around for a thousand years? What if loyalty is being withdrawn from Britishness rather than transferred, like a side bet, to Scottish nationalism? Problem: the British constitution was not created for the twentieth century, far less the twenty-first. It was built, chiefly, on the property interests of a small group in the seventeenth and eighteenth centuries without any real democratic assent and grew from their struggle with royal power.

The constitution was not made, in its essentials, to accommo-date universal suffrage or democratic systems of election. More than that, its fictions and its forms are all but designed to circum-vent representative politics. Westminster's second, revising, house is a wheezing compromise and likely to remain so, while the party system of the Commons is a parody of freely elected government meant to detach members from their constituents.

All this has long been recognized, criticized and defended. Critics observe that the British system falls short of any reasonably accurate definition of democracy. Defenders point to stability, continuity and durability, forgetting that dictatorships often meet these same criteria. The argument, at its extremes, is between purity of expression and pragmatism, between those who say British democracy does not work well enough and those thankful that it works, in its fashion, at all.

But the point (and the problem) remains: this is not, in its essentials, a system designed for a world in which people take rights to equality before the law and in the ballot box for granted, a society in which deference is mostly a joke. The British constitution was not designed for an era distrustful of elites, castes and conventions agreed between themselves by small groups of the powerful. Above all, the constitution did not evolve – the favourite euphemism – in expectation of a century that would produce, all but simultaneously, the Labour movement, women's suffrage, the mass media, neo-republicanism and challenges to the sovereignty (meaning the legitimacy) of Westminster itself.

Yet those opinion pollsters who bother to ask discover two things: that a third and upwards of voters believe Britain is not actually a democracy at all and that perhaps three-quarters believe we tolerate a voting system incapable of producing governments which reflect the views of most people. It is no secret, meanwhile, that turn-outs at elections have been falling steadily for fifty years. There is a case for saying that the age of mass (if not class) politics has alienated the majority from a system of government designed for the convenience of the few and still operated, whenever possible, for the benefit of the few.

Britain has no sacred piece of paper enshrining its fundamental laws. Instead, its constitution is the system itself, the entire, tangled ball of string, and its history is its character. The constitution is, above all, a collection of rules for the distribution of power among a self-selecting minority. For all the chatter about the people's this and the people's that, the majority scarcely participate and believe, it seems, that they have no real stake in their own polity. Perversely, all the talk of the pride we are supposed to take in our democracy has bred a deep cynicism.

What might that do to the British identity when the British system, the British way of doing things, is supposed to be part of our inalienable heritage? Consider: a Commons committee appointed to scrutinize the work of the executive produces a damning report on the Foreign Office's role in the export of arms to Sierra Leone. The event should be part of the constitutional mechanism, numbered among the checks and balances. Instead, the prime minister dismisses the report with something approaching contempt. And why? Because he can. He can because Tony Blair's party has a huge majority in the House of Commons. Yet this Labour landslide was achieved with fewer actual votes than John Major attracted for the Conservatives in 1992. Margaret Thatcher was, similarly, a minority taste in her time. And why? Because our skewed electoral system is preferred – allegedly for reasons of stability and continuity – by the people who benefit most from it. They happen also to be the only people with the power to change the system.

But then, part of our tradition's glory is parliament's second chamber, there to scrutinize and revise, to check and balance in the people's name. The small difficulty, for those interested in democracy, is that the largest faction in the Upper House got there by being born; the rest attained the ermine through patronage. The executive, in turn, controls the means of reform and can make of the Lords what it wishes, a hash not least. These are but three examples of the ways in which the British system alienates the majority who have been brought up to believe they should have a say, unlike their forebears, in the way they are governed.

But what else was Scotland's demand for home rule if not a wholehearted rejection of the constitutional settlement? After all, interspersed between the Scots and unrepresentative government there is, for now, merely another thicket of bureaucratic centralism called the Scottish Office.

Scotland has made the change. It has identified the failure of Britain as it most immediately affects the Scots. It has gouged a little more power from the British constitution by insisting on closer representation and the repatriation of some of the means of government. This is held, even by Unionists, to mark an erosion of British identity. But if you leave the question of national identity aside, what have the Scots said about the nature of our politics that could not be said by anyone in Britain? What does all this mean for England's sense of a British identity?

The Government came to office promising it would make good democratic deficits. Scotland would have its parliament, Wales and Northern Ireland their assemblies. The Lords would be reformed and representation restored to London. Bureaucratic secrecy would be broken down through freedom of information and the regions of England would have such authorities as they desired.

It has not worked out that way. Labour has been caught between the principle of devolution and the instinct to retain control. A constitution that was already incoherent has been treated, to paraphrase the economists, to a series of asymmetric shocks, unbalanced still further by what appear, often, to be *ad hoc* solutions to local political problems. Thus, for reasons never explained, it was unthinkable for Scotland to have a parliament without legislative powers yet perfectly acceptable for Wales to have a talking shop and Northern Ireland, come the day, to enjoy a kind of nursery assembly. In any case, the relationship between these bodies and Westminster (West Lothian's question and the rest) is left in obscurity.

Meanwhile, the idea of English regional government bobs up and down on the tide of received opinion while London is granted a super-quango. Back at the ancient heart of things, Lords reform begins to look like a fudge, a populist gesture to allow in the commonality while ensuring that the Upper House does not acquire any sort of popular mandate. Elsewhere, freedom of information legislation (the little we are allowed to know of it) does not sound precisely comprehensive. Piecemeal is the kindest word to apply to Labour's reforms.

It is all very British, and at its heart is an intellectually messy, utterly British notion: that the Westminster parliament, supernaturally bonded with the Crown, is sovereign in all things. It was this concept that got Tony Blair into such a fankle while campaigning for devolution. It is this concept that stifles any idea of popular democracy or coherent reform. Yet on this bedrock rests the British system and identity. When you try to talk or legislate around it – by arguing, as Labour has, for Scotland's right to a parliament – you are generating constitutional nonsense, not dissolving it.

But see how things work: under the constitution, sovereignty underwrites the supreme power of governments regularly elected by a minority of the voters, far less of the people. This sovereignty makes a mockery of home rule. Above all, the sovereignty of Westminster (circumscribed these days only by European obligations) turns the political executive (these days a single individual) into an elective dictatorship. Tony Blair did not become all-powerful simply by clever use of the media, mastery of his party, or charisma. The British constitutional settlement, our nineteenth-century antique, all but demands a maximum leader.

Mr Blair himself may believe sincerely that this is wrong, that power should be devolved from the centre. In practice, and in power, he is entangled in a contradiction. The doctrine of the sovereignty of parliament does not allow him the impulses he claims to feel. All this, nevertheless, is held to be the core of British identity, more important than family ties, picture-book royalism, wars or shared culture. We are subjects, still, of a constitutional monarchy with an unrepresentative parliamentary system driven by an almost mystical belief in its own self-preservation.

It is many things but it is not democratic. It does not connect people with power and it does not give an equal voice to all. Whether it can be saved from itself, with time running out, is the real challenge for Unionists.

6 March 1999

Spare us convoluted excuses for dithering . . . Call to delay referendum is a rush to exploit mourning

IAN BELL

There are people who will vote on 11 September who were babes in arms the last time Scotland tried to make a decision about home rule. The argument itself has staggered on, endless year in and weary year out, for even longer. Say what you like about the Scots, we know how to kick a political theory around.

That being so, the undignified rush to exploit mourning for Diana, Princess of Wales, as an excuse to postpone the devolution referendum is as disingenuous as it is depressing. After twenty-five years thundering away on the subject, it seems, Tam Dalyell, MP, will be cruelly deprived of his sacred democratic rights if he is denied even a week in which to tell us what fools we are. Terrible, is it not?

But hands up, nevertheless, all those who do not know precisely, in grim, relentless, repetitive detail, exactly what Tam thinks? Who has just emerged from a very deep mineshaft? Who has just been rescued, twenty-five years on, from a desert island?

This is not to deny that some people are astoundingly ignorant of the issues. There are people walking around who think devolution is God's answer to Charles Darwin. The point is that there are always people who are at all times astoundingly, proudly ignorant of most things.

The difference, as it applies to home rule, is that those who are still in the dark must have made a real effort of will to keep themselves that way. How, realistically, could you have set about avoiding the issue? By never once opening a newspaper? By never once switching on a television? By never entering a pub?

The people who remain oblivious are the sort who have taken care not to care. One more week of ritualistic insults will make no difference to them. If they do not care by now, they never will. The same could be said of every electorate in the world.

Equally, it is specious for some to pretend that we are losing a week in which slumbering Scotland could be galvanized to grasp its destiny. If Scots cannot be roused by now, cattle prods would not help. On this occasion, at least, there has been no shortage of pride, passion and detailed information. Indeed, the level of public involvement has been unprecedented – one good reason why sane people simply want the issue settled.

We are glutted with argument. Were the debate to be extended to next spring, as Mr Dalyell demands, apathy would vitiate the entire exercise. The Linlithgow MP probably knows as much. The circumstances may be tragic but a break from a dull and dogged campaign is perhaps just what voters need.

Consider the alternative. Postponement would require the recall of parliament. Time would also be needed for postal votes to be organized. An extra month, perhaps six weeks, would be required.

Who contemplates that with relish? Who really wishes to hear more of arguments which are in grave danger of becoming arid and self-defeating? Besides, you do not convert the undecided simply by repeating the same few points endlessly. The truth of the home rule campaign – and one reason why it has seemed so dull – is that there is damn all left to add.

It is odd, in any case, that demands for a postponement of the referendum or a resumption of the public argument are being heard both from the Yes and the No camps. This speaks of a certain panic on either side, one spooked by polls (which only show an emphatic, as opposed to a crushing, Yes, Yes vote), the other side fearful that its last chance to spread gloom and uncertainty is slipping away.

Any number of weird and convoluted excuses for delay have been emerging as a result, few of which seem to appreciate the country's mood after Sunday's tragedy.

One – Mr Dalyell's – has it that Scots are 'bewildered' by the implications of the home rule proposals. How so? Did not the Government's white paper become a best-seller even as it was being dissected by every newspaper and broadcaster in the land? Was not every household caught in a blizzard of leaflets? Have there not been headlines, comment, television debates and radio rows on a daily basis? One can only stand in awe of anyone who proposes to surpass all that in a week.

But then, the people demanding a postponement of the plebiscite, from either side, show an alarming lack of confidence in their arguments. On the one hand there is Mr Dalyell and sundry No campaigners, proposing to achieve in a few days what they have failed to achieve in twenty-five years. On the other there are Yes supporters who agree that the public knows nothing and add that Diana's funeral is somehow a threat to home rule.

This last, disreputable argument runs as follows: the funeral for the princess will show Britain coming together in grief. This, in turn, will become a kind of advertisement for the unifying virtues of Britishness. Ergo, people will be less keen on home rule.

It is a bizarre and tasteless gambit. First, it drags the death of the princess into politics. Second, it appears to presume that devolution is somehow an attack on the Union between Scotland and England when the Yes campaign proposes the precise opposite. Third, it suggests that the will of the Scottish people is far from settled and might somehow dissolve in one emotionally charged weekend. See us? Fickle, or what?

And all this just to secure a few more days of a campaign that has begun to bore those who care while failing utterly to reach those who refuse to give a toss? All this as a paltry distraction from extraordinary national grief? All this from people, Yes and No, who claim to believe passionately, and as matters of principle, in the causes they evince?

Spare us, Lord, the Scotland that needs just a wee while longer to dither a little more. Spare us the Scotland affronted by raw human emotions and desperate for an excuse to avoid them. Spare us Scotia's sophistries. Spare us our betters.

And, Lord, let's get on with it.

3 September 1997

THE ENGLISH

Victims of a crisis of confidence

GAVIN ESLER

I have begun to worry about the English. Some of them, a minority, thankfully, are developing the least lovely characteristic of my fellow Scots – the chip on the shoulder. The sense of being a victim. The national anthem of whining. And like all family rows, it starts with apparently trivial things.

'Why is it,' an old English friend demanded to know, 'that the English cheer on the Scots during the World Cup, but the Scots never cheer on the English?' I have heard this before, but never, as in this case, from someone utterly uninterested in football.

Another friend, a Londoner, and a long-time Labour supporter, was particularly aggressive. 'Too many Scots in the government,' she insisted. 'It is like being colonized.'

Well, you are the experts, part of me wanted to exclaim, but I bit my tongue. Then a third old friend, a woman with a slight grasp of history and an even more tenuous grasp of football, wondered why the Scots never support 'the British team.'

That old confusion again – English, British, Scottish. As an expatriate Scot married to an Englishwoman with two American-born children, I find all this particularly unsettling. I love the English, despite their funny ways, or maybe because of them. My father-in-law, a delightful heart-of-oak Englishman, is still puzzled by my lack of enthusiasm for warm beer and cricket, which he assumes is a genetic defect.

A few years ago, when England were playing Norway, he

demanded to know which team I supported. 'Make it more difficult,' I suggested. 'How about England playing Iraq?'

He has looked at me strangely ever since, and in the interests
of marital harmony, I have avoided all further displays of Celtic
humour. But, recently, it has begun to get serious. There was
English newspaper coverage of the kicking to death of the teen-
ager, Mark Ayton, in Balerno, and the suggestion that his English
accent played a part in the attack on him. The innuendo was that
the Scots and the English are western Europe's Albanians and
Serbs, just one step away from ethnic cleansing.

Now, I know nothing of the precise circumstances of the Ayton
case, but I do know Balerno. I was brought up in the Edinburgh
suburbs near by – and there were always teenage boys who needed
no excuse, no English accents, to start some nasty inter-village
fighting.

Then, last week, one distinguished columnist in *The Times*
wrote about Scottish politics as if trying to figure out the differences between the Hutu and the Tutsis. (The Tutsis are the big
ones.)

Another *Times* columnist talked about the 'over-representation
of Scots in the government' by pointing out that the four top
jobs – prime minister, Lord Chancellor, Chancellor of the Exchequer and Foreign Secretary – are held by Scots.

I cannot remember *The Times* being so exercised by the fact
that the same four offices were held by Englishmen or women,
presumably because (Malcolm Rifkind excepted) *Times* colum-
nists generally assume this to be the natural order of the universe.

One has to wonder why a newspaper owned by Rupert Murdoch, once an Australian before he decided to become an American, is so hung up on mere details like nationality. Perhaps it is
because the Canadian-owned *Daily Telegraph* is similarly
obsessed.

Whatever the cause, nine members of the Cabinet do indeed
have roots north of the Border. Many sub-Cabinet appointees are
from Scotland too, and there is growing irritation against what
one friend described as the army of squat Scots in suits driving

the New Labour revolution. Again, I do not remember similar anxieties about, say, the unrepresentatively high number of farmers in previous governments. But behind this, I scent an unlovely and unaccustomed feeling of English victimhood.

Certainly, to judge from my conversations about the World Cup with numerous London cab drivers, and the cabbies' political soulmate, the Conservative MP, Alan Clark, English fans who get into trouble abroad are victims. The foreign police – remember Heysel, Dublin '95, Rome '98? – don't understand them. Louts from Tunisia or Argentina travel across whole continents to have a go at the fragile, but patriotic, little darlings.

Now, it is not obvious where this sense of victimhood may be leading, but it extends to some English irritation at Scottish pride for the good behaviour of Scotland supporters in France. My friend Mark – a Partick Thistle supporter, and consequently a very sad case indeed – tells me there really is a conspiracy at work.

He claims every Scottish supporter in France knows nothing so much annoys English nationalists as the spectacle of men in kilts not behaving badly. Consequently, even the roughest hooligan from Ibrox or Parkhead is an angel in France. I like this idea very much. After all, it was a Frenchman who remarked that the best revenge is living well. For nationalist-minded Scots, perhaps the best revenge now is behaving well.

22 June 1998

Common culture,
but divided loyalties

ALLAN MASSIE

When you step between fighting dogs you are apt to get bitten. Nevertheless, the temptation to take part in the Neil–MacWhirter scrap* is irresistible. Our editor-in-chief writes of 'Scotland the self-deluded'; Iain MacWhirter calls the boss's piece 'overstated and alarmist'; heady stuff on both sides.

Is Scotland anti-English? MacWhirter says no, and he is right. Is the public expression of Anglophobia more frequent and apparently more acceptable than it was, as Andrew Neil suggests? Undoubtedly. That is the worrying thing.

Racism and xenophobia exist in every society, but in a decent and self-respecting society, people don't say publicly what they may occasionally think. They don't give vent in a crowd to expressions they would be ashamed to state as individuals. If you heard a chant of 'if you hate the f. . . . . . . Jews, clap your hands', you would be worried about the health of the society that found this acceptable. Substitute 'English' for 'Jews' and you have a Tartan Army chant. That is, or ought to be, worrying.

Like Andrew Neil, I am puzzled and dismayed by the weakening of a sense of being British. I was brought up feeling comfortable

---

* In columns in the *Scotsman*, Andrew Neil, then the paper's editor-in-chief, and Iain MacWhirter, one of its main political commentators, found themselves at loggerheads, over whether Scots are anti-English.

in a dual nationality, both Scottish and British, sometimes one uppermost, sometimes the other; and to take pride in both. This may have been because of the influence of the Empire and two terrible wars. It was also because the centuries of Union had created a common culture, neither uniquely Scottish nor uniquely English, but British.

Scots sometimes talk resentfully of the English influence on Scotland, but the Scottish influence on England has been at least as strong. The dogma of Mercantilism, subscribed to by generations of English political economics, was blown away by the writings of Adam Smith. The greatest moral influence on early Victorian England was exerted by another Scot, Carlyle. We speak a common language; till very recently the King James Bible supplied both Scots and English with words for moments of high emotion.

I once asked Alex Salmond if he didn't feel at all British, and he said he didn't; yet he can think of himself as a European. I can do that too, but I am less European than I am British, and it seems odd to me that any Scot as admiring of Scotland's nineteenth-century achievement as I know Salmond to be can so easily slough off his British cultural inheritance.

Scottish cultural nationalists like to play up our links with Europe, which are indeed strong, although no stronger than England's. But not even French culture is part of our being as English culture has been for centuries, even before the Union. Our greatest Renaissance poet, Dunbar, regarded Chaucer as his master. Sir Walter Scott found that the two writers he most often quoted were, first, Shakespeare, and, second, Burns.

It is axiomatic in Scottish political argument now that the sense of Britishness was weakened by Margaret Thatcher, who imposed on us an alien dogma. This puzzled the Lady, who thought she had got her ideas from Adam Smith (with a bit of help from the Aberdonian Dr Madsen Pirie).

It puzzled, and puzzles, me too because so much of what she said was the sort of thing the grown-ups used to say when I was a boy in Aberdeenshire. It was nineteenth-century Scottish

Liberalism, which, as Michael Fry, journalist and Conservative candidate, has written, 'had an ethical basis. In voting Liberal, Scots voted for a view of man as a free, independent being – and for not much more.' That was a view of man that fitted my farming forebears, staunch Liberals and adherents of the Free Kirk created by the Disruption of 1843.

So, unlike many, I never found Thatcherism un-Scottish. It represented one strand in Scottish tradition, even if no longer the dominant one, which was now collectivist. Now, encouragingly, I find Scottish members of a Labour government – Gordon Brown and Gus Macdonald, for instance – who have moved some way from collectivism to Scottish old-fashioned Liberal Thatcherism, which says you stand on your own feet.

Where I am with Andrew Neil is in his criticism of the line taken by so many Scottish Labour politicians in the 1980s, when they told us we were being 'cheated out of our democratic rights', and so, as he puts it, 'disaggregated the Union for their own partisan purposes'. In doing so, they prepared a rod for their own backs, stoked the fire that now singes, and may yet consume, them.

So we have the absurd spectacle of the very Scottish Labour Party being scorned by the SNP as a branch-office controlled by London, whereas the reality is that we have a British government dominated and directed by Scots.

And so to devolution. Here again, I am with Andrew Neil, and against Iain MacWhirter. It may seem odd that those of us who argued against devolution should now wish the Scottish parliament to have more powers than it is to be granted. It is odd, but it is not illogical. We tried to persuade our fellow-Scots that the Union was not only valuable but best preserved in unitary form. We failed.

But still, valuing the Union, and accepting the democratic decision that there should be a Scottish parliament, we wish a new settlement that will bring stability, and benefit both Scotland and the United Kingdom. And we can't believe that creating a parliament with the power to spend but without the responsibility of imposing taxes can either make for good government or prevent recurrent and damaging friction between London and Edinburgh.

We think the devolution scheme in its present form will work to the benefit of the SNP, and that the best way of preserving the Union is to make the Scottish parliament more responsible.

The authors of a pamphlet issued by the (Tory) Tuesday Club say flatly that 'a parliament which does not tax is a sham parliament'. So it is logical for Unionists to say now that, since there is to be a parliament, it should be a real one; that a sham parliament is indeed an exercise in self-delusion.

24 August 1998

Strains begin to show

IAN BELL

For some of us a devolution backlash, so called, cannot come soon enough. If resentments have begun to simmer in the south the sooner they are brought into the open the better. Equally, if the home-rule settlement is flawed (and it is) we should face the fact and deal with it. Most of all, we need to understand how a devolved Scotland should comport itself when feelings in England run high.

Clearly, the process has already begun, with certain English politicians getting their retaliation in first, well ahead of the creation of the Scottish parliament. The row over the tuition fees to be imposed on English students studying in Scotland begins to look like a case in point. The rude noises being made over the Barnett formula and relative levels of public spending are another. Scotland may think of itself as a special case; in parts of England it is deemed a sight too special.

On one level, of course, the noises from below the Border are a monumental folly. Anyone in England who wants to hold the Union together should think twice before noising off about whingeing Jocks – and then say nothing. After all, if we are unwelcome in the partnership we have a clear, logical alternative. English politicians may not consider themselves propagandists for Scottish independence but that, often, is their function.

Equally, Scots might do well to rid themselves of the delusion that England will pay any price, forever onwards, for the pleasure of our company. Some in the south would happily see the back of us, and make no bones about it. They are content, increasingly, with the idea of England and with English nationalism. What does a Tory back-bencher care, these days, about Scotland? Besides, how might someone in England draw up the balance sheet? Their taxes pay for our public spending, they might say. They will subsidize our little parliament, they might add. And are we grateful? When the subject of Scotland impinges on the consciousness of England it is generally in the form of a grievance.

This is not a reaction to be found only in the Home Counties. In the hard-pressed areas of the north of England the appearance of special treatment for the Scots, whether in inward investment, public spending or devolved parliaments, has begun to rankle. More importantly, the resentment is being voiced.

Consider the row over tuition fees and the four-year Scottish degree. From our side it seems that a clear threat is being posed to Scottish institutions, the degree itself, or both. Juvenile nonsense about rich English snobs littering Edinburgh and St Andrews aside, it seems obvious that Scottish universities are to be handicapped in the competition – for that is what it now is – for customers. Meanwhile, the incentive to offer the four-year degree is being eroded. Labour having sold out the point of principle in the argument over fees, the damage in Scotland is to be compounded.

Think of it, however, from an English point of view. Why should English authorities subsidize Scottish universities, particularly when they insist on keeping their odd degree structure? Why not provide a compelling reason for English students to make their way to York or Durham, to the economic benefit of those areas? If institutions must compete, why should there be special treatment for the Scots, especially when money for education is tight?

Besides, have not some in Scotland developed a taste for being rude to English students? Are they not constantly complaining that too many English voices can be heard in Scottish universities? If they want a cure for 'Anglicisation', here it is. And let them continue to delude themselves about the innate superiority of Scottish education while they are at it.

So runs the refrain, but it is one that is finding an echo in many areas of public life. Last week, for example, Sir George Russell, the chairman of the Northern Development Company, denounced the Barnett formula* as unjust and unnecessary. From his point of view a prosperous Scotland has used blackmail, to all intents and purposes, to gain a bigger slice of the public spending cake than it deserves.

As many others have pointed out, not all of that cake is identified. The south-east of England, in particular, enjoys numerous undeclared subsidies. But with the Treasury select committee preparing to sniff around the Barnett formula, inward investment being 'reviewed', and a growing suspicion that sections of the Cabinet are unhappy with the deal granted to Scotland, home rule begins to look a little problematic.

Quite simply, an old consensus is falling apart. The idea that a price must be paid to keep Scotland in the Union no longer goes unquestioned in England. It is, if you like, the mirror image of the belief that Scotland would be better off independent. But it is being voiced in the face of a constitutional settlement explicitly intended to hold the United Kingdom together. A Scottish response depends entirely on your attitude towards that proposition. The accurate answer probably is that separation is inevitable sooner or later. Nevertheless, an alternative suggestion might be that the fact of home rule, with all its anomalies, will inevitably put pressure on the British constitution as a whole. The complaints we are hearing from the south of England might be the first signs of these strains, in other words.

Thus, a Nationalist would be quite content with growing English resentment – the more, he might say, the better – and live in hope that the likes of Jack Straw, the Home Secretary, will

* The so-called Barnett formula was devised by Joel Barnett, a former Chief Secretary to the Treasury. It was intended to be a stop-gap measure and simply allocated to Scotland and Wales an agreed proportion of any government-authorised change in public expenditure acorss the UK.

persist with his attempts to put the Scots in their place. One good backlash deserves another. Keep the insults coming, says a Nationalist, the quicker to drive Scotland to independence.

But where does that leave supporters of devolution, meaning the greatest number of Scottish voters? If they are serious about staying within Britain, do they accept that it is legitimate for English politicians to have a say in Scottish home rule; that it can ever be right for English MPs to cut public spending in a devolved Scotland by scrapping the Barnett formula?

Besides, if devolution is to be such a boon, is there any justification for special treatment? Are we entitled to maintain a sense of grievance, reacting to every slight, real or imagined, while insisting on subsidies? If home rule is really meant to keep Scotland within the Union, why does it increasingly look like an excuse for an argument?

Some of us predicted that outcome long ago, of course. The real point might be different. Devolved or independent, Scotland must develop a way if relating to, and working with, its southern neighbour. Language and attitudes need to change, here as in England. Taking a few cheap shots at English students who actually want to be in Scotland is not the way to do it. That brand of patriotism is the last refuge of the puerile.

3 November 1997

National pride perverted

ANDREW NEIL

The pavements outside London pubs blessed, or cursed, depending on one's view, with Sky television are littered with signs tempting patrons over the threshold by reminding them that they can watch all England's and Scotland's World Cup matches. The assumption is that, apart from the usual bunch of red-and-white-daubed yobs who give English football a bad name, the bulk of London's pub-goers have an interest in watching both teams and seeing them do well.

Apart from expat Scots who live in London, of course, the vast majority of fans will be supporting England for as long as they remain in the competition. But if – and it is admittedly a very big if – Scotland survives to the later stages and England does not, it is Craig Brown's team that will attract the cheers in London pubs when they put one past their opponents.

Not necessarily so in Scotland, where dislike bordering on hatred of the English is fast becoming the nasty side of our renewed nationalism and risks poisoning the moment when Scotland takes charge of its own domestic affairs. Given its head, this trend could turn a proud, tolerant, outgoing nation within the United Kingdom into an isolated, bigoted outpost consumed with hatred for our neighbours to the south.

The second part of *The Scotsman*'s opinion poll, to be published tomorrow, will reveal that barely 50 per cent of Scots would cheer England were Scotland to be knocked out. In the eighteen-to-thirty-four age group, the supposedly young, forward-looking part of our population, more than half would support their opponents. It is a sad testimony to the irrational mood in Scotland that, in an England v. Iraq contest, a sizeable minority of Scots would be supporting Iraq.

These depressing statistics will come as no surprise to anyone who has listened to invective chanted from football stands; but Scotland's growing problem is that resentment of all things English is no longer confined to mindless yobs. It is endemic in large sections of the middle class, who pervert the proper emotion of national pride, especially at sporting occasions, by assuming that vitriolic anti-English sentiment is one of its essential components.

The first signs of infection were when the posh folk at rugby internationals took up 'Flower of Scotland'. Embarrassed at first, and haltingly unsure of the words of this supremely irrelevant ditty, which encourages the national predilection to hark back to the past, even occupants of the royal box got the hang of it after a few seasons and eventually sang with gusto. They sang most loudly when England were the opponents. The Hampden roar against the auld enemy had been doucely transformed into a more upmarket Murrayfield drone.

Those who refuse to face up to this unattractive aspect of a modern Scotland on the verge of home rule will dismiss this either as wrong or irrelevant. It isn't wrong. In any match in which England is involved, the voice of too many Scots will be heard in approbation only when they fail. It isn't irrelevant. For intolerance of our English partners in the British nation reaches beyond the fevered ninety minutes of a football or rugby match and now infects everyday life in sometimes alarming ways.

Last year, a nineteen-year-old boy in Balerno, hardly the Harlem of Scotland, was assaulted and killed by three others who chanted 'English bastard' as they finished him off. They were not football rowdies acting in a drunken post-match frenzy, but middle-class children from respectable families. It was deemed by some a more tragic incident because it turned out he was Scottish anyway. There is an evil hidden assumption in making that point: had he been English after all, his assailants could have pled the fact in mitigation.

Anti-English sentiment is not always demonstrated so brutally; but it sours the atmosphere in many other ways, a drip, drip, drip of intolerance that has settled deep in the Scottish psyche. 'White settlers' in the Highlands have been grumbled about for years behind the twitching curtains of established locals. But Scottish Watch and Settler Watch are two movements proud to peddle their intolerance in racist terms, inciting direct action to drive any English foolish enough to interpret a Highland welcome in a literal sense back across the Border.

They make the absurd allegation that the English are taking over Scottish institutions. Throughout the Union, the takeover has more usually been the other way as it is today: even a cursory glance at Tony Blair's Cabinet should convince any fool that that argument, were it to be taken up, would come more convincingly from the mouths of the English.

In the long drive towards a Scottish parliament, spurred on by the ulterior motives of the SNP, anti-English sentiment has been harnessed, mostly covertly but sometimes overtly, in the cause of home rule. SNP recruiting literature directed at students is not only openly anti-English, it can be foul-mouthed, puerile and offensive. How can any party which expects to be taken seriously, as Alex Salmond's does, think it smart that even its most youthfully indiscreet student supporters use the language of anatomy and excrement as a weapon in political debate? The shrewd and sensible Mr Salmond should rein these idiots in.

The Scottish Labour Party, too, must shoulder part of the blame. Their sustained attack on Margaret Thatcher's government over her eleven years in power was largely inspired by a genuine hatred for her policies, most of which as New Labour it has had to swallow and even advance; but the attack was sharpened by lampooning her 'Englishness' and, thus, irrelevance to all things Scottish. Now in government, it is reaping the seeds of the nationalist whirlwind it sowed in opposition.

Sane voices must be raised to counter the anti-English cacophony that now risks doing real damage. Why should anyone with pride in Scotland and all she stands for tolerate activities and language amounting to racism which, if practised against any other identifiable minority, would result in prosecution?

Indeed, in one case, that of Graham Power, the deputy chief constable of Lothian and Borders police, the jury is still out over whether or not, for the purposes of discrimination, Scots and English can be defined as distinct races. That it has come to this is shameful.

Scotland, always keen to trumpet a self-perceived reputation as an outgoing, internationalist nation, risks deceiving itself. If, as today's poll tells us, 52 percent of Scots favour independence (I would relish that being put to the test of a referendum), such self-deception could help forge a flawed nation, unrecognisable to those of us who have always been first and foremost Scots, while proud of our British tradition and seeing our English partners as friends.

The English, the vast majority of whom bear us no ill will, have every right to be puzzled. Prejudice dressed as patriotism is not a banner Scots have ever waved before. Nor should we now as we stand on the brink of home rule.

5 June 1998

In search of Middle Scotland

ALAN TAYLOR

I was born just in time to witness the Coronation of Queen Elizabeth II and the conquest of Everest. Judging from the photographs in old copies of the *Illustrated London News*, the former owed more to Hollywood than history or heritage, a Cecil B. De Mille extravaganza with the entire nation enlisted as extras. The latter, I see now, was an attempt to demonstrate to the rest of the world that Britons, with a little help from Sherpas, could still get to the top when they really put their minds to it.

Re-reading the magazine, I got a strong whiff of jingoism, of euphoria and of desperation. Both events were greeted with arrogance, with the idea of Empire still potent. The coverage was so gung-ho it was nigh hysterical, as if the country was trying too hard. But the thought lingered that if Britain could put on such a show and scale the highest mountain, it was not yet on its uppers. The future was not as bleak as everyone had been led to believe.

Little did we realize then that both of those landmarks were part of the same watershed. Having survived the war, Britain had changed, and changed utterly. But change came agonizingly slowly. Any sense of triumphalism soon faded in a post-martial hangover. Growing up in a small Scottish town, I was not aware that I was living in a time warp, but I surely was. As Ian Jack relates in his book *Before the Oil Ran Out*, 'we lived with old times; concurrently in the 1910s and Twenties as well as the Fifties'.

No one in our house mentioned the war, or if they did I never heard them. I had an uncle who fought and died in it and I once saw faded pictures of him in uniform and of the cemetery in Italy where he is buried. Beyond that and Commando comics, the war, the Second World War, was as remote to me as the Crusades or the sacking of Rome. But there was, I believe, a residual sense of Britishness, as if the war had been the mortar that kept Britain as a unit, in the same way that Britishness had been cemented by the Great War at a time when nationalism was beginning to flex its muscles.

Nor was there any sign of disintegration. My family was not overtly political and what pride we took in Scotland was low-key. Our sense of Scottish history was patchy and we knew very little about Scottish culture. We were aware of the tradition of invention and industry, knew that Carnegie had emigrated to America and introduced capitalism, though we could not have put a name to it at the time. We knew, too, that as the archetypal Scot on the make he had found his wealth burdensome and had used it to underwrite libraries and church organs and other good causes. On Sundays, our impossibly old minister, Rev. Mackay, reminded us grimly that there was as much chance of a rich man entering the Kingdom of Heaven as a camel passing through the eye of a needle.

The only occasion on which we were conspicuously Scottish was New Year. Back then it was special because such celebrations were so rare. There was whisky and black bun and shortbread. Teuchter music played insidiously and we sang along to the 'Scottish Soldier' and marvelled at the White Heather Club dancers. If this was Scottish culture you could keep it. I yearned to defect to the south where, in the heart of Middle England, a place as mythical and mystical to me as Tolkien's Middle Earth, everyone wore pinstriped suits and bowler hats and maintained their composure with a stiff upper lip.

Scotland in the fifties and even the early sixties was a grim place. Those who could escape did, many of them ex-servicemen who had discovered not all of the world was grey and damp and depressed. With modest pensions they could live well in the

Mediterranean. The poet Alastair Reid was one of them, becoming a professional itinerant. Returning to St Andrews in 1970, he had an opportunity to take stock of Scotland. 'Something,' he reflected, 'was always chiming. Punctually at five thirty in the evening, the streets emptied; shop locks clicked shut almost simultaneously up and down the street. It felt like a place that had taken care to deprive itself of surprises.'

Here, if it exists at all, in an affluent town with an ancient university and a rural hinterland, is Middle Scotland, which Tony Blair says is just like Middle England, with the same hopes and fears, values and standards. Only I find it hard to equate Blair's idea of what Middle England represents with what I know of Scotland and its people. Blair's Middle England is forged in the image of David English's *Daily Mail*, with its base sense of values and parochialism worn on its sleeve like a decoration for bravery.

The 'genius' of David English, who was publicly endorsed by Tony Blair and whom the obituarists inexplicably eulogized as the greatest journalist of his era, was apparently to discover the prejudices of Middle England and pander to them. Thus the *Mail* revelled in xenophobia and homophobia. It embraced Thatcherism with a vengeance and made greed a virtue. It turned single mothers into pariahs and any minority group into hate figures. It rejoiced in classlessness but swiftly created an underclass. To be homeless or jobless or fatherless was to be an outcast.

It gave its support unquestioningly to the Government and saw nothing amiss when the SAS killed three IRA suspects in a Gibraltar street, turning them instantly into martyrs. It wanted better schools and hospitals, but the notion that it might be necessary to raise taxes to achieve this made it froth at the mouth. It liked to rant on about the bucolic countryside, but shouted down anyone – from fell-walkers to Swampy and his ragged army of ecological warriors – who wanted to preserve it from the developers. The fox was public enemy number one.

The *Mail* turned anger into a commercial proposition. Sales rose exponentially under English and Blair was among the first to recognize the potential in the phenomenon: pander to Middle England and Labour might yet win the election. With assurances that they would not be any worse off than under the Tories, Middle Englanders turned on honest John Major and sent him bumpily to the boundary. For New Labour, the *Daily Mail* formula proved efficacious in every way.

Tony Blair is under the impression that Scotland – Middle Scotland – was also 'on message', that it voted for Labour – New Labour – with the same agenda as its counterpart, Middle England. The evidence for this, as John Curtice noted yesterday in *The Scotsman*, is risibly thin. Scots are more relaxed about tax increases if they will result in better schools and hospitals. They do not like to see sections of society demonized. And, crucially, they have a stronger and more cohesive sense of self-identity: Scottishness is not the albatross it was for the generation before the war.

How this transformation came about is hard to pinpoint. Perhaps it's true, as the late John P. Mackintosh intimated, that with a dual identity there is always the possibility of opting out and choosing to be Scottish if pride in being British wanes. Over the last several decades there has been a gradual erosion of the feeling of Britishness in Scotland which has become stronger as a sense of Scottishness surfaces. Rather than being submerged by three centuries as Britons, modern Scots have a more palpable sense of themselves than previous generations.

No one grasped this better than John Smith, Blair's predecessor, who was in tune with the Scottish psyche in a way that the prime minister never can be. Smith personified a middle-of-the-road Scotland, recognizable to any post-war Scot. Smith was in his teens in the fifties and though he was older than me, I doubt if there was a huge difference in our upbringings. Council housing was the norm, and not far from where I lived there were sooty tenements with their ill-lit closes and dark secrets.

No one in our neck of the woods would have dreamt of going to a fee-paying school even if they'd had the money. There was a boarding school on our doorstep and the boys who went there looked like aliens. The streets were our Hampden and Wimbledon. Social life centred round the church. My father was a kirk elder and still is. He was also leader of the Life Boys, a position, it seemed to me, of great and grave eminence. My mother went to the Young Wives' Club or the Women's Guild. There were coffee mornings and summer fêtes and the annual Boys Brigade camp to Chirnside or Dollar; the names changed but the fields were always mined with cowpats.

Two brothers from the Red House home orphanage were Life Boys. Much later I learned that one of their fellow boarders was the child murderer Robert Black and I felt sick at the thought that he lived so close to us and that I might have known him. At Christmas we went to the Eastern Star Christmas party. In the summer we went to seaside B&Bs or hired a caravan. Our first car was a Ford Popular, our second a Ford Anglia. After church and Sunday school we'd often drive to Innerleithen where we had relatives. It seemed to take an eternity.

Lately, I have been reading accounts of the lives of John Reith and John Logie Baird, and though they were born at the end of the nineteenth century, their upbringings do not appear hugely different from mine. Presbyterianism was the backbone of society. There was a strong sense of stewardship and community. Anyone who got above himself was swiftly taken down a peg. Selfishness was one of the top sins; charity began somewhere in Africa in a place probably discovered by David Livingstone or Mungo Park.

This was a Middle Scotland of the mind; its actuality is much more difficult to identify. When such values have been drummed into you *ad nauseam* they're not easily supplanted. What is amazing, however, is how they survive today in such a secular world. Maybe it's in the genes. But there does seem to be a difference in attitudes north and south of the Border, if the various political surveys are to be believed. Scots do seem to be more altruistically inclined than their southern neighbours.

This is particularly true of young modern Scots, which may be why so many émigré Scots in the media find the new-found appetite for separatism mystifying. Their generation saw the

Union as a means to an end. They were in the mould of the eighteenth-century Scots who were determined to exploit the new Union. In her book *Britons*, Linda Colley writes: 'As shrewder English politicians recognised . . . Scotland's loyalty to the Union and Scotland's manpower would have to be paid for by giving its titled and talented males increased access to London and its plums.' But what pertained for nearly three hundred years no longer holds. Plums, these days, are ripe for picking all round the globe, not least in the European Union, the burgeoning Empire of the twenty-first century. Nor do young Scots hark back to the war, when it was absolutely crucial that Britain put up a united front. Thus they have no nostalgia for a Britain which gave its blood, sweat and tears to combat fascism.

Nor, indeed, do they have the same reverence for the royal family, which earlier generations had blindly venerated, and which Middle England still holds in awe. The Diana cult, for example, is regarded by many Scots with bemusement and suspicion. The Church of Scientology is more sympathetically received. Any references to the People's Princess are meant ironically. It is seen as what it is, a meaningless and cynical soundbite aimed by the Downing Street spin-doctors at weepy Middle England. If it was meant to bind the country, it succeeded only in loosening the stays still further. Given the opportunity, the likelihood is that Scotland would opt for republicanism.

How this translates into votes is the tricky question. Tony Blair has said there is no difference between those in the north and south of Britain who voted for New Labour. At best this is naive; at worse it is ignorant. For pro-Union devolutionists it is a dangerous stance to take.

Better by far for the Government to recognize national and regional differences and rejoice in them while playing on the benefits of a United Kingdom. The more we are made to appear the same, the more apparent will be our differences.

Middle Scotland, if there is one, has spoken.

18 July 1998

The two tartan armies

IAIN MacWHIRTER

All right, so it's a cliché: football politics – the national psyche dissected on the terracing. Every time Scotland figures in international football championships – Euro 96, the World Cup in 1994 – pundits get their scarves out and pontificate on what it all says about the 'national mood'. And why should I be any different? The tradition goes back to 1978, when the rout of Ally's Tartan Army was supposed to have been such a national humiliation that Scots lost confidence in the devolution referendum.

So here are this column's top five footie questions of the moment: How many Scots will jeer English defeat? Does Tony Blair support Scotland? Will the SNP's showing in the opinion polls increase or decrease? Is there a sign of greater national identity following the referendum? Can Scotland suffer inevitable defeat with grace?

At a gathering of Scottish MPs in Westminster after the Brazil game, the assessment was, well, pretty predictable: 'It's Scottish history, isn't it?' Spirited defence, brilliance against the odds, and then defeat by an own goal. Scottish football expressed the Scottish character in its own special way.

But it's more than a game, of course, and this year, we're told in the nation's press, there is a more sinister undertone to football-terrace nationalism. There has supposedly been an outpouring of ethnic hatred lately as the SNP has risen in the opinion polls. An evil force is abroad, painted blue and singing anti-English songs. Caledonian xenophobia is on the march!

Comparisons have been drawn between the SNP's campaign against Scottish Widows and the Nazis' assault on the Jews on Kristallnacht. The murder in Balerno of Mark Ayton, singled out by thugs allegedly because he had an English accent, is being used as evidence of incipient race war. Actually, one of his attackers was English, and it is not at all clear that this was a racist attack. Nevertheless, we're warned that Settler Watch could be about to start burning cottages and that the soliloquy from *Trainspotting* about 'English wankers' is a manifesto of ethnic hatred.

Jings, crivvens! Alex Salmond and his blackshirts are poised to exploit the outflowing of national sentiment in the World Cup; to inflame these dark forces; to recruit naive footie fascists into his blitzkrieg assault on the British state. The National Front surely had nothing on this.

So when I encountered the tartan horde in Glasgow airport on Sunday, I was braced for the worst. Maybe they'll think I'm English too – after all, I come from Edinburgh, which is almost as bad. Look down, avoid eye contact, keep smiling. What I encountered was a crowd of tartan clowns in floppy hats and face-paint which looked about as threatening as student rag week. Down in London I came across them again, massed around the Eurostar terminal at Waterloo and looking considerably the worse for wear. But so far the lager seemed to be remaining in the bellies of the beast. Any large crowd of drunken young men – whatever their nationality – is liable to turn nasty, and the police were ready for them.

I draw no firm conclusions from this, except that some 10,000 Scots have clearly acquired a fine sense of their own absurdity. They looked so daft, with their redhead wigs, tammies and Saltire lum hats, that it was difficult to look at them without laughing – not a reaction that might have been advisable in the past. There was a time when gatherings of the Tartan Army would have held a real menace for anyone not decked out in the national colours.

In the seventies, the Scots had a wholly legitimate reputation for football violence, as anyone who remembers the Scotland–England matches can testify. Many middle-aged Scots still have bits of English goalpost on their mantelpiece – or claim to. In those days, Scots on and off the pitch were brittle, prickly and deeply insecure. Many still are, of course. But there is an irony about this latest assertion of national identity in Paris which cannot be other than encouraging.

Of course, you might say that nowadays Scots have little choice but to laugh at themselves. After all, our role in these championships is to get gubbed – with whatever dignity we can muster, but gubbed nevertheless. The Scots have learned to accept that, in this sporting sphere at least, the glory days are long past, and that Scotland is a small nation with a very mediocre football team. Many Scots now seem to regard their team with affectionate disrespect, rather as Glasgow media folk have adopted no-hope Partick Thistle as a kind of mascot. 'Don't come home too soon' – this is ironic football fanaticism, where the point is that you don't win.

Indeed, it is intriguing that while Scottish football nationalism has become laced with self-effacing humour, English football nationalism has become markedly harsher and more menacing than it used to be in the seventies. Prompted by xenophobic tabloids, there was real nastiness in the attacks on 'Krauts' and 'Scuttle heads' two years ago during the Euro championships. It almost made you glad when England missed the all-important penalty in the shoot-out with Germany. Not, of course, that you'd ever see this column indulging in such expression of anti-English sentiment. Far from it. Some of my best friends . . .

But in the end, who cares? Football has become a ridiculous, overblown spectacle, far removed from the proletarian opera it once was. And the days when you could discern any real political significance from the performance of the players or the fans are gone. There are other things to worry about than whether twenty-two overpaid Scots, many of them expatriates, can kick a ball about a field better than anyone else. Independence for a start. The recent opinion polls seem to indicate that something seismic is taking place in Scottish political opinion. Many, perhaps most, of those young Scots in their kilts getting drunk in Paris are convinced that Scotland should and will become independent within the next decade or so. And this has nothing whatsoever to do with football. Even as national pride in sporting prowess has weakened, the sense of Scottish identity has hardened – emerged in a more enduring form.

Of course, we still don't know exactly how solid is this new constituency for Scottish independence; it could be merely an expression of cultural Scottishness which will evaporate as the hard practical choices emerge in the campaign for the Scottish parliament next year. Or it could be that since the September referendum Scotland already feels that it is another country, and that the momentum will propel Scotland into some form of independence in Europe. This is a question which we simply cannot begin to answer at this stage in national development.

But as for those footie questions at the top of this column, the answers of course are: lots; only in Scotland; neither; no; and yes – we've had plenty of practice at being gubbed, after all.

11 June 1998

Something rotten in Utopia

JOYCE McMILLAN

Once upon a time, in the aftermath of the 1992 general election, I sat talking to a woman, English by birth, who was an ardent supporter of the campaign for a Scottish parliament. She was telling me why she had decided to make her home north of the Border. 'Believe it or not,' she said, 'when I was a child my mother used to stop me from playing with other children in our street because they had runny noses and common accents. Now can you imagine a Scottish mother ever saying anything so snobbish and silly?'

I thought about the housing scheme in Renfrewshire where I had spent most of my early life, and about the day-to-day struggle of most of the mums there to do exactly what this woman's mother had done, to keep their kids away from the scruffy ones and the snotty-nosed ones, and to get them to 'talk properly', which meant not in Scots. But I also saw, quite clearly, that there was no point in protesting. For this woman had woven her politics, and a key piece of her identity, around a pure piece of nationalist myth-making, the idea of a little Utopia free of snobbery and greed, which she called 'Scotland'; and when that kind of myth takes hold, and acquires such emotional importance as a source of political hope, facts that don't fit the picture might as well not exist.

Now this week's *New Statesman*, in a headline over a despairing piece by the London-based Scot John Lloyd, has described Scotland in 1998 as being 'awash' with anti-English feeling; and so, in a certain sense, it is. But as Lloyd himself concedes, this is not really a matter of Scots being any more inclined than they ever were to mistreat English people as individuals, to rejoice in England's defeats, or to bully English 'new kids' in the school playground. What has happened, rather, is that the national myth of Scotland as a better place, a kinder place, a more communitarian place – and of England, by reverse image, as a place where 'they' are less friendly, more devious, more snobbish, and more materialistic – has now taken such a grip on the popular imagination, in the run-up to the Scottish parliament, that English people can no longer ignore it.

Of course, if you ask Scots in the grip of this argument whether they really mean that all this is true of everyone in Newcastle or Manchester, or of their own English colleagues and friends, they'll generally say: 'Of course not; I don't mean them.' But in a world where politics increasingly resembles a television game-show, people apparently have no difficulty in maintaining good relations with most real English people they meet, while continuing to believe, in the world of virtual reality, that 'England' is a kind of national shop of horrors; and of course, there is no way that English people, hearing this kind of talk, are not going to feel both excluded and insulted by it, and increasingly inclined to express hostile feelings in return.

And the problem about this disturbing state of affairs is that it's almost a crime without a culprit, and therefore difficult to remedy. Some blame the SNP, although in fact the record of that party in denouncing anti-English prejudice and including English-born people in its inner councils is exemplary. The big thinkers of Scottish civic nationalism might have guessed that some people would find it hard to distinguish between the idea that our English connection is a problem, and the idea that there's something problematic about the English; but it's hardly their fault if the man and woman in the street can't handle the idea of national self-determination as pure principle, and insist on stuffing it with moral and pragmatic content in a way that is either fanciful or racist.

Some are inclined to blame the UK's traditional first-past-the-post electoral system, which fed the myth of 'Labour Scotland' and 'Tory England' throughout the eighties. Some blame Margaret Thatcher for starting the rot with her determination to show the whole of Britain that there was 'no alternative' to free-market policies, red in tooth and claw; she played the dangerous game, in a democratic system and a Union state, of seeking to deny voters a genuine choice of social policies, and drove them instead to seek an alternative in the politics of identity and schism.

And then there are those – legion nowadays – who blame the Labour Party, for its careless use of quasi-nationalist rhetoric in the late eighties, for its cultural and intellectual failure to think through its constitutional reform programme in terms of a radical New Unionism, and above all for its over-enthusiastic endorsement of Margaret Thatcher's 'no alternative' approach to market economics, which once again has left Scots of the Left with no Utopia to dream of except a Scottish one. Of course, their dreams are largely fatuous; socialism has never been embraced by a majority of Scots, and is unlikely to be now. But we seem to have reached the stage where the myth of kindly socialist Scotland will have to be subjected to a 'reality check'; in other words, only in attempting to put it into practice will we find out how much, or how little, of a myth it is.

So where do we go from here? Well, the pragmatist in me suggests that the longer the debate about Scotland's constitutional future goes on, the more dangerous racist talk it will generate; and that in the interests of damage limitation, we should therefore cut to the chase, have the blasted independence now, and start work on building friendly civic relations with all our neighbours, including the English. The woman of principle, on the other hand, says that this is spineless capitulation to a reactionary spirit of schism and divisiveness among the ordinary citizens of the world which has to be fought wherever it rears its head, even when the battle promises to be bloody and futile.

But in the meantime, here is what I know. I know that the sense of alienation many Scots experienced from Westminster government during the Thatcher years was not a matter of being Scottish, but a matter of being human. It was a feeling shared by millions in England, not only those geographically far from the south-east, but ethnic minority groups, human rights campaigners, professional associations, men and women of the decent Left everywhere; and they expressed solidarity with Scotland's aspiration for home rule because they saw it as part of the struggle against the worst, most centralizing aspects of Thatcherism. Now, it seems we Scots are in a mood to forget those links for a while, to cast the English as the problem, and to make the break. Some say it's just a phase we're going through, a necessary stage of history. But if that's true, it's not a phase people of genuine goodwill can be expected to enjoy. We may have to live through it; but liking it is another matter, and too ugly by half.

14 August 1998

THE BLAIR FACTOR

A Nation with its
Own Identity

PETER MacMAHON

Tony Blair bursts into the Cabinet room at No. 10 Downing Street. Followed by his two closest aides, his long-time personal assistant Anji Hunter and jocularly intimidating spokesman Alastair Campbell, he shakes hands, smiles that smile and heads for the table.

Shirt-sleeved and tanned, he enquires about the state of Scotland and picks up a copy of this paper to see for himself. Where, he asks, after leafing through the pages, is the editorial section? The prime minister has been getting a hard time on some editorial pages of late, particularly over his policy on the single currency.

Satisfied that *The Scotsman* had not, that day at least, followed suit, he orders tea, sits down and gets on with the business at hand.

It is often said that Mr Blair does not like Scotland and that the feeling is mutual, although there is little to support the assertion. The prime minister has made it his business to travel north of the Border frequently, including trips to the Hebrides, where he opened the Scalpay Bridge. He has fond memories.

'I loved it. It was a great visit. People were really friendly. We had a fantastic time. Midges slightly difficult – as your pictures indicated. What is different about a visit like that is that you get to meet people and talk to them at some length, whereas usually you go round the place and you don't get the real chance to talk to people.'

The Labour MP Calum Macdonald once described the Scottish National Party as midges – always with us as an irritant. The main task for Mr Blair and Labour is to swat them away by the time of the first Scottish elections on 6 May.

So first to a question which Donald Dewar had some difficulty answering in the recent *Scotsman* debate: What can a Scottish parliament do in Scotland that a Labour government at Westminster can't deliver?

'The answer to that is very simple,' the prime minister replies. 'That you can do things that are distinctive without being divided off. The Scottish Labour Party can take different types of policy initiatives, can be different and maybe sometimes more imaginative or bolder in initiatives it takes on education or the health service or crime.

'For example, Donald Dewar's announcement of a drug enforcement agency for Scotland – we've not yet got to that position in England . . . we may get there. You can put forward policies that are distinctive and different.

'It's a democratic but it's also a practical argument. I think you will find naturally that the process means that on education Scotland can find its own way to do things and, although strictly the Scottish Secretary can do that now, he is still bound into a very Westminster style of government. If you look at it in a different context, when you get a mayor for London, he or she will have a different type of agenda.'

It is, at least, one answer. Mr Dewar take note. But what of the bigger picture? It is often said that Mr Blair has embarked on a massive raft of constitutional reform – Scotland, Wales, Northern Ireland, reform of the Lords, a mayor for London and much more – without knowing where the final destination is.

He treats that argument with contempt. 'Where we end up is perfectly obvious. I never understand it when people say this to me. We end up with a system of government that is more accountable, closer to the people and where we've removed some of the idiosyncratic and less justifiable aspects of the British constitution.

'It is absurd that in one of the major cities of the world [there is] no London-wide government, in exactly the same way that it is ridiculous that hereditary peers, the vast majority of whom support only one political party, namely the Conservatives, have ownership of the upper house of our legislature.

'So when people say "Where does it all end?" it's perfectly obvious where it ends. It's like putting the European Convention on Human Rights into British law. It makes government more accountable, brings government closer to the people, gives us decentralization of services and makes the system fairer.'

Does this lead to the House of Lords being the 'constitutional glue' for the United Kingdom?

'That's now in the hands of the Royal Commission and they should be allowed to get on with that,' he parries.

'We're not going to stop at the first stage, we're proceeding to the second stage – let me underline that – but even if we did stop at the first stage it would be a far fairer system than at the moment. I am giving up the right to appoint cross-benchers, independent peers. At the moment I have all the patronage in the House of Lords. I am going to be the first prime minister in ages who is giving up this power of patronage.'

There is an edge in the reply that shows a certain sensitivity to the criticism over 'Tony's cronies' and the Upper House.

In a typical piece of seventies-style Blairspeak he sums up his constitutional perspective: 'Decentralization is where it's going to be at.'

The Government is still left with the problem of where it ends. Will there be a federal Britain, perhaps evolving as the English regions demand elected devolved bodies? If the north-east region, which he represents as an MP, asks that its development agency be transformed into an assembly, can it do so?

'Of course they can. We have said that already but we're not going to push it on people. You've got unitary local government in Scotland, it will require changes in local government too. The position is just less advanced in England than it is in Scotland.

'But, believe you me, when you go to the north-west or the

north-east or you go down to, say, Cornwall, people are talking about greater democratic accountability.

'People in London think that it is ridiculous that they have no system of proper accountability for issues like transport, pollution, the local environment, how we co-ordinate jobs and inward investment into London. This is the debate about which Scottish devolution is perhaps the most prominent part, but it is a debate about the whole nature of how we govern the UK in the future.'

So is it about an evolving federal system? How does he feel about the idea of an English parliament, as floated by the Tories, as the answer to the constitutional questions?

'I don't think there's any desire for that at all, I really don't. I think people are happy with the idea, in England, that Scotland is a nation with its own identity and there had to be a different partnership, a different type of Union for the future between Scotland and England.'

So the future is not federalism and it is not an English parliament. There are, it seems, still questions unanswered.

But on to another. Would it be too much to ask who is going to be Secretary of State for Scotland after 6 May when Mr Dewar has said he will stand down if he is elected First Minister?

'Correct.'

If he will not say on the personal level – and it is virtually certain to be Mr Dewar's deputy, Helen Liddell,* who is highly regarded by the prime minister – will there be a Secretary of State for Scotland at all? There has been a growing feeling that eventually there will be a minister for constitutional affairs with responsibility for Northern Ireland, Scotland, Wales and possibly London.

Politely but firmly he says: 'I have nothing to say to add to what I have already said on that.'

He refuses to be moved further. 'As we set out in the [devolution] white paper, over time, we would look at the position. That is the position and that remains but there will need to be a Scottish Secretary of State, I've no doubt about that.'

---

* In fact, it was John Reid who became Secretary of State for Scotland.

So does it, say, make sense to have a constitutional affairs minister as things evolve?

'It does in the future but we have to examine the case for that.' A little ambiguous but there is clearly long-term change in the air.

So to another ambiguity. The prime minister has famously brought Liberal Democrats into Cabinet committees and has, it is said, flirted with the idea of bringing them fully into government. With the election system for Holyrood likely to produce coalitions in Scotland, is he relaxed about a Lab-Lib deal?

'Em, we're obviously going out to win every seat we possibly can and every vote we possibly can and the question of coalitions waits another time. As Donald Dewar has said, we're not going to start speculating on that. People can make the speculation.'

Relaxed, quite clearly, but what of the broader Lab–Lib love-in? At his first Labour conference as leader he spoke of making the next century the century of the radical and teased his party about what he was up to with the Lib Dems. What did that mean?

'I mean that in the end what the Labour Party stands for, for me, is not some tribal allegiance. It stands for certain values and it stands for two particular concepts, which are progress and justice.

'I think that we should always be willing to understand that there will be people from outside our own political tribe who share those concepts and who would be what you would call modern social democrats. Some of those are in the Liberal Democrats and there is never any harm in admitting that you share a heritage.

'When I look at our political heritage, of course I would look at Keir Hardie and Nye Bevan, but I also look at Keynes and Beveridge and Lloyd George.'

Asked in the Commons about whether Paddy Ashdown would be asked to join the Cabinet, the prime minister resolutely refused to say. People inferred from that that he would like to see Lib Dems in the Cabinet? That smile again.

'They shouldn't infer anything from that really.'

One way or the other?

'No. I've always said let us begin with the dialogue of ideas. It shouldn't be about dealing out posts, it should be about sharing ideas.'

So he is not saying 'No'?

The laugh and another dazzling smile. 'I'm not saying "Yes" either.' He could, of course, just have said there will not be Liberals in the Cabinet.

Mr Blair has been stung by criticism from the *Sun* and other Rupert Murdoch-owned newspapers over the perception that he is leading Britain, by stealth, into the single European currency. Lord Healey and Lord Owen have joined in that criticism.

'They are perfectly entitled to their view. There should be a debate. What is important is that their position is not to go in yet and they would like a longer timescale than the one I'm talking about.

'My response to that is to say what we should actually do is determine the timescale by the conditions. The question is, provided the conditions are met, "Is it the right thing for Britain to go in?" and all that they are saying is "It requires more time to assess that".

'Well, that is a very different thing to talking about a thousand years of history and being opposed to it in principle.'

Mr Blair, faced with a concerted campaign by some papers, said he did not give 'two hoots' about being described in the *Sun* as 'the most dangerous man in Britain' over his pro-single currency stance, but did not deny that he had tried to win over Mr Murdoch.

'I'm always engaged in trying to persuade people of the strength of the Government's case, no matter who it is, but in the end the Government decides the policy of the Government, not newspapers, not anybody else, because that's the right way.'

What if the convergence conditions happen before the next election?

'They can't. There's no way that you will have convergence

before the next election. It can't happen as a matter of economics and that's the reason why, back in October '97, when we could see that it wasn't going to happen in a short timescale, we said "Look, in order to give certainty to people, we're not going to be doing this before the next election but we want to be in a position to make a judgment early in the next parliament".'

How can convergence suddenly happen, if it is not right in the run-up to the general election, six months or a year after the next election?

'It doesn't suddenly happen. The question is whether there is a path of economic convergence that can take place and you need some time to judge it.

'But if you start ruling it out – I don't know if this is what David Owen and Denis Healey are saying ... Denis Healey is saying he thought the whole thing would collapse – well, there are a lot of people who said the whole thing would never happen but they have been proven wrong and I think we shouldn't base policy on the basis that the whole thing is going to collapse because I don't think that's very likely.'

Is it not right that his colleagues in Europe regard this more as a political rather than an economic matter?

'Yes, but I have constantly said this – and you can track this back to speeches I made even before I became Labour leader. I've always said this about the single currency and I just underline it so that people listen to it. It can't be conceived of except politically, I accept, but it can't be made to work except economically and the two things have got to go together.

'Now my view of the political issues are that they are very considerable indeed, but if it is in our economic interest to go in and it does enhance our power and standing in the world, then we should be prepared to do it.'

So will Labour's manifesto position be to join the euro and does not the election therefore become the campaign on the single currency?

'No. Because people will know that they will have a separate vote on the euro.'

Asked about the forthcoming European summit, where Britain will be under pressure over its rebate as part of attempts to reform the Common Agricultural Policy, Mr Blair said he was not in the same position as Margaret Thatcher, who was frequently said to have 'handbagged' other leaders.

'The reason why I have said I am not negotiating away the rebate is because the rebate is justified. I'm not doing it, banging the metaphorical handbag or anything else, I'm putting forward a perfectly reasonable argument. We have to have a rebate.'

With Scotland, Europe and other issues like Northern Ireland ahead, the prime minister has his hands full. The problems are many, the decisions never easy. From the evidence at Downing Street, Mr Blair is loving every minute of it.

3 March 1999

Time for passion, Mr Blair

IAN BELL

There is not a lot of time left for those who still don't know. Years of agitation and a week of national mourning leave us with one hundred hours – give or take forty winks – in which to sort out our uncertainties, stiffen our spines, and make sense of modern Scotland.

We arrive at this point in large part thanks to Tony Blair's Labour Party. Had it not been so easily spooked by Michael Forsyth's pre-emptive campaign against the 'tartan tax', home rule would have been cut, dried and delivered on 1 May, that being the day on which Scotland chose the party promising devolution as its party of government.

Instead, Labour elected to stage a referendum. Then it entangled itself in a farce over the number of questions to be asked in that referendum and the reasons for asking them. Having insisted for years that a simple general election decision was to be the end of the matter – as it is, generally, in all of the great affairs of state – the party leadership decided it needed insurance.

The effect has been predictable. Even in abject disarray, even when politically quarantined by the voters, the opponents of home rule have fastened themselves to the issue of taxation and refused to let go. Many of their arguments have been spurious; several have been downright dishonest. Nevertheless, those defending the status quo have managed to infiltrate into the debate the vision of a dangerous, poverty-stricken future for an unstable Scotland.

Few have asked why a Tory Party that has been so thoroughly

discredited after years of incompetence could have quite so much gall. Fewer still have asked why these avowedly patriotic Scottish Tories have such a low opinion of their country's ability to run even a small part of its own affairs. The clients of the old order have got away with something very like murder – and Labour has helped them to do it.

That being so, Mr Blair and his party will bear a heavy burden of responsibility over the next four days. Quite simply, they got us into this particular difficulty. It falls to them to ensure that the climax of the debate, and the vote which follows, are as convincing as they should be. If Blair's personal standing is as high as polls claim, he has something of an obligation to risk a little of it before Thursday.

Opinion surveys suggest that the contest over tax-varying powers will be tight. Given the horrors predicted by devolution's opponents, this is scarcely surprising. No politician likes to campaign in favour of the power to tax, and few voters swoon when parties begin talking about other people's money. Nevertheless, the interesting thing about recent polls is not that they show a hardening of opinion against tax-varying powers but that they indicate growing doubt. More people are less sure than they once were, nothing more. Given that the debate has dragged on for so long, it is hard to blame them. So what might Blair do?

It would be a mistake to repeat his general election strategy under which Labour candidates were forbidden to admit that they had even heard of this thing called taxation. When the horrible stuff was brought to their attention, Blair and his people treated it as a social disease that they, being upstanding types, would never contract. Tax, for New Labour, was a very dirty word.

In a campaign dedicated, in part, to securing tax powers for the Scottish parliament, this makes little sense. Labour has already talked as though the only good reason for the Edinburgh body requiring the power to tax is so that it can promise never to do so. Scepticism, to put it mildly, has been the result, and it has made the parliament look like an exercise in futility before it is even born.

That being so, Labour might do well to keep things simple. If Scots want a real parliament, Blair might say, they must therefore want a responsible parliament. Taxation powers are the ultimate expression of political responsibility. Is Scotland so immature that it balks at responsibility?

Equally, the Labour leader could make the simple but often forgotten point that unpopular administrations are administrations asking to be kicked out. If the majority group in the Edinburgh parliament turns out to be irresponsible it lies with voters to kick them out. That – and he should claim no original thinking here – is what democracy is all about.

This said, Mr Blair might then try another plain and simple gambit. Anyone voting No on Thursday, he might gently observe, would in effect be voting Conservative. Remember them? he might ask. Remember what you thought of them only a few months ago?

The Tories are the only party now opposed to reform, he would remind the hard of thinking. Given the result on 1 May, a No vote would amount to nothing more than a Tory vote. Even those sceptical about home rule might balk at handing William Hague his first victory. Voters are contrary – how many will admit to being entirely self-deceiving?

Beyond that, there is the potential problem of the turn-out. Much nonsense has been talked about the 'Diana effect', so called, a timid, patronizing little idea which presumes that one tragedy deprived people of their political appetite and all their wits. If anything, many might actually find politics a welcome relief from the events of the week just past.

If there is a risk of a low turn-out, nevertheless, the cause is more likely to be boredom with the referendum campaign than with anything else. Even those with a professional obligation to take an interest have found it stale, ritualistic and perilously light on content. People have been going through the arguments as they would through revolving doors.

Hence the real service Mr Blair can perform. If home rule matters at all it matters as an issue of principle. We want devolution, if we want it, because it is right. Matters of principle, in turn, should generate passion. If home rule is right for Scotland, we should want it badly.

Equally, if Mr Blair harbours a deep belief in constitutional reform (and I am not absolutely convinced) the next few days should be accompanied by an explosion of passion on his part. We know he is capable of it. Passion, indeed, was one of the things which got him elected. He insists he believes in an Edinburgh parliament with tax-raising powers. If so, he must begin to fight for it with the passion this old, weary argument has always demanded.

In any case, the Prime Minister cannot afford the embarrassment of a No vote of any sort at this stage in his administration. The stakes this week are much higher for Scotland, meanwhile, than they are for him. Labour marched us up the referendum mountain; will it dare march us down again?

8 September 1997

QUESTIONS OF IDENTITY

A Retreat to the kailyard

ALLAN MASSIE

Scotland small? asked Hugh MacDiarmid, indignantly. 'Our multiform, our infinite Scotland small?' Well, yes and no. The journalist Kenneth Roy, editor of the admirable little magazine (little in format if not ambition) *The Scottish Review*, is the author of two books about Scotland – *Travels in a Small Country* and *Conversations in a Small Country*; and I am not convinced he employs the adjective ironically.

Of course we have people who would deny smallness, and even make big boasts. In his introduction to an anthology of new (i.e. recent) Scottish writing, the novelist Duncan McLean declares: 'We are trying to write new stories, written in the language of the day, about the ideas and problems that confronted us here and now . . . The best England could offer was pastiches of Victorian novels . . . and cobbled together patchworks of half-grasped argots, ad-talk, and transatlantic idioms . . .'

Setting aside the suspicion that this indicates that Mr McLean doesn't really have a very wide acquaintance with contemporary English, which is rather more varied and ambitious than his description would suggest, what follows in the anthology suggests a Scotland that is decidedly small, all but confined to the housing-scheme kailyard. Just as the novelists grouped together as the original Kailyard gave the impression that the whole of Scottish life was in small country towns and rural parishes, where the most important question was whether the young minister had found, or would find, a suitable wife, so now the lion cubs of

Scottish literature would – it sometimes seems – have us think that everything which is significant in Scottish life today is to be found on the fringes of our society, among drop-outs and junkies, whom they view with exactly the same sentimentality with which the old Kailyard writers were charged. If either view of Scotland – that is, old Kailyard or now – could be thought right, then MacDiarmid was wrong, and Scotland was, and is, small; indeed, very small.

Perhaps it is. Mr Roy, in his Editor's Letter in the new issue of his magazine, declares himself 'repelled by the absurd triumphalist posturing of large sections of the Scottish press as we approach our date with destiny' – the last phrase is certainly intended ironically. He is 'taken aback by the self-satisfied tone of the devolution so-called debate' and so has devoted 'a large section of this pre-referendum number to an attack on the complacency of Scottish attitudes', one of which was reprinted in this newspaper yesterday. Well, complacency is usually a sign of small-mindedness. So it is good to find him, in his words, 'having a go at a few sacred cows – deevolooshun for one'.

What Mr Roy calls 'the absurd triumphalist posturing' and the complacency reminds me of nothing so much as Aesop's frog who wanted to be a bull. Let us assume for the moment that Mr Dewar is wise in his judgement of the likely consequences of the establishment of a Scottish parliament; and that it satisfies the national aspirations of the Scottish people, and draws the sting from nationalism itself. What then? Well, it would certainly show that the Scottish people are easily satisfied. It would show that MacDiarmid was in the wrong when he questioned the idea that Scotland was small.

Consider what is on offer: a parliament where the most important issues will not be the sort of things that occupy the attention of leaders of other nations. The list of powers reserved to Westminster makes that quite clear. It is formidable. They will be: the constitution of the United Kingdom; UK foreign policy, including the ability to conclude European Union and other international agreements in both reserved and devolved areas; UK defence and national security; the protection of borders, including designation of the UK's land and maritime borders and fisheries limits; immigration and nationality; extradition; the criminal law in relation to drugs and firearms, and the regulation of drugs of misuse; the stability of the UK's fiscal, economic and monetary system; common markets for UK goods and services, including company law; employment legislation; social security policy and administration; regulation of certain professions; transport safety and regulation; and a whole rag-bag of other measures presently subject to UK regulation.

So, what's left? You may well ask. The detailed list is quite long, but a catalogue of headings will suffice: health; education; local government, including social work and housing; economic development and internal transport, the former being very limited; law and home affairs. And that's all, folks.

It is hard to see that there is anything here which requires the creation of a separate Scottish Executive. It is hard to see that there is anything which could not be competently handled at Westminster using the Scottish Grand Committee as developed by the last two Secretaries of State, Ian Lang and Michael Forsyth, possibly even making still greater use of that body.

But no: we are told that a separate, extra layer of government is desirable. We are told we need an extra 129 politicians at Edinburgh to oversee these areas of government. Nobody would suggest that health and education and Scots law are not important matters; but are they so important that we need all this?

Moreover, is it realistic, sensible or honest to describe the opportunity to vote on the creation of this wee subsidiary parliament as Scotland's Day of Destiny? Or is it just a case of Aesop's frog puffing himself up?

Scotland small? Some will conclude that this modest reform proves it is. If it gives satisfaction, if the Scottish people are happy to accept that a parliament and executive with such limited powers really represents a Scottish government, then we shall have demonstrated that we are indeed small and small-minded.

If, however, people are not fooled by what is on offer, they will soon be discontented with the reality; then pressures for full separation will intensify.

Scotland is big and manifold within the United Kingdom, playing a full part in its government. Scotland could be big and manifold as an independent state, playing a full part in the European Union. Either is a credible and creditable future.

But what is on offer on 11 September is neither credible nor creditable. It is a retreat into the Kailyard. I can understand why a Nationalist should vote for it, as a first step to the breaking of the Union. I can understand why a Unionist should reject it. What I find ridiculous is the suggestion that making Scotland smaller will serve Scotland well; and yet that is what is likely to be the immediate consequence of the proposed measure. Scotland the small, Scotland the inflated local authority unit.

Mr Roy speaks of 'absurd triumphalist posturing'. He is quite right. He might have added 'dishonest', for there is little doubt that many will suppose on 11 September that they are voting for a real Scottish government, and not just for the old Strathclyde Regional Council on a wee bit bigger scale.

27 August 1997

Fabric of a nation

JOYCE McMILLAN

On one thing, it seems, they are all agreed; that some time this weekend, when the debris of six years of building work is finally swept aside, and the lights switched on for a triumphant weekend of opening celebrations culminating in Monday's royal opening by the Queen and glittering black-tie ceilidh, Scotland will take possession of one of the most beautiful and distinctive new public buildings it has seen in half a century.

The new Museum of Scotland – designed by architects Gordon Benson and Alan Forsyth for one of Edinburgh's key city-centre sites, next to the Royal Museum in Chambers Street – looks, from the outside, like a small, elegant post-modern castle of glowing golden Elgin sandstone, tucked compactly into its wedge-shaped corner site. But inside, it opens out spectacularly into a range of beautiful, varied, soaring, and unexpected spaces, illuminated during the day by great splashes and shafts of natural light that seem to flow around the building like well-channelled water; and despite the difference of opinion about design that led the Prince of Wales, a few years ago, to distance himself from the project, it's impossible to spend much time in the new museum without feeling that this is a building which finally transcends the debate between traditionalism and modernity.

For unlike a modern functional building such as the new Scottish parliament – which will be system-built at the foot of Holyrood Road for less than half the price – the Museum of Scotland has essentially been handmade on site, inch by inch and stone by stone. The results show in the beautifully finished quality of the building's smallest details; and Mark Jones, the overall director of the National Museums of Scotland, unfolds the thought that this is because museums and art galleries are the new cathedrals of our time, complex, beautiful and highly worked buildings that have become our key places of contemplation and reflection, places where communities – national, local, international – talk to themselves, and try to understand more about who they are.

But that, I'm afraid, is where the atmosphere of agreement and consensus around the new museum is likely to end; for as soon as the remains of the feast have been swept away, and the public begins to troop through its beautifully articulated spaces, all hell is likely to break loose in terms of public debate about whether this museum, so far as its contents are concerned, is indeed talking to Scotland about itself in the language that Scotland currently wants to hear. Of course, all national museums, insofar as they present a vision of the nation to the public and the world, are – and should be – open to robust public debate about whether the vision they present is the right one.

But this new Museum of Scotland seems to have come to birth through a collision between two completely different sets of priorities; and the tension between them, although sometimes creative, raises real problems of theory, practice and presentation for the whole project. For in the first place, the new museum was conceived – as long ago as the Sixties – simply as a practical and modern replacement for the inadequate Museum of Antiquities exhibition space in Queen Street. Ask David Clarke, the high-powered archaeologist who is director of exhibitions, when he first heard of the idea of the new museum, and he'll say it was in 1968, when he arrived in Scotland as a young curator. The original project was cancelled after the IMF crisis of 1976, only to be revived again, suddenly and unexpectedly, by Malcolm Rifkind in 1989; so that for Clarke and the other curators, the new museum was always bound to be, first and foremost, a chance at last to get their hands on the kind of exhibition space they had always wanted.

Clarke is also a rigorous theorist of material culture, who despises any attempt at ethnic myth-making around material objects, focuses tightly on the objects themselves, and hates reconstructions, dioramas, mock-ups that speculate about how scenes from ancient life 'would have looked'; and this is the intellectual background to what Mark Jones calls the 'basic agreed approach' behind the whole Museum of Scotland project, which is that it will not attempt to create a 'Scotland's story' illustrated by material objects, but will focus on exhibiting and explaining the objects themselves, and let 'Scotland's story' emerge as it may.

And it's not difficult to see how this severe curatorial approach, which effectively allows the whole content of the museum to be shaped by the accidents and happenstances of an uneven collection started by a group of Edinburgh antiquarians in 1780, might run headlong into conflict with the fierce demands and expectations of a post-modern nation on the brink of a new political age; a nation which has probably, at some deep level, only found the money for this project because of a resurgent sense of national identity and pride, which is likely to assume that something called 'The Museum of Scotland' will indeed tell 'Scotland's story' in a fairly explicit and comprehensive way, and which – perhaps most importantly – has become used to seeing history served up in the form of increasingly spectacular reconstructions and video 'experiences', rather than through objects resting quietly in exhibition halls or in glass cases, however gorgeously lit and displayed. To put it bluntly, it's hard to imagine how many visitors, raised on a popular idea of Scottish history that is all William Wallace, Mary Queen of Scots and Bonnie Prince Charlie, will cope with a Museum of Scotland that has nothing to say about the first, and just a few small pieces of jewellery said to have belonged to the second; although the Jacobite rebellion, upstairs in the 'Scotland Transformed' section that covers the long nineteenth century from 1707 to 1914, does a little better.

For the truth is that the idea of not 'telling Scotland's story' in such a museum is almost impossible to sustain, given the need to set the objects in a historic context that will make them interesting and meaningful to a general audience. As Neal Ascherson has shrewdly observed, the pretence has already collapsed, so far as some of the museum's publicity and marketing is concerned; and my guess is that, as this museum matures, the pressure to boost up the collection in areas where it seems to be weak in reflecting important aspects of history – in other words, to let received ideas about Scottish history begin to shape the collection, as well as vice versa – will become almost irresistible; as will the pressure to create some displays in a more spectacular, populist form.

But that would, in a sense, be a pity; because there's no doubt that for those willing to leave their expectations and assumptions on the doorstep, and to spend an hour or two in quiet, concentrated contemplation, the collection shown in this museum will be a revelation, a magnificent treasure-trove of objects that sometimes confirm our ideas about history, and sometimes – as in the elegance and lightness of the objects in the Reformation Church gallery – challenge them in seriously important ways. Understanding that no such exhibition can ever be wholly apolitical or objective in its presentation, the museum has avoided the big overarching theory, and made space for a multiplicity of voices, for five great slices of Scottish material history, each presented by a very different curatorial hand. So it begins in the basement with a good, old-fashioned display of geological and natural history, showing – for even rocks seem to carry political messages these days – how England and Scotland once cruised the world on the edges of two different continents, separated by a great ocean, followed by David Clarke's superb exhibition on 'early peoples'; moves upstairs to Hugh Cheape's inevitably controversial section on the Kingdom of Scotland 500–1707, and George Dalgleish's physically spectacular display covering the years from the Union through industry and empire to 1914; and ends on the sixth floor with the already famous twentieth-century gallery, in which modern Scots – some well-known, some less so – have been invited to choose and show the material objects that changed their lives in the twentieth century, from Carmen rollers to a photo of Kirsty Wark's Saab convertible.

So what is it that these key men – and a few women – behind the Museum of Scotland finally hope it will do, for the hundreds of thousands of people who will walk through its halls in the coming years? It's safe to say their hopes are not political or nationalistic, in any simple sense. But what they have tried to do, and have perhaps succeeded in doing by avoiding the traditional formulas of Scottish history, is to create a record of Scotland which finally puts Scotland itself, its people and their material culture, right at the centre of the story; and that fact alone, combined with the obvious record of Scottish achievement represented in the museum, should, Mark Jones believes, generate 'a certain sense of quiet pride' in Scots who visit it.

'The museum doesn't define Scottishness in terms of England,' says the archaeologist David Clarke. 'It looks at the thing in itself, and I think that makes it very strong.' For Mark Jones, it's about 'reworking the mental map, and understanding that the idea that the centre of the world is always far away from Scotland isn't right'. And for Jenni Calder, who has created most of the text and print that accompanies the exhibition, the hope is to have created a space that Scots will want to come back to. 'I hope they'll feel that it's their own,' she says. 'And that it's really their history, presented in a way that allows them to embrace it.'

And maybe that's the key. For on my last visit to the museum, as the final exhibits were being brought in, I found myself standing for ages with my hand resting on a nineteenth-century handloom from the row of houses in Kilbarchan, once weavers' workshops with rooms above, where my parents still live; and where my grandmother, as a little girl, once ran around helping her father to operate a loom identical to this one. And it made me feel – not more proud to be Scottish, for there are finer and lovelier objects in the museum to do that; but somehow more aware of the huge diversity and complexity of Scottish life, and of how each of us, our family, our story, however we came to be here, has a right place in it, strongly bound to all the rest.

And if the new Museum of Scotland can do that, or something like it, for all the Scots who visit, then its effect on the life of the nation will not be spectacular, or sudden. But it will go deep, in helping to shape a nation fit to make choices on a basis of self-knowledge, confidence and self-respect, rather than on that old superstitious fear of being left behind on the edge of someone else's world; and whichever way our decisions finally fall, that is surely something to celebrate, not only this weekend, but for years to come.

28 November 1998

A dual sense of identity

ANDREW NEIL

Those of us who are proud to be Scottish and British have become strangers in our own land. There was no conflict about being both in the Scotland in which I grew up and was educated in the fifties and sixties. The mood is very different today; the past two decades have seen the rise of an increasingly separatist Scottish identity and a concomitant decline in British identity north of the Border. It is a dangerous brew which threatens the very existence of the United Kingdom.

My generation (and many before it) was brought up to revel in its dual identity. We had no doubt where our loyalties lay on the football or rugby pitch, especially when the enemy was England, and took great satisfaction from Scotland's all-too-infrequent victories. But those of us who followed cricket cheered when England scored one of its even rarer victories over the West Indies or Australia and in general we liked to see Brits win, whatever their home nationality. These days, if England played Iraq, you could count on a substantial and voluble minority of Scots to be backing Iraq.

At school I learned to take pride in my distinctive heritage and history. I could reel off the long list of Scottish folk heroes, pioneers, entrepreneurs, philosophers and inventors. For a small, cold, mostly barren country on the periphery of north-west Europe we seemed to have made a disproportionate contribution to the intellectual and economic progress of mankind. No doubt that helps to explain why, at the age of ten, I was a Scottish

Nationalist, as were most of my classmates. But we soon grew out of such childish notions.

As we learned more, it was quickly apparent that Scotland had flourished most when it had voluntarily joined forces with England (we took great pride from the fact that Scotland, unlike Ireland or Wales, had never been permanently conquered by the English) at the start of the eighteenth century. The Union gave Scotland a far bigger canvas on which to map out its prosperity and allowed Scots to exploit their talents on the international stage.

By the end of the nineteenth century, Scotland was probably the richest country in the world; Glasgow was the unrivalled second city of the Empire and Scots had played countless crucial roles in the building of the British nation-state and its global empire – without ever having to lose the culture, history, education and religion that made us different from the English. Those born to be Scottish and British had been truly dealt a privileged, winning hand by fate.

Not in today's Scotland, where being a 'true' Scot involves disparaging the very notion of Britishness. Britain is increasingly depicted as an irrelevance, a historic interlude from the age of imperialism, a conspiracy to keep Scotland in supposedly colonial shackles, an impediment to the creation of a separate Scottish identity. You cannot feel more Scottish, we are told, unless you feel less British.

The Scottish media are drenched in such drivel. The blethering classes who dominate their columns and letters pages never miss a chance to put Britain down, to play up every imagined English slight to our Scottish sensitivities; to predict a more mature and civil society and politics for Scotland if only there was more self-government (which means glossing over the cesspit of waste, incompetence and corruption that is Scottish local government); to boast of a superior Scottish nationalism in a manner which they are the first to condemn whenever the English, Germans or Americans parade their own narrow nationalism.

Behind all this lurks a pervasive and growing anti-Englishness.

The *bien pensants* of Scottish nationalism deny this but it is there for all to see, the nasty underbelly of contemporary Scottish attributes. The Scottish tabloids – even those edited by Englishmen – think it is good for sales to have regular swipes at the English. The foul-mouthed, anti-English rant of an Edinburgh heroin crackhead in *Trainspotting* has been made into Scotland's Gettysburg Address by fashionable bletherers.

Children with English accents are bullied in the playground. A so-called comedian at this year's Edinburgh Festival begins his act by announcing that his jokes are not for the English snobs in the posh seats in the front. Even the Scotland bourgeoisie begins every rugby international at Murrayfield with a morose, anti-English dirge, 'Flower of Scotland', which some would like to make our national anthem.

The English have every right to be mystified by this outpouring of denigration and hatred. After all, they elected, by a landslide, a government dominated by Scots. If anybody should feel discriminated against and excluded from power and influence in today's Britain, it is the English. Nor has the near-monopoly of Scots in the top jobs (prime minister, Chancellor, Foreign Secretary, defence, now social security) undermined New Labour's continuing popularity south of the Border.

Last year's general election also at least gave Scotland the government it wanted after eighteen years of Tory rule. So the result should have been good for the Union on both sides of the Border. But there is no pleasing Scotland in its current curmudgeonly mood, as the Blair government is currently finding out to its cost.

Allan Massie, one of the few sane Scottish commentators still given space to write, has attributed the decline in British identity among Scots to the end of the Empire and the absence of external threat to those islands. Scotland was content to be subsumed into a greater whole as long as there was an empire to build, exploit and defend, and foreign foes who threatened our liberties to see off. Now there is no Empire and no foreseeable prospect of being invaded, there is less point to Britain, and the Scots are returning to a pre-Union nationalism which they think can be preserved within the warm and welcoming embrace of the European Union, just like Ireland.

There is something in this; there may be a certain historic inevitability about the decline of British and the renaissance of Scottish identity. But it need not be terminal for the Union. There is a more immediate reason, however, why it might be: throughout the Tory years, Labour unwittingly encouraged Scotland's nascent fissiparous tendencies. A party that thought all it had to do to keep Scotland happy was deliver devolution is instead reaping the whirlwind it sowed in the eighties.

While England reluctantly swallowed the Thatcherite market medicine for four consecutive general elections, Scotland remained steeped in a sullen collectivism. Scottish Labour politicians told the Scots that they were being cheated out of their democratic rights, that England was foisting an alien and permanent Tory government on Scotland; the wilder fringes of Scottish Labour even joined with the Nationalists in urging non-payment of the poll tax, thereby creating a culture of non-payment of council taxes which exists to this day.

By disaggregating the Union for its own partisan purposes, Labour played into the hands of the Nationalists. It encouraged the idea that Scotland was a distinct political entity from the rest of the UK whose interests were being ignored by London (despite the over-representation in Westminster and the over-spending north of the Border). The horde of Scottish Labour worthies who feared they might be denied office for ever in London began talking in more nationalist tones; they warmed to the prospect of a ministerial car in Edinburgh.

There was much wild talk of Scotland's democratic deficit. It came at a time when there was already something of a Scottish cultural renaissance underway. Politics and culture combined to produce a separatist genie which even a Labour government dominated by Scots cannot shove back in the bottle.

Those of us who feared that devolution would not assuage nationalist sentiment but turn out to be the slippery slope to separatism have a good chance of being proved right. That is scant consolation if the consequence is that your country gets dismembered. Nor does it take into account the fact that the election of yet another Tory government last year, while Scotland stayed stubbornly Labour, would equally have put the Union in jeopardy.

Those who want to save the Union need to do two things: first, accept that devolution is a done deal but build on what Labour has delivered to create a new Unionism; and second, restate in clear and certain terms the case for the United Kingdom and a British sense of identity.

Labour's gimcrack plan for a parliament in Edinburgh is likely to encourage separatism rather than dish it. It allows for a substantial devolution of power in home affairs, but all the money will continue to come from a block grant from London. It would be hard to imagine an arrangement more tailor-made for exploitation by the Nationalists than this. Every time there is a shortfall in spending they will blame miserly London. Tension between Edinburgh and Westminster will become an everyday occurrence, making what was supposed to be a permanent constitutional settlement unstable.

The only way to resolve this is to go much farther than Labour proposes: the Scottish parliament should be responsible for raising all the money it plans to spend. Then the Scots can indulge in their supposed love of high taxes and big-spending politicians (or more likely flood the A74 south to England when Edinburgh overtaxes them). And only when there is some clear correlation and connection between what politicians promise to spend and what they have to raise in taxes will Scottish politics grow up.

For too long Scotland has enjoyed Thatcherite levels of taxation and socialist levels of spending. Home Rule worth the name would make the Edinburgh parliament self-financing for all the areas under its responsibility. It would also mark the beginning of a new Unionism, one that recognized the new, enhanced Scottish identity but based on the belief that there was still enough residual support for the concept of Britain to make it worth continuing with the United Kingdom.

That support would grow if more politicians and opinion-formers put the case for Britain. Too many are too quick to denigrate the very idea: even Lord Rothermere dismissed Britain in the *Daily Telegraph* last week as a 'third-rate power'. His words are music to those who would split us asunder. He should know better.

Britain remains a power to be reckoned with. We are the fifth-largest economy in the world, with fine and feared armed forces and a global influence that comes from membership of the European Union, the UN Security Council, Nato, the Commonwealth – and our special relationship with America. The United States, of course, is in a league of its own. But Britain remains in the top half of the world premier division.

We have also become something of a success story: in many ways, Britain is better equipped to face the demands of the Information Age than any of our European competitors. Germany and France are a decade behind us in the privatization and deregulation essential to compete in the global economy. We would do well to dwell more on our successes, for it would reinforce our British identity; people don't desert what the rest of the world admires, and it was a pervading sense of British failure which gave separatism its first boost in the seventies.

That peculiar mix of English, Welsh, Scottish and Irish, augmented by immigrants from all over the world, still makes Britain special: the whole is greater than the sum of its parts and without the United Kingdom we would all be diminished. We would certainly all count for a lot less in the world. That is well understood by European federalists in Brussels: a Europe of a hundred regions and small nations would be far easier to control than a Gaullist Europe of strong nation-states.

So there is still all to play for; I do not subscribe to the view that the dissolution of the United Kingdom is inevitable, though many in Scotland – and a growing number of English Nationalists as well – would like us to think so. But the old Unionism of the unitary state is gone. A new Unionism will have to be forged within a much more devolved, even federalist United Kingdom. That can only be achieved if the case for Britain is restated clearly and convincingly. Do both these things and the Union can be saved – and I might once again feel at home in the land of my birth.

15 August 1998

A guid Scots word in your ear, Donald

PETER JONES

Our estimable Secretary of State, Donald Dewar, used a splendid Scots word the other day. Writing the bill to give legal flesh to the bones of the Scottish parliament white paper was not, he said, a downhill 'skoosh'.

It is possible that anyone not brought up with a Scottish education might not know what this meant, although the word gives enough of a clue from its mere sound (i.e., as language scholars say, is sufficiently onomatopoeic) to reveal the meaning, which is of course: something that is 'easie-peasie'.

One of the joys of following Dewar's career is that his speeches and pronouncements are studded with words like this. Guid Scots words like 'dreich' and 'scunnered', which are far more expressive then their English equivalents of 'dull' and 'disgusted', fall readily from his lips; much to the dismay of the shorthand writers in the House of Commons, much to the delight of people like me who regard such usage as greatly needed re-enrichment of our everyday speech.

Re-enrichment, because as the *Edinburgh History of the Scots Language*, published today (Edinburgh University Press), at the stoatin price of £150, makes plain, an awful lot of Scots words, language and grammar have gone out of use.

This is not simply because too many dominies used to beat it out of the weans in the misguided belief that it was lower-class filthy talk, but also because newspapers such as this as well as the British Broadcasting Corporation have made dictionary phonetics and received pronunciation the norms to follow.

The Scottish parliament might yet change this. Hopefully, this would not be done through legislation which would inevitably impose diktats which would be resisted, but simply through usage. If politicians used Scots words in their speeches, perhaps even in their soundbites or slogans (which is, incidentally, one of the few Gaelic words to have made it into the English language), they would get reported and thereby become more commonly used.

This might sound like a plea for a political drive towards some kind of linguistic ethnic purity to result from devolution. It is not; indeed I would abhor any such tendency. And in fact, as the *Edinburgh History* makes it stunningly clear, there never has been any such thing as a pure Scots language, despite what some people might think.

Scots words are a hoovering up of flotsam and jetsam from all sorts of languages: from Scots Gaelic (for example, all the terms for Highland dress); from Irish Gaelic (a good many words in Galloway dialect such as 'spalpean' for a naughty boy were brought in by Irish labourers); from Latin (such as 'dominie' for a teacher); from French (the Scottish chicken dish 'howtowdie' derives directly from an old French word and recipe); from Norse languages (including widespread terms such as 'skelp' and 'skirl'); from Dutch ('haar' for fog is among the most obvious); and from Romany ('barrie', meaning good, is steadily spreading among Lothian and Fife children).

Arguably, Scots itself is not even of Scottish origin, being a much-moulded variant of Northumbrian English, which spread northwards through migration. This is why, in the Geordie dialect of Tyneside, you hear words such as 'toon', 'hoos' and 'bairn' (for town, house and child), words which were not brought south from Scots but were rather there first before they moved northwards to Scotland.

As for poor old Pictish (presumably the Picts, the original inhabitants of Scotland, did have their own language before they were conquered by the Scots immigrants from Ireland), nothing much survives in Scots apart from possibly 'mounth' (meaning, a bare upland area).

In any case, the latest academic research on Scottish politics appears to show that efforts to base political campaigning on the idea that there is an ethnic cleavage between the Scots and the English would be doomed to fail.

Lindsay Paterson, Alice Brown, David McCrone (all Edinburgh University) and Paula Surridge (Aberdeen University) have found no evidence to support the idea that Scottish voters rejected the Tories and backed devolution in this year's election and referendum as some kind of anti-English gesture.

According to their surveys of Scottish voters, the electorate backed constitutional change simply because they thought there would be benefits to be derived from it. This is why, they argued at a recent conference in Edinburgh, there was such a high vote in favour of the tax-varying power in the referendum. People recognized, it seems, that while they might have to pay higher tax, they would benefit by getting better education, a better health service, and so on.

It seems to make sense, though there is further work to be done. But if this is true, the future for the Scottish National Party seems bleak, for its electoral appeal has always been underpinned by the idea that England has been doing Scotland down in some way.

Well, we'll see about that, but meantime, here's a suggestion for Dewar: instead of styling the leader of the Scottish administration 'First Minister', how about a using a guid Scots word? What's wrong with 'heidyin', Donald?

26 November 1997

Switch-off time for Ukania

GEORGE KEREVAN

Your columnist shared a disreputable left-wing youth with BBC *Newsnight*'s pugnacious anchor, Gordon Brewer, the thinking woman's Jeremy Paxman. Gordon has just returned to Scotland, after many years' absence, in order to make a Who-Are-the-Scots-Now? documentary. He treated me to a drink at the new Museum of Scotland – coffee, since it was licence-payers' money – and gave me the *Newsnight* third degree. Gordon wanted to know how myself and a generation like me had ceased to be British. Now the cameras are turned off, I've thought of all the right answers.

The country Gordon and I were born into was an invention of the Second World War. Its Golden Age lasted from 1940 till the early sixties. We are living through its death agony. Call it Ukania.

Ukania was a collective amnesia of the English middle classes arising from two seminal events. The First World War physically annihilated their sons, especially in the shires, shattering their personal confidence. The Second World War ended their Empire. The ideological cement of the new Ukania was therefore a retreat into nostalgia that stopped the English middle classes facing up to post-war economic and political downsizing. As exemplified in a hundred black-and-white war movies and a thousand BBC costume dramas.

Just as Hollywood's utopia of small-town America was invented by immigrant Russian Jews, this British Erewhon was the product

of the new mass media and their north of England working-class
writers. Often the first of their family to go to university, they
rationalized their insecurities by inventing comforting fantasies
of Ukanian life, such as *Coronation Street* and *Dixon of Dock
Green*. Gordon Brown has attempted to defend the social basis
of the Union by recalling paramount shared British experiences.
But such shared experiences derive from watching these same
television programmes in the days when there were fewer channels
to zap.

For Ukania did not have a national purpose. It was not a
land of opportunity for the individual like America, Canada or
Australia. It was not a France with a secure cultural identity based
on language that united bourgeois, peasant and Paris Red Belt.
Periodic attempts to give Ukania direction – Wilson's White Heat,
Forsyth's 'I'm Backing Britain', Blair's Cool Britannia – always
seemed crass and synthetic because they were.

The core myth of Ukania – or at least the one believed in the
Home Counties – was the camaraderie and classlessness of the
Second World War perpetuated into the post-war world. Ukania
had won and could cling to a comforting sense of national moral
superiority while the economy collapsed. Premature non-
Ukanians – genuine imperialists such as Alan Clark – realized the
truth that winning the war meant subservience to America. But
the war had a deep influence on the working class. My mother,
born of a large Glasgow family in the harsh inter-war years, was
catapulted from a humdrum life into the RAF. For her, and
many like her, Churchill's war provided the best years of her life.
Besides, the Establishment kept British wartime casualties low –
they fought till the last Russian, Australian and Canadian.

It was not my mother's generation who turned Nationalist.
Understandably seduced by the comfort of a cod-liver-oil welfare
state, after the vicissitudes of the Hungry Thirties when a tenth
of Scotland emigrated, they gave the Conservative and Unionist
Party an absolute majority of the Scottish vote in the 1955 election.
But my mother never believed in Ukania, though she was a devo-
tee of *Coronation Street*. Till her dying day she hated Churchill

as a man who shot at Welsh miners. She bought us Yuletide presents but reminded us it was a foreign custom – in her day my grandfather went to work on Christmas Day.

My generation, born in the aftermath of the Second World War, were brought up Ukanians. We made Airfix kits of Spitfires. We read comics like the *Eagle*, where stiff-upper-lip Dan Dare refought the Second World War against the Mekon without the need for Lend Lease. (Though Dan's middle name was MacGregor from his Scots mum.) We were the first TV generation. What we saw was newly minted Ukania: the Coronation, *The Army Game*, *An Age of Kings*, and TV news with a pronounced metropolitan bias (and accent).

But the same television that invented Ukania also gave my post-war generation a vision of something beyond the Noël Coward world of True Brit mythology. We watched *That Was the Week*, men on the Moon, bodybags in Vietnam, the hypocrisy of Profumo, British troops imposing internment in Northern Ireland, the endless possibilities of a wider world. Worse: STV appeared and its announcers started speaking with the same accents as we did in the playground – yet God did not strike down our television aerials.

Reality first intruded into Ukania in 1957. The old Scots heavy industries like shipbuilding, artificially resuscitated by the war, went belly up in the face of competition from a revived Europe. The return of mass unemployment sent hundreds of thousands of disillusioned Scots (like my Uncle Bob) on another round of emigration. The Ukanian economy proved not to extend beyond the Midlands car factories. In 1959, Labour got its first Scottish majority.

In the sixties, the post-war TV generation, from Paris to Perth, revolted. We were collectively rejecting post-war regimentation in favour of the world of boundless possibilities viewed through the small, flickering screen. Nostalgia held no interest for us. We were going to the stars and the man in the engine room had a (bad) Scots accent. We saw ourselves as Scottish, as European, as internationalists – not Little Englanders.

In Scotland, tens of thousands joined the SNP. Some, like myself and Gordon Brewer, rejected orthodox politics for a romantic flirtation with Trotsky. Nobody joined the Ukanian Labour Party. Then came Thatcherism. As the substance of the Ukanian myth became threadbare in the real world of global economic competition, Thatcher hunted the scapegoats within responsible for the collapse of her British idyll. It was the first stirring of a post-Ukanian English nationalism. Even the Scottish middle classes rejected Ukanian citizenship.

For a time, with the 1979 SNP badly split, Scottish Labour seemed the only political alternative. But it was a Ukanian Labour Party that eventually resulted in milk-and-water Thatcherism complete with Union flags to welcome Blair into Number Ten. And the Peter Mandelson memorial dome.

When technically did Scotland cease to be North British? Probably in 1919, when that earlier Imperial Britain died from exhaustion at the end of the Great War. The subsequent Ukanian interval was an aberration based on Home Counties delusions of grandeur. And some very good television programmes.

4 January 1999

Playing the Scottish card

ALLAN MASSIE

In a letter to this newspaper, Mr Steven Laidlaw poses the question: 'What defines a Scot?' He has been prompted to do so by the selection of Matt Elliot for the Scotland football squad, and remarks that 'while exiled in England, I remember watching Matt Elliot play for Oxford United and am amazed, as no doubt he is, that he is now "Scottish"'.

Since Elliot is, like Laidlaw indeed, one of the great Border names, some of us might be more surprised to find an Elliot who wasn't considered Scots. Walter Elliot, the pre-war Secretary of State for Scotland, used to enjoy pointing out to Americans who talked of old feuds with England that 'the English have hanged more Elliots than the total of all the people killed in the War of Independence'. This was (probably) an exaggeration, but a pardonable one.

Of course, the descendants of Scots who have moved south of the Border and settled there do often come to consider themselves as English, whatever their family origins. I doubt if my friend Auberon Waugh would thank me for claiming him as a Scot, though the Waughs hailed from Berwickshire and he is also a direct descendant of the great Lord Cockburn (no Celt, but of Saxon-Norman origin, as Evelyn Waugh observed in his autobiography). On the other hand, there are numerous families, originating from Scotland, but settled in England for several generations, whose members nevertheless continue to define themselves as Scottish.

In contrast, Compton Mackenzie, the novelist, who would have been a candidate for the title of 'most famous living Scot' forty years ago, began adult life as a very English writer – though he had been a sentimental Jacobite as an adolescent. The Mackenzies had gone south some five generations previously. Compton Mackenzie decided to become a Scot in middle life, and was to be one of the founders of the SNP. But he was a Scot by adoption rather more than by heredity. There wasn't, I think, any Scots blood on his mother's side.

If Mackenzie was Scots by adoption, Muriel Spark, our greatest living novelist, describes herself as being 'Scots by formation'; her father was Jewish, her mother English, and she has not lived in Scotland since she was a young woman, but her Edinburgh childhood and schooling made her indisputably Scots. She writes the most lucid and elegant English, but with an unmistakable Scots tone of voice.

'Scots by formation' is a good phrase, and may be a good definition. It certainly accords with the 'civic' rather than 'ethnic' nationalism which the SNP has espoused. It permits immigrants from any background to be Scottish, even if they retain traces, or more than traces also, of some other national inheritance. Scots-Italians in one generation become Italian Scots in the next. Ricky Demarco and the late lamented Emilio Coia are both identified completely with Scotland without losing certain qualities characteristically Italian. In this they differ or differed from cosmopolitans, who belong nowhere in particular. The same could be said of the Contini brothers, who run Edinburgh's most agreeable shop, Valvona & Crolla; it contrives to be at the same time authentically Edinburgh and authentically Italian. I once asked their uncle Dominic – another delightful man, now departed – if he had been on holiday. '*Si, si,*' he replied, '*giu la costa* – Gullane, ye ken.'

It may be argued that in the world today sport is more effective than anything else in keeping ideas of nationhood alive. Yet most sporting bodies have been flexible in their interpretation of qualifications – and are more so now than ever. Mr Laidlaw, in his letter, observes that 'the sport of bowls uses mere residence as a qualification'. Football was quite strict till recently, that fine Edinburgh-accented Hibs centre-forward Joe Baker, for instance, being denied the chance to play for Scotland because he was born on the wrong side of the Border. Now, as the case of Matt Elliot confirms, the SFA takes a liberal view of definitions.

Rugby has done so almost from the beginning, those who were then known as colonials (i.e. Australians, New Zealanders and South Africans) flitting in and out of the home countries' national sides. Soon after the war we had a Scottish captain, Doug Keller, who had actually toured Britain the previous year with the Australians. More recently, our 1990 Grand Slam captain, David Sole, was born in Aylesbury, son of an English father and mother; but, schooled in Scotland, he was certainly Scots by formation and will. Something similar is true of our present captain, Rob Wainwright. Though he was born in Perth, both his parents were, I think, English; it would be hard to find a more committed Scot . . .

The easy conclusion to come to is that anyone is a Scot who thinks he or she is; that it is all a matter of self-definition, and that heredity, birthplace, formation or simply adoption may be the determining factor. This conclusion is not only easy, it is sensible. (Adoption must include residency, even though not everyone resident in Scotland may consider themselves to be Scottish, just as there are many Scots in England and elsewhere who continue to think of themselves as Scots.)

Yet, if this conclusion is sensible, it does not follow that it is politically satisfactory, or sufficient. The devolution referendum demonstrated its limits. Then there was a good deal of annoyance expressed by Scots resident in England that they were allowed no say in a question, the answer to which might, indeed must, affect the future relations of Scotland with the other parts of the now United Kingdom. The ruling, which was actually the only practical one, was that their wishes were irrelevant, since they would not be directly affected, at least immediately, by the establishment of a parliament in Edinburgh; the point being that that parliament wasn't going to be able to legislate for non-residents.

Consequently, people resident in Scotland did have a vote, even though they might not regard themselves as Scots and their residency might be merely temporary. The question was dramatized by Tam Dalyell when he asked why Gary McAllister, the Scotland football captain, should not have a vote, while the English internationalist Paul Gascoigne did. Many thought there was something vaguely right in the question, and vaguely unsatisfactory in the answer. Yet it was not possible to see how any other course could have been followed.

In reality, there is no such thing as a 'pure' nation anywhere in Europe. What we recognize as nations are formed over time from a myriad of strains. Germany still imposes an ethnic test for citizenship, but this is fairly absurd, and becomes more absurd the farther back in time you go: when Frederick the Great became King of Prussia, half the population of Berlin was made up of French-speakers, descendants of Huguenots expelled by Louis XIV.

Nationality, and questions of nationhood, are fascinating subjects about which to speculate; nationalism, on the other hand, is a political force, ideology or movement that has only a tenuous relationship with nationality.

12 November 1997

The Scottish psyche deconstructed in Six Parts. No. 1: Meanness

ROBERT McNEIL

So, there was this Aberdonian. His cousin tells him to send a telegram if Grannie, who was ill, passes away. 'And remember,' he was told, 'you get twelve words for sixpence.' Granny duly died and Andrew duly sent his telegram: 'MACKAY—OTEL, LONDON. GRANNIE PASSED AWAY TODAY. ABERDEEN 2 DUNDEE 1. ANDREW.'

I know. You're laughing so much I can feel your tears dripping on to the page: unless you're from Aberdeen, of course, in which case you wouldn't waste the water.

Seriously, this stuff about mean Scots is beyond a joke.

Here we are, time after time, giving more than anybody else to charity appeals: we're the ones in the London pubs with the open wallets; we spend vast amounts on the accoutrements and jiggery-pokery of the computer age; and yet the stereotype sticks of the dreepy-nosed misery in the tartan bunnet standing up a fifties dour back close adding another padlock to his wallet.

How did this come about? How come it sticks? And why us? Well, in the following scientific exposition, based on sound principles of logical positivism and some other stuff, we will see that Scots are sometimes mean; and so is everyone else.

Take the English, for example. The meanest people I have ever met have all been English.

I have mentioned the observation to several people and they have all enthusiastically agreed, joyful at being able at last to speak the truth, and recounting experiences which we all found broadly similar. They mostly revolved around rounds – of beer or tea or whip (you know, as in charity or people leaving work and whatnot). The English were always the ones trying to work out the change, and asking: 'Now who had the dry-roasted peanuts?'

I also happen to believe that there is a grain of truth about meanness in the north-east of Scotland. Based on what? Based on scientific observation of an Aberdonian in a Chinese take-away in Lerwick a few years ago. It was one of the most embarrassing scenes I have ever witnessed in my life.

There is nothing much to record other than that he refused to believe that the cost of his main meal did not include the rice, and indicated that the restaurateurs were trying to pull a fast one on him on account of the fact that it was obvious he had never experienced anything so exotic as a Chinese take-away in his life. 'Does it come wi' neeps?' one half expected him to ask. Even when the obvious was pointed out to him on the menu, he refused to give ground, pointing to another dish and exclaiming: 'But yon wan says the price includes rice or chips.'

I can't recall if he buckled in the end or if the Chinese people gave him complimentary rice cooked in sputum, but I do remember feeling that here was a stereotype made flesh and bloodyminded, and a reminder that where there is smoke there may very well be a conflagration.

But let us move to another scene, in Aberdeen itself. A party of English commercial travellers in a hotel are opining on the meanness of the Scots. One approaches an Aberdonian at a nearby table and asks him: 'How do you tell the difference between an Aberdonian and a coconut?'

The Aberdonian shakes his head, fixing the Englishman with a steely stare.

The punchline comes: 'You can get a drink out of a coconut.'

The Englishmen guffaw and the Aberdonian smiles gently. 'No bad,' he replies, appearing to take no offence. 'Here, would you like a drink now?'

The Englishman is delighted. 'That would be very sporting of you.'

'Weel,' says the Aberdonian, 'away and buy a coconut.'

Unfortunately, that's a madey uppy story (culled from that fine repository of humour, *Scotland's Laughing*). But with luck, it will have restored some dignity to the Don.

We Scots have all – from Haroldswick to Gretna Green – been lumped together as makers of muckles from mickles, bawbee hoarders, thrifty, stingey, parsimonious tightwads for whom prudence is the most cardinal of virtues. You don't have to be John Maynard Keynes to apprehend that the thrift thing had its roots in our old national poverty, sustained through many years of the Union with England. These days are gone now, and there are signs that the daft old prejudice is going too.

Cheek is all the meanness gibe is about. I think most Scots are like your humble scribe, hopeless with dosh, not really caring to get rich, proud when poor; prodigal when quids in.

The Government keeps scaremongering that we'll be poorer under home rule. I doubt it, but who cares anyway? A Scotsman was told he had just won £1 million, a penthouse suite, a luxury sports car and a pet dog.

'What breed?' he asked.

It's all a matter of perspective. Money: here today, gone tomorrow. I leave you with Richard Armour:

> That money talks
> I'll not deny,
> I heard it once:
> It said, 'Goodbye.'

The Scottish psyche deconstructed in Six Parts. No. 2: Pessimism

ROBERT McNEIL

'Oor first breath is the beginning o' daith.' The old Scots proverb is hardly a recipe for starting out with a sunny outlook on life, realistic though it may be.

Imagine: you're born in Harthill in late November. For the first few months of your life it's freezing cold. The skies are grey. Everybody is snorting or blowing into handkerchiefs. Your food is probably plain or cholesterol-laden, dooming you to die younger than if you had been born elsewhere.

As a people, we are rubbish, accursed by God – and probably Jehovah, Allah, and Thor as well. Given a rotten climate, we are physically the least prepared for it. Look around any Scottish street in the thankfully multi-cultural nineties on a cold day. Oriental people, black people, Mediterranean people; everybody looks well enough. The Celtic Scots are the shivering ones, the ones with the thin, blue, hairless skin, the red noses streaming with snot, the folk born into a meteorological scenario for which they are the least fitted. And you want us to be optimistic? It's hard to stay optimistic when all your picnics are cancelled.

If our climate is rubbish, so is our political outlook. We can't even move towards home rule without everybody telling us that we're too rubbish to manage it. And the people telling us that are oor ain folk. We poo on our own doorstep, while the world looks on and thinks: 'What is wrong with these folk?' We look, frankly, feart. We lack faith in ourselves. Perhaps it is our dour taciturnity that stops us getting excited at anything so prosaic as home rule. After all, what's the point? We'll be deid soon enough.

Calvinism might partly be blamed for all this. I remember, one Sunday, driving past a Presbyterian kirk in Skye. It was white and plain, and a balding man with a grey face and hollow eyes was looking out of a window at the falling rain. A cameo of misery. The man was not beyond redemption. He could, theoretically, still have saved himself from his soul-destroying, heart-eating, spirit-sapping creed. He could have taken his gaze from the window, stood up, shouted: 'Away with all this! Let's live!' He could have skipped down the aisle, flung wide the doors of doom, jumped on to the rough gravel and raised his arms to the sky, letting his remaining hair get soaked, until the sun came out to dry it and the buds opened and trees came into leaf, as he sang, 'Things can only get better!' But, every day, in every way, they won't. And he wouldn't. And so we leave him staring disconsolately out of the window at the drizzle until it is time to die.

But it can't all be down to Calvinism, lodged in the collective psyche like a maggot in the haggis. There are plenty of pessimistic, kent-his-faither, doom-mongering Scottish Catholics in my ken. Nothing rosy in their rosaries. Life? It's a sin, so it is.

You may have heard of the Fifer who saw St Paul's Cathedral for the first time, and remarked: 'Man, it would haud a terrible lot o' hay.' This take is culled from a splendid old volume called *Scotland Laughing*, by W. B. Burnett, which was published in 1955. Since then, we have all been open to wider, more cosmopolitan attitudes, New Ageism and whatnot. They cut no ice with the true Scot. He or she sees the depressing number of positive thinking books on the market and says: 'Positive thinking? Tried it once. Didnae work.' It's too much effort and too unnatural. In Caledonia, the light of hope is at best a Swan Vesta in a tar-painted cellar, where we dine on butter-side-down toast, and sip flat Irn Bru from a half-empty glass.

I know this all probably sounds like an extended exercise in misery – 'Hallo, ma name's Sepulchral Dirge fae Dunbar and ah'm no very happy at all' – bringing to mind the honeyed words of P. G. Wodehouse: 'It is never difficult to distinguish between a Scotsman with a grievance and a ray of sunshine.' But it needs saying. Sure, independence may write the epitaph on the gravestone of our pessimism. But I hae ma doots. Perhaps we may say, paraphrasing several claimants to the original epigram, that an optimist is a Scot who thinks this is the best of all possible countries; a pessimist is one who knows it is.

13 March 1999

The Scottish psyche deconstructed in Six Parts. No. 3: Health

ROBERT McNEIL

Snot. It sums up graphically, lumpily, swimmingly, the state of Scotland's health.

We must have a greater gross national product of snot than any country in the world. Indeed, one suspects a misspelling on our nation's birth certificate.

It's a disgusting state of affairs. From September to May, great snorting, gobbing gobbets are propelled on to cloth and paper; dignified men with degrees in Brainy Studies minutely examine the content of their hankies – even at the dinner table; most women in Scotland may be found dabbing hankies to their hooters every five minutes or blowing pantomime raspberry noises through their beaks with never a thought for the ludicrous impression it creates.

They paste make-up on their coupons and dab their bodies with scent, and then they go out into society and make fart noises through their faces. Ludicrous.

If only we could find a use for this nasal effluent; to fertilize fields, or power motor-cars, or fill in the cracks between bricks; we would be a wealthy nation indeed and need never fear the prospect of poverty, famine and drought which our betters in London, most of them Scottish, keep telling us must follow, should we opt for independence.

A snot-based economy could dominate the world, allowing us

to capitalize on our hitherto most under-employed asset. To wit, our ill-health.

The climate is the culprit, of course, but – historically at least – poverty has played a part in our wider sickness, as has the fact that a lot of Scots are slobs.

That said, this is not a siren call from the get-ye-doon-the-gym brigade. So much of this health malarkey is just so inappropriate. You get home, having battled through sleet and slush, the wind having gouged lumps out of your face. You sit down with a cup of strong tea and a plain chocolate Hobnob – heart-warming, cheering – and open your paper to find an article by a nutritionist telling you to eat more lettuce. In January.

Well, not us, matey boy. Give to us a peppery pie, cheery with grease, sodden with meat grey and formless. Once, when I was a child, I got a daddy-long-legs in a pie. We never complained.

The smell of the chippie on still winter nights. The thrill of the cake, the sweet caress of sugar on tongue, the welcoming lips of the fried onion ring. We will never surrender such joys.

Sadly, there are signs that some people are letting the national side down by taking up exercise. This is all right in the privacy of one's home but the distressing sight of such folk puffing and peching down the streets of our cities has been a depressingly common one in recent years.

It is not just the blatant narcissism that most excites our revulsion, but the contemptible fear of dying that the jogger so ostentatiously displays. We are all scared of dying but most of us contemplate the prospect in quiet panic at home rather than advertising it in gaudy lycra on the streets.

The Scottish Health Services' Report of 1935 'deplored the passing of the old staple foods of porridge, salt herring and potatoes and the substitution of shop bread, tinned foods, tea and sweets, and other goods purchased from shops or, more commonly, the traders' vans'.

Ah, the melancholy tinkle of the ice cream van on our council estates. How it transports us back to our humble origins.

The past is another country kitchen. Listen to this from Ian

Finlay, in his book *Scotland* (1945): '"High tea" is the traditional Scottish evening meal, and a healthy meal it was when it included such items as fresh herring or kippers, eggs, oatmeal bannocks, fresh butter, home-made jam and a scone to finish with. But replace those foods by fish and chips, canned meats and pickles, new bread and bakers' scones and cakes, as the last generation has done, and you have the key to the digestive troubles which undermine the health of so large a section of the Scottish community.'

Some of this is mince. Supermarket white bread is superb. Tatties, porridge and herring. Who's going to eat them when you can have crinkle-cut chips, coconut-flavoured ice cream, and chocolate bars the size of doorstoppers? The answer is: we are rich enough to have them all now. Tatties, porridge, herring, chips, ice cream, chocolate. I love them all.

In the past, under-nutrition was a problem, co-habiting with its partner, disease, in overcrowded slums. Now obesity abounds as acrylic-clad blobs with inside toilets waddle round huge food halls, piling fare into overstuffed trolleys. That at least is the thing we notice. Plenty of other people are picking at Seaweed Surprise or slurping nettle soup. Some Scots even eat fruit.

We are, at any rate, a society whose collective historic health is in transition. The snot, like the relatively poor, will always be with us. But we will live longer, grow taller and broader, and breathe more easily. We may never love lettuce, and ever love pies, but the day may come soon when the sick Scot must die.

20 March 1999

The Scottish psyche deconstructed in Six Parts. No. 4: Style

ROBERT McNEIL

I may as well state straight away that you'll never catch me in a lycra balaclava, leather kilt, or Tommy Hilfiger tweed jock strap. No sirree, bub.

Fashion is a foreign country. I don't so much have style as sartorial serendipity. In other words, if I'm neat, it's by accident. I'm happy to admit that, from the appalling haircut to the cheap desert boots. I look a right plonker. But I'm comfortable and, anyway. I don't give a hoot.

I habitually wear a cardigan. I have not set foot in a hairdresser's for nearly a year. I have a beard. I wear cords. When I dress for work, sometimes people say: 'You're looking smart today.' I know they're really thinking: 'At least his flies are done up for once'.

Show me what everyone else is wearing and I'll don something different. It's egotism if you will, but I despise the mob mentality. That makes me the perfect objective commentator on style among my fellow Scots, most of whom, at least among the under-fifties, look frankly laughable.

Q. What do you call an Airdrie girl in a white shell suit?
A. The bride.

Here's another question: what do you call a bloke with shaven or short broon hair, baseball cap, pasty face, baggy breeks with the crotch at the knees, and a hooded blouson giving him the air of a medieval serf? Answer: Scottish.

Street fashion, prole vogue, call it what you will, has accentuated the ugly for several years, partly in response to the new brutishness of women, partly in response to the right-wing political agenda.

No one has taken up this ugliness with greater enthusiasm than the Scots. I don't know why this urge towards uniformity is so pronounced in a country so apparently wedded to liberal values, creativity, and the cultivation of the intellect.

Northern Ireland – our nearest equivalent, minus the liberal values, creativity and intellect – is the same. I have never been anywhere supposedly in the United Kingdom where you got Ku Klux Klan looks for having hair over your collar. These are insecure, conservative people, with scary mob values.

It is traditional to contrast our naffness to the stylishness of the Italians. Fair dos. In Edinburgh, certainly, you can see their Mediterranean panache every summer. They might block the pavements as they stand in groups of at least three hundred chattering like amphetamine-fed starlings, but at least they look tastefully trendy as they do it.

They have avoided the Scottish and British rush to embrace the unattractive. The contrast could also be seen in the World Cup, at which our team was undoubtedly the ugliest, closely followed by England's. It has been thus for some time, with our less brutalized womenfolk swooning for the Latin players, their flowing locks and sensible strips a gigantic contrast to our shaven-headed borstal boys, whose outfits had been over-designed by sports clothiers to whom subtlety is a dodgy stranger.

That horizontal band round the shorts, that purple lightning stripe on a white background; and now the pink away strip. It's enough to make a grown man greet: as if the team's performance were not already sufficient reason.

Footballers, club-goers, disco dancers, even our best attempts at fops: they all look ridiculous. I suspect the reason Scots are not stylish is precisely because they are fashionable, in the shallow sense, often wearing clothes inappropriate to their climate, culture, and complexion. Look at the Scandics. They wear anoraks but have managed to make them modish. Theirs are blue and yellow, whereas the Scots – who should by rights have excelled at anorak design – usually go for dour olive green or navy blue.

Bizarrely, and I think reflecting the moves towards greater national identity and presence in the world, elements of our traditional dress are now to be seen adorning the science-fiction torsos of the catwalk models.

The kilt in particular has been embraced by the likes of Vivienne Westwood, a wacky lass previously best known for her bondage outfits. According to Mrs Westwood, 'clothes should be the badges of culture and civilisation!'

Jackboots, togas, powdered wigs and top hats; all certainly expressed something, but in the long run meant nothing.

Yves Saint Laurent, the French fashion designer, once said: 'Fashions fade, style is eternal.' So the kilt will undoubtedly slip down the thighs of haute couture before long and revert to being the sole preserve of the professional Scotsmen and the wedding-day nationalists.

The very idea of the kilt as fashion accessory brings to mind the withering words of Charles Murray:

> *Foreign fashions, lad, allure you.*
> *Homespun happit I would be:*
> *Bring nae mair, for I assure you*
> *Ferlies only scunner me.*
> *Fancy tartans, clanless, gaudy,*
> *Mention them nae mair, I say:*
> *Best it suits your service, laddie.*
> *An' my drinkin', hodden-grey.*
> (†Strange sights).

Of course, the gap between the rarefied fantasies of the fashion designer and the workaday world of the great unwashed is a vast one. No one in their right mind is going to wear a steel corset or a ceiling-high hat to go and watch the dog-racing.

So for the moment, tug the toggle on your anorak, twang the suspenders on your socks, and pray that the current ugliness will pass, and something new – perhaps kin to the liberating force and sense of sartorial elation of the sixties – will return.

27 March 1999

The Scottish psyche deconstructed in Six Parts. No. 5: Timidity

ROBERT McNEIL

Listen to these words, supposedly uttered by Calgacus, the Caledonian king, before the battle of Mons Graupius against the Romans in AD 97 (as recorded by Tacitus, who doubtless made most of it up): 'The enemy have no wives to fire their courage, no parents ready to taunt them if they run away . . . See them, a scanty band, scared and bewildered, staring blankly at the unfamiliar sky, sea and forests around them. The gods have given them, like so many prisoners bound hand and foot, into our hands.'

We were, of course, gubbed. Calgacus was clearly the Ally McLeod of his day. We have never learned. Swaggering one minute, staggering the next. Here's tae us/Wha's like us/Gey few/ And they're a' deid. Nae wonder.

Scottish aggressiveness is well known and, like all these bulging generalities, largely mythical. But it is not entirely to be dismissed. Aggression comes from fear which comes from uncertainty and poverty and lack of self-confidence, all of which for three hundred years at least we have had in abundance. Indeed, before that, we always had an eye for a fight, and a somewhat shameful history of supplying soldiers to nutters and tyrants around the world, not to mention by appointment to the British Empire.

In the Middle Ages, mercenaries were one of our greatest exports. In the First World War, 'The ladies from Hell!' – so called because of their kilts – inspired pride through their valour and ferocity; though in retrospect, they seem a bit dense, often having marched implacably towards the enemy guns to be predictably slaughtered. It was not like cattle gormlessly approaching an abattoir. The Scots soldiers did not have the excuse of bovinity. They knew what awaited them but still marched on, taking the feudal urge to obey orders a tiny bit too far.

At other times, with better-thought-out strategies by the British Army officers, they did manage to break through and, according to recent revelations – such is the fast-moving news agenda of war – a berserker streak seemed to break out among some, who killed enemy soldiers as they surrendered. And who's to say any of us would have acted any differently? I, at any rate, would have surrendered at the first sign of trouble.

I'm not proud and would wave the white flag when confronted by an unarmed duo of walking wounded from the Kaiser's Own Loyal Milkmaids. But I could have killed people too, what with my brain unhinged by all the noise and flashes of light and mud and disease and rats and corned beef eaten straight from the tin. I doubt I would have killed, because I am squeamish and highly principled, but I could see how less sensitive Scots might be induced to plunge bayonets through the flesh and bones of fellow human beings stuck in the middle of a war ordered and run by idiots.

It is instructive to read the works of observers from earlier this century, who produced wonderfully unreal books with ludicrous generalizations ('Oh yes, everyone in Fife is either a farmer or a miner; they have, for the most part, maroon eyes and tend to wear highly patterned socks'). Many of these have drawn distinctions between Highlanders and Lowlanders, claiming the former were poetic, romantic, gentle (hence all the inter-clan massacres), while the latter were pugnacious, even violent, the reason being they had been forged into a tough shield by the frequent military incursions from south of the Border by various bampots from evil Edward I onwards.

According to Ian Finlay, author of *Scotland* (1943): 'The hard core of the Lowlander contains, pent up within, an inner core of smouldering, dark violence which has been the dominating force in Scottish history and which underlies most of the outstanding achievements of the Scottish people. Its presence imbued the Lowlander with the energy that made him the really dangerous fighting man, ferocious in his dourness, as implacable as he was slow to rouse.'

Oh aye. Geez a brek. One suspects this may be a case of: 'A blate [timid] cat makes a prood moose'. There certainly are aggressive Lowlanders, exemplified perhaps by the swaggering clowns who parade their atavistic bigotry every July on the streets of Glasgow and Edinburgh. But most folk are timid as titmice, unless roused by the likes of Braveheart.

Scotland's history and, more particularly, her later historic helplessness, has helped to engender a weird martial reverence for medieval heroes, folk who fought for freedom, supposedly, until the yoke was on us. It has remained on us ever since, though quite comfortable it has been – and soon to have an artificial fur lining at Holyrood – giving us an excuse to make a song and dance preserving our national identity while lacking real power and responsibility. The result? Morose, petulant, childish prickliness.

Edwin Muir, in *Scottish Journey* (1935), tells of a typical Scots character in this regard, an old carter in Glasgow who had once been a renowned ploughman: 'After drinking for some time in silence he would flap his great hand on the counter of the public house and roar: "Wallace, the hero o' Scotland!" If nobody paid any attention to this, he would drink for another half-hour and flap his hand on the counter again: "D'ye ken what the English did to him, the dirty b******s? Libbed [castrated] him!" After that he would growl to himself for a time over his beer, but then, as he grew merry, he would tell stories of his feats at ploughing matches as a young man and of his prowess with the women. When he got really drunk he would bellow out in a voice that had once been good an old song beginning: "Fareweel, fareweel, my native hame".'

Says it all, really. That sort of thing still exists to a degree.

Braveheart has partly resurrected it but only among a very few of our more impressionable compatriots. Independence will kill it for good but, in the meantime, easy self-confidence is not displayed by banging bar-room tables. And timidity may be displayed in more ways than one.

For example, was there ever a nation that mumbled as much as the Scots? It happens because we don't know which language we're supposed to speak. Most of us had to ditch our glottal stops to get on; to modify harmonious 'didnae' to bump-along 'didn't'; to call our tea 'dinner' and our dinner 'lunch'. Some even went the whole hog and now speak uncomfortably of 'dinnah', but without the necessary chutzpah.

London rule has constricted and repressed our vocal cords. The word, if it is a word, 'Eh?' must be the most frequently uttered in Scotland. By contrast, in offices, hotels and airport lounges all over the country all the English people are effortlessly throwing their voices, so that you can hear their sensitive telephone conversations on the other side of the room. Their raucous laughter in Edinburgh's pubs damned near shatters the windows. And hats off to them for it.

We may be full of smeddum; we're thrawn and gallus tae. But it's a fat lot of use if we enunciate like bashful schoolboys brought before the headmaster for smoking behind the bike shed. Freedom! Eh?

3 April 1999

The Scottish psyche deconstructed in Six Parts. No. 6: Perfection

ROBERT McNEIL

His hair flaming in the wind, he marches manfully down the heather-covered hillside, muscles rippling, sword dangling from his side, rain and sweat mingling on his ruddy, finely chiselled face. Stopping only to stroke the neck of an adoring horse, he strides into the village.

Smoke rises from the simple, thatched homes. The sound of hammer on anvil punctuates the laughter of children and the good-natured gossip of the womenfolk. 'Aye, Rory, this'll be you,' says an old man. 'Aye, Lachlan, this'll be me,' replies the other. 'It is time,' says the old man. 'It is time,' concurs the other.

He enters a long, low hut and takes down a leather bag from a wooden peg. Mysteriously, ethereally, hissing steam billows from a chamber at the far end of the hall. A strange heat fills the room, a portent, perhaps, a wreath in which to wrap the sacred purpose of the coming journey. From the hills beyond the village, Rory hears the howl of a wolf. An eagle circles the clouds above, its pin-prick eye gleaming fiercely.

Rory walks fearlessly towards the source of the hissing steam. It envelops his body, healing, cleansing. He stands under a powerful shower of water, removes a bottle of Head and Shoulders from the leather bag, scrubs his body vigorously with jojoba liquid soap, dries himself, ties his hair into a pony tail, dons suit, tie, cufflinks; he takes his briefcase, passes through the connecting door to the garage, gets into his car and drives to his insurance office in the middle of Edinburgh. His car bears a sticker saying 'Alba'.

These, I suspect, are the two sides of the modern Scot, the Jekyll and Hyde of the millennial Caledonian psyche, seamlessly merging. Hollywood history married to the dour demands of reality, with the best man a melancholy folk-singer.

Yes, behold the contrasting dream and reality of the modern and, to coin a word best lisped, mythanthropic Scot. William Wallace in accounts. Conal the Librarian. *Highlander III – Renewing of the Bus Pass*. Here he is, Archie Typal, the perfect Scot of his own imagination, his sedentary soul perpetually pricked by a thistle. One foot in the brave.

Wha's like us? Everybody. Except they're better at it than we are. Football, style, self-confidence and health. We lag in them all. But all that can change. For I have a dream. A dream in which all Scots, black and white, can strive towards the promised land, the pine-forested, heather-carpeted, snow-capped peaks of wur nirvana.

We stand on the brink of a new Mclennium. Constitutional change offers much more than dreary realpolitik. New creative forces will be unleashed. Art, literature, philosophy: all are bound to prosper as the sun slowly spreads over the time-hallowed uplands of self-determination.

We can be a born-again country, without the goofy-eyed stares of the Christian and the renewal-of-man fanaticism of the communist. We have a chance to inspire, to be the world's first thoroughly decent country.

The psychology of individuals suggests that acting like someone competent eventually makes the actor competent. Without such self-bluffing, newspaper offices, to take one immediate example, would fold immediately. Nations too may take up the self-fulfilling pretence: let's act like we're a bright and humane country, leading the world by example, and we shall become that country. Make it so, Mr Salmond. Warp factor 11, Mr Dewar.

Think of it. We could have all the attributes of Norway without whaling, England without arrogance, America without

McDonald's. Multi-ethnic, multi-skilled, michty me, we could be the most splendidly unassuming little place in the world, quietly creating wealth, looking after the elderly, helping the Third World. In our perfect Scotland, the fainthearts, bigots and fatcat economic blackmailers will fade away.

But hold on a minute, I hear you say. Who's going to do all this? Who's going to clear up our massive council dump estates? Who will scrape off the 'God and Ulster' tattoos, burn the accordions, thwack sense into the shaven heads? Who will make our blobs healthy, who will instil culture into our massive lumpenproletariat, who will teach our team to score goals? And who – which man of magic? – will teach us to speak clearly and with confidence?

A pony-tailed accountant leaves the office and gets into his car. He drives home to Caledonian Crescent, in the leafy suburb of Dreamtime. As he gets out of the car, he hears the throaty bark of next door's poodle, while on the guttering of the roof a sparrow twitters and throws him a glance. Crossing from the garage to the house, he discards his suit with a sense of urgency and gets into the shower. As the steam rises, he feels himself being reborn. He leaves the shower and enters the long low hut, where he dons his kilt and straps on his sword.

Stepping outside, he finds the village just as it was when he left. An old man sitting in a doorway says: 'How did you fare?' Rory shakes loose his hair and looks thoughtful. At last he replies: 'It was bloody awful. And you can sod this for a game of Highlanders an' all. Pass me a fag and a pie.'

10 April 1999

FOLLOW MY LEADER

Donald Dewar: The real architect of Holyrood ready to reap his reward

PETER MacMAHON

The Scottish parliament should be mental. That is the considered view of Her Majesty's Secretary of State for Scotland, the cerebral and cultured Donald Dewar, the man who seems destined to be Scotland's first First Minister.

His gangly frame is sprawled across most of the seats at the back of his comfortable battle bus as he begins the final week's campaigning. Dewar is musing on how it will work, and an incident during a presentation by the parliament's Catalan architect comes to mind.

'One of my favourites is Enric Miralles' famous exhibition board with its "Parliament is a mental place". I don't think he is very familiar with the language of Scotland. But maybe it will be a mental place. Maybe people will be prepared to do a bit of thinking.'

Thinking is something the man who has made it his life's work to bring a devolved parliament to Scotland does a lot of. He thinks deeply not just about the nuts and bolts of establishing the first parliament in three hundred years but also about the always difficult interface between Scottish national identity and politics.

In common with most sensible politicians, Dewar has never denied that Scotland could be independent if it so desired. 'But I've always said that in my view it was unwise to go down that road.'

Though he may warn of the dangers of independence the man the polls predict is First Minister-in-waiting is a self-confessed 'cultural nationalist', steeped in Scotland's culture and learning, as Scottish as it is possible to be.

He outlines what marks him out from the man he almost unfailingly calls 'Mr' Salmond, in that slightly old-fashioned, respectful, lawyerly way.

'The difference is that I come from a Scottish background. I am marked by my Scottish cultural experiences. I've been brought up in a separate legal system which doesn't allow me to practise law outside Scotland – it's built on a totally different philosophical base.

'I think all my experiences are shaped by a consciousness of being Scottish, whether it be in terms of my philosophical approach to life or my practical experience.'

Warming to the theme, he continues: 'Probably since the late 1880s Scotland has become prouder and prouder of the differences. I draw an enormous amount from the literary traditions of Scotland – to be fair I draw a great deal from the literary traditions of the United Kingdom as well – they overlap, obviously.

'But it doesn't follow from that that you've got to endorse political nationalism at a stage in the development of political structures when nationalism looks a more and more archaic and outdated concept.

'And indeed Mr Salmond's admissions about the management of an independent Scottish pound just make that point.' The SNP leader last week conceded that sterling would continue to be the currency of an independent Scotland before it joined the euro.

Dewar adds: 'If you say to me: "Do you want to maintain the difference in Scotland?" of course I do and that's what devolution is all about, a parliament that reflects Scottish values, Scottish solutions; trusts Scottish people – that's what Labour has delivered.

'But that doesn't mean I have to support an independent Scottish army, the dismantling of our entire national institutions, the apportionment of the national debt and so on.'

He is sceptical about what he sees as the SNP's reluctance to talk about independence. 'The Nationalists took a very early decision not to campaign on their main plank. They have been anxious to talk about issues where they feel the record of the Government is weak.

'They have been very, very reluctant to talk about independence, about whether we should have relations with the rest of the United Kingdom or not. Every time you try to tackle that there are great shouts of negative campaigning.'

Despite his reported reservations over the running of the Labour campaign by Gordon Brown and a team of advisers mainly drawn from Labour's London headquarters, Dewar is unrepentant over the accusations that Labour's first, anti-independence party broadcast was a masterpiece of scaremongering, negative campaigning. 'It was trying to raise issues because we have to break into the public consciousness with some of the real questions. But the second one was very constructive, very positive.' The arguments used in the broadcast were 'absolutely first class'.

How does he react to the taunts that this is a Millbank-run London-pulling-the-strings campaign? 'I get very tired of it.' Is it true? 'No. But people just go on saying it. I can't stop them saying it.'

The campaign does, though, have all the hallmarks of the Millbank machine, something which the SNP has focused on. Dewar becomes scathingly sarcastic.

'You mean it's efficient? Oh, dear me, the Labour Party is efficient and we must attack it for its efficiency. Come on. We have national experience. We've had some help in the way in which you organize the basics. All parties draw on their reserves.

'I find it lunatic ... people say to me "What a disgrace it is that Gordon Brown's helping". The story would be if he wasn't. Supposing you were saying why has Gordon Brown not been around? I would be fighting to think of an explanation. I would have to say flu or something.'

Perhaps feeling the criticism that he is not in charge, he adds: 'This battle bus keeps constantly in touch but I took a decision that I would be out as a campaigning figure and I think it has been a good decision, it has been a happy experience.

'We have been coming back every night for strategy discussions but clearly there are people minding the shop while I am away.'

Dewar, a home rule campaigner for decades, is not convinced by the argument that devolution has let the independence genie out of the bottle. 'It is the oldest fallacy in the world, that if there is a very strong move for reform the best way of defeating it is offering nothing at all. That is what the Bourbons thought. It doesn't seem to me to be a very sensible approach to modern Scotland.'

But devolution has not killed political nationalism, as George Robertson, Labour's former shadow Scottish Secretary, said it would. 'I am not in the business of killing people. People are entitled to their views.'

He is angered by the SNP's 'Scotland's Party' presumptions. 'I object to the arrogance of saying they are Scotland's party and the very clear implication of much of their propaganda that those that don't accept their political ideology are somehow betraying Scotland or are not true Scots. I think I am every bit as legitimate an interpreter of Scottish opinions as Mr Salmond or any of his colleagues.'

There has always been a suspicion that Dewar is rather more 'old' than his party's Scottish New Labour campaign suggests. 'I am told I am a great Brownite. I see it as an integrated team. I've got immense admiration for the prime minister's work on behalf of the party and his sense of direction in politics. I think they're both essential.'

So would he be prepared to differ from the London leadership on policies in the devolved areas for which the parliament is responsible? Yes. He takes education as an example. 'To the disappointment of some journalists, they come to me and say ' "Why aren't you doing a David Blunkett?" ' The answer is because we have got a different education system in Scotland and we approach radical change in a rather different way. That is true of the health service.'

He adds: 'The point about this is that over a period of time we want to develop our own lines reflecting the needs of Scotland

and the wishes of Scotland. We're building a machinery which I hope will put to bed for ever the system and the inflexibilities and the insensitivities which produced the poll tax or education vouchers.

'We will have a parliament which reflects Scottish priorities which will be trying, no doubt at times falteringly, but I hope effectively over a period to deal with some of the problems of Scotland. That's the whole point of devolution.

'I don't think suddenly Scotland is going to be totally different. You have to look back over a period in terms of change, a new confidence. We start with a parliament which is very, very new.

'We don't know how many MSPs Labour is going to have but let's say for the sake of argument that it will be between fifty and seventy. Of that there is going to be only a handful who have been in a national parliament but what there are going to be is an enormous number of new faces, some very bright people. Not by any means all of them but some very bright and a lot of very good women.

'We're going to have to settle down. We're going to have a big education job to do. I don't mean that in any way patronizingly. I think the new approach, the lack of preconceived notions, will, I hope, make it exciting and a place for change.'

So if he is excited why is the nation so laid back about these 'historic' elections?

'I think maybe it is something of a tribute to Scotland that we are a tolerant and civilized political system and it is not the tradition to exchange abuse. Maybe this is the Nationalists' trouble – I don't think that there is nationalist fervour which defies logic and argument is a common characteristic of the Scots.

'I certainly believe that rational argument is the best way of conducting election campaigns. No doubt I sin many times but that is my basic position.'

So the sinner repents. It is now for the people to judge his repentance.

4 May 1999

Jim Wallace: The man who would be kingmaker

PETER MacMAHON

The longer they are in the public eye, the more politicians are caricatured. Alex Salmond is Smart Alec. Donald Dewar is Big Donald. David McLetchie, well, he has not been around long enough. Jim Wallace is the Mr Nice Guy of Scottish politics.

'I don't think there's anything wrong with being nice,' the leader of the Scottish Liberal Democrats says carefully as we talk on his election battle bus. However, the man who could be the kingmaker of Holyrood if no party has an overall majority on 6 May clearly resents the implication that being nice equates with being a soft touch.

'If anyone mistakes niceness for a lack of determination then they would be seriously mistaken. You don't enter the Liberal Party or Liberal Democrat politics embarking on an easy road to power so you have got to have a sense of commitment to what you believe in and a sense of determination to try and achieve it.

'So if I am sometimes characterized as being nice then I'm not going to disavow it but don't be mistaken, I'm quite determined to win the things that are important for Scotland. That's why I am throwing myself wholeheartedly into this campaign.'

It is the Liberal Democrats' misfortune that the electorate do not see them as the party of determination. The wishy-washy Liberal jibe has always jarred. So where is the evidence to demonstrate that the party which now stands a chance of sharing power in a coalition has what it takes? Wallace cites his struggles with Labour in the constitutional convention before the last election to achieve proportional representation for the Scottish parliament, his securing the compromise of 129 seats for the parliament and winning the argument for the 'reserve powers' model for devolution as a demonstration of his toughness and determination as a negotiator.

He recalls the convention days. 'I don't think there is any evidence at all that when push came to shove we got shoved. Looking at the [devolution] scheme it bears greater resemblance to what Liberal Democrats have been arguing for than where the Labour Party started out.'

Wallace is realistic enough to recognize that the Liberal Democrats' only hope of power is in a coalition but says that is a function of the new politics which proportional representation brings. 'It is very unlikely that any one party will win an overall majority despite what the Labour Party might say and therefore every party, if it is going to have power, is going to have to share power.

'I believe that the way of ensuring that the parliament is successful is to have effective and stable government and that inevitably means that there ought to be some coalition.

'Between now and polling day our task must be to make sure we are in there with as many seats as we possibly can muster because our hand will be much the stronger the more of us that are there.'

If they are not wishy-washy, it is often said that the Liberal Democrats are a party of protest, not a party interested in power. Wallace positively bristles. 'That's absolute rubbish.' He says that the role Liberal Democrats have played in the United Kingdom political arena in pushing Labour into constitutional reforms such as proportional representation for European elections, human rights legislation and even possible change in the Westminster voting system proves it.

From local to national government, the lesson is the same, he says, making it clear that he is looking to be in office at Holyrood rather than opposition. 'When we have had an opportunity to take power we have not shirked it. You are in politics to get your ideas and policies into practice and I would value that opportunity.

'There's often plenty to protest about. It doesn't mean to say we're not going to protest but equally I am quite determined that as a party we should think of ourselves in this election as a potential party of government.'

One of the great mysteries in the new politics is just how a coalition would be formed. We are not used to it here but Wallace makes the point that the process is commonplace in Europe. Parties fight on their manifestos, put them to the electorate, wait for the outcome and then construct a programme for coalition government, he says.

So, it's as easy as that? Not if you listen to those who say that coalitions give voters government they did not vote for. Wallace says: 'The more voters vote for the things in our manifesto, the more likely they are to get them. The emphasis is on what we do and what we try to achieve rather than which posterior is on the back seat of a ministerial Rover.'

Most of the coalition talk centres on Labour and the SNP so does he rule out a deal with the Tories? 'I cannot conceive of any circumstances . . .' he begins, but it is pointed out that this was the formulation used by Michael Heseltine when he ruled out standing against Margaret Thatcher and subsequently did. Wallace laughs. 'I really mean that I cannot conceive of any circumstances where that ever would become a likely possibility,' he says.

Back to reality. If he does form a coalition, it must be important that he gets on with his potential partner. Does he like Alex Salmond? There is a very long pause. 'It's . . . I mean . . . I don't find Alex someone who you would bump into and say "let's go for a pint". Equally – and Alex has mentioned this before – Alex and I once partnered each other in a round of golf against two representatives of a leading oil company. Once I got past the bunkers on the first four holes at Gleneagles our partnership worked quite well and we did win.

'I have never found Alex a particularly outward-going, social sort but relations between us have always been cordial. They have never been acrimonious.'

He agrees that you don't have to be the best of pals to work together.

What about Donald, the man who is likely to lead the largest party at Holyrood and therefore the leader Wallace has said he would go to talk to first? 'Donald I have known a lot longer. I was probably first introduced to Donald when I was still practising at the Bar. Again, Donald is not someone you would say "let's go for a pint" to either.

'I have always had a fairly good relationship with Donald. I think the fact that we're both lawyers ... without our conversations ever having to descend to the legal. There is the way our minds work that you know what each other is getting at.'

So another oft-made criticism of devolution, that the Edinburgh parliament would be run by lawyers, will be true.

Scottish politics has also been attacked for being obsessed with the process of constitutional change, so what about real, concrete proposals? If there was one thing he could achieve in the four-year term of the parliament, what would it be? Wallace is typically honest. 'Clearly education is our number-one priority. I think one of the problems of answering the question is that very often investment in education takes some time to come through. I am not trying to avoid the question, it would have to be seen to be making steps in education, raising standards in education.'

An even more fundamental question. In Scotland with a left-of-centre Nationalist party, a right-of-centre Tory Party and the Labour Party (wherever they are), what is the point of the Liberal Democrats? Wallace splutters, 'What is the point? I'll show you a thirty-seven-page manifesto. It is to drive the agenda. There are a number of issues where we have actually come forward with policies well in advance of other parties who have adopted them late in the day.'

However, to emphasize the quest for real power, he adds: 'I don't think we should be content to be a glorified national think tank, far better that we're actually in there in government implementing them at the right time and in good measure.'

Though his remarks about the price he would extract from Alex Salmond are revealing of a nervousness that Labour may pull off the feat of winning an absolute majority, Wallace reveals that if he does make it into power he will be the first Liberal in office in a law-making parliament in Britain since Archie Sinclair, Churchill's air minister in the war. Just thought we might like to know.

A feature of this election campaign for Wallace is that for the first time he is accompanied by his wife Rosie, leaving their two daughters at home in Orkney under the watchful eyes of his mother and the New Zealand au pair. 'It was Rosie's idea,' Wallace says.

Rosie chips in: 'In elections Jim can't get home by teatime because we live in Orkney and it's lonely if you are away four days on your own. So I thought I would come along. It beats going to Safeway's and going to work.'

Wallace laughs and recalls the fact that he has been away from home for long periods at Westminster: 'It is nice to have her along – you can relax together in the evening. We got married the month after I was elected so we never actually lived together.'

Rosie adds that the campaign has become their 'trial marriage'. Michael Moore, the Liberal Democrats' campaign manager for the election, has even told Wallace that he is far less tetchy as a result of having his wife along. Wallace, who spent yesterday in his bus on the Clyde estuary and took a quick trip over the water to Dunoon, says he relishes campaigning.

'Every time I have campaigned and have to knock on doors, I have always found the first door difficult but once I get into the stride, I enjoy it.'

He will be hoping that his efforts will see him knocking on the door of the parliament's temporary Assembly Hall home with a mandate to demand a place in Scotland's first government for three hundred years.

15 April 1999

David McLetchie: High hopes of the low-profile Tory Election '99 campaigner

PETER MacMAHON

The Scottish Tories are moving on up, moving on up. Nothing can stop them. So the Conservatives, with their M People election theme tune, would have us believe. M in the Tories' case stands for McLetchie, David, the party's first Scottish parliamentary leader, the man with the lowest profile of any of those seeking to be the first First Minister of Scotland.

Mr McLetchie has been criticized for being boring, for lacking charisma and for being the ideological heir of his right-wing Tory friend, Michael Forsyth. Not long ago, there were even Conservative whispers that so poor was his performance, Mr McLetchie would not be their leader at Holyrood.

The Edinburgh lawyer, who had never held elected political office, would, we were assured by his enemies in the party and his political opponents alike, be eaten alive in the brutal cut and thrust of a Scottish election campaign.

It has not turned out like that. Mr McLetchie, forty-seven, has held his own against the experience of Donald Dewar, Alex Salmond and Jim Wallace. This is not to say that he has no political problems.

As well as his low public recognition there is the more fundamental difficulty of leading a party which the voters of Scotland rejected at the last general election.

Mr McLetchie talks as he relaxes in the back of the leather-seated Tory people carrier – they do not have a battle bus – at the end of a hard day's campaigning in Glasgow on Wednesday. He is on his way to campaign in his targeted Edinburgh Pentlands seat, once held by Malcolm Rifkind, though he demonstrates his status as an 'ordinary guy' by making clear he will get home in time to watch the Manchester United game on television.

He is frank about the way he viewed the job after his election. 'At the outset one was a bit daunted at the prospect of leading a national campaign for thirty days, but we're halfway through now and I am enjoying it much more than I thought I would. Personally I feel I am growing in confidence and getting stronger the longer the campaign goes.'

He is dismissive of those who had written him off. 'I never doubted my ability to compete head to head with people like Donald Dewar and Alex Salmond and Jim Wallace. I always knew I could do it.

'I just had to demonstrate that to others. A lot of the criticism I don't think was personal to me. I don't think there was any personal malice. I think there was frustration in the party in terms of making progress. William Hague has to put up with ten times worse than I do.'

As for talk of a challenge: 'I have been leading the party in the campaign and I expect to lead the party in the parliament. Any leadership challenges in the Scottish parliament are far more likely to come for Donald Dewar and Alex Salmond than me.'

A good vibe, but what of the serious business of the parliament where, thanks to the proportional representation system, there will be visible elected Tories after two years in the wilderness. One of the first tasks will be to elect a First Minister.

The proposed system involves an elimination ballot of all MSPs, so it could come down to a straight fight between Mr Dewar and Mr Salmond. If Labour does not have an outright majority and it has failed to woo the Liberal Democrats into coalition, the Tories could therefore have a crucial role to play in assisting Mr Dewar into power, no doubt to Mr Dewar's great embarrassment.

How will they vote in such a ballot? 'We don't know what the overall arithmetic is going to be, nor do we know the order of elimination of the parties.

'We're not in the business of furthering the separatist agenda of the SNP, so it is almost inconceivable that we would ever vote for Alex Salmond as First Minister for Scotland or for the SNP to form an administration.'

Is this the grand Unionist coalition with Labour that has been spoken of and which has been much derided by the SNP? 'We have quite clearly said that we don't believe in coalitions. We're not talking about having coalitions with Labour or the Liberals or anybody else.

'We wouldn't enter a coalition. We certainly would not be entering coalitions with the SNP and we're not particularly enthusiastic about coalitions with Labour because that would mean having to sign up for a four-year programme.

'I don't see why you can't have an administration which might be a minority administration putting forward proposals and seeking support from other parties for them on that issue-by-issue basis. That creates much more honest and open opinion, rather than back-stairs deals done within a cabinet.'

There is still a huge credibility gap for the Scottish Tories and their leader, who campaigned hard for a No, No vote in the devolution referendum.

Does he wish this whole devolution thing had not happened? 'Yes, of course. I would rather we had won the argument in the referendum but we didn't and we just have to respect the decision that was taken. The decision we had to take was do we pick our ball and say "We're no' playing" or say we have this new important, law-making institution in Scotland which will materially affect Scottish life, do we have any distinctive Tory ideas for this parliament?

'The answer is: yes, we do. Even people who voted No, No

accept that the parliament is for keeps. There is no going back.'

It is a message that many voters will find almost as hard to take as the admission in the party's manifesto that they got things wrong at the last election.

'There certainly was a large degree of hostility at the time of the 1997 election and that hostility has largely evaporated. People are prepared to listen to our ideas and give us a degree of respect again. We may need more people to positively love us but there are a lot of people who acknowledge that a Scottish parliament needs a Scottish Conservative presence.

'There is a vacuum in Scottish politics which I would characterize as the lack of a right-of-centre political voice. All the other parties, by and large, position themselves to the centre-left.'

But would not a radical Scottish Tory Party follow the example of the Conservatives in the 1980s and offer the Scottish people a tax-cutting agenda, using the 'tartan tax' powers to offer a reduction in income tax north of the Border?

'That's something we can consider for the next term. For the first term I don't think that would have credibility. I think what people want to see is constitutional and financial stability in the first term of the parliament.

'For us to have said we would take a penny off or two pence off, that would have been seen as irresponsible and opportunistic.'

His explanation of why people deserted the Tories at the last election is simple. Labour's skilful 'time for a change' campaign was one reason, but he adds: 'The party was seen to be divided and riven by sleaze and scandal, no longer the strong united party that we had been.

'A lot of the sleaze allegations which beset individuals in the last parliament hammered away at that sense of respectability that was always associated with the party by many of our core voters. I think that was very damaging.'

In Holyrood there will be a tough code of conduct for the MSPs. Mr McLetchie says: 'We will crack down very hard on any member that breaches either the letter or spirit of these rules.'

Tory MPs south of the Border have increasingly railed against the 'overfunding' of Scotland compared with England. McLetchie, not surprisingly, does not agree.

'I think Scotland gets a good deal out of the Union and I am not in a position of rocking that particular boat.'

What will he say to Tory politicians who say that the overfunding should end? 'You do what every politician would do by standing up for the interests of your own country or community as you counter these arguments as effectively as possible to get yourself the largest slice of the pork barrel.'

However, he concedes that there will have to be a debate over issues like the 'West Lothian question' at Westminster. 'I am relatively relaxed if Scottish MPs did not have the power to vote on domestic English affairs which are within the province of the Scottish parliament. Most people in Scotland would see that as only fair and reasonable.'

What would the Tories' first action be in the parliament? Mr McLetchie does not hesitate. 'The first bill we would introduce would be to abolish university tuition fees because it is an enormous tax burden on families and a tax on learning. It would demonstrate our tax-cutting credentials.'

Then there is the Heart of Midlothian (Prevention of Relegation) Bill 1999, though on that he intends to seek cross-party support from a fellow Jambo,* Alex Salmond. It is probably as near to a coalition as they will get.

Mr McLetchie has appeared at his most tetchy when asked about his close friend and ally, Mr Forsyth. 'I'm not Michael Forsyth. I'm not Malcolm Rifkind and I am not Ian Lang. I'm David McLetchie. I'm my own person.

'I'm a great admirer of Michael's. He is a long-standing friend of mine, as everybody knows, but I judge people as they are and I expect people to judge me as I am. I am not a surrogate for anybody.'

Does he miss him? 'I would much prefer to have Michael

---

* A 'Jambo' is a nickname for a supporter of Heart of Midlothian Football Club.

Forsyth in the House of Commons, even on the opposition benches.

'He enlivened Scottish political life in his fourteen years in parliament and I think he is a loss. For all that some people have characterized him as a hate figure he actually won the respect of political opponents right across the spectrum for his abilities.'

Can he emulate his friend and rise to the top? Not this time around. The polls show the Tories will do well to be the third party in the parliament.

During a visit to the Calton Athletic drugs recovery group in Glasgow on Wednesday, Mr McLetchie posed playing pool with a couple of young lads. Winding up the picture opportunity, his ever-present spin-doctor, Gerry O'Brien, asked the youngsters: 'Is there any hope for him?'

He meant McLetchie's pool-playing ability. 'Not much,' one replied.

He could have been talking politics.

23 April 1999

Alex Salmond: Convinced of victory against all the odds

PETER MacMAHON

It's all gone pear-shaped. The election is as good as lost for the Nationalists. The polls show Labour could win an overall majority. It's gloom, doom and leadership crisis time.

Alex Salmond looks me straight in the eye. 'I think we're going to win it. I think we're going to win the election. I believe that will happen.'

Certainty and self-belief are attributes which any leader must have to survive in the brutal, judgemental and egocentric world of politics. Salmond has all these attributes, in spades.

Whether he is putting on an act for a demoralized party, it is hard to tell. More likely he has, like other politicians cast as certain losers, convinced himself that he can secure victory by the sheer force of his impressive will.

It has not been a good campaign for the SNP. It has found itself under heavy pounding from Labour's mighty Millbank machine, transplanted temporarily to Scotland.

Salmond himself came under attack for opposing the NATO intervention on Kosovo, the 'penny for Scotland' plan has allowed Labour to cast it as the party of high taxes and its Liberal Democrat suitors appear to want to form a coalition only with Labour.

So Salmond should be downcast, depressed and feeling pain from his bad back, but his spirits appear high. How is he? 'Great, just great.'

After suffering a big setback when opinion polls last week

showed its vote was in freefall, the party adopted a new strategy. Out went the regular press conference. In came more campaigning around the country and the publication of its own newspaper as it does not believe it gets a fair showing from the Scottish press.

Salmond is bitter about the newspapers, including, it must be reported, *The Scotsman*. The *Daily Record* has also attracted his fury amid claims that it used a nine-day-old picture of an angry Sean Connery lunging at a photographer to try to discredit the SNP.

So how was the world's greatest living Scotsman after his exposure to Scottish media which even shocked the star's tough Hollywood agent Nancy Seltzer? 'Sean is on great form. I think the *Record*. . . he just found that extraordinary, the nine-day-old picture. But he got himself into a very humorous resolve about it.

'The thing I admired was that he knew he would take a lot of flak but he insisted on doing it – his idea, actually, because I wouldn't have asked him to put himself in that position. It was his initiative, his wish and his determination and I think the world of him for it.'

Was Connery angry? 'There was a steely resolve. He was going to say something and no matter what anybody else said, and I thought he delivered.' Salmond lapses into a passable Connery impersonation. 'They tried to provoke me, they sucssheeded.'

Provoking Salmond is a little more difficult than provoking 007, though he was clearly a little irked by a remark made by Jim Wallace, his potential coalition partner, in his *Scotsman* interview. Asked if he liked Salmond, Wallace said the SNP leader was not the kind of guy he would go for a pint with, but nor was Donald Dewar.

Quick as a flash Salmond retorts: 'Well, it looks like he is not in a coalition, then. I would go for a pint with either of them.'

Even Donald? 'Yes, though I am not so certain I would go for a pint with Robin Cook.' It was Cook who branded him the toast of Belgrade after his Kosovo statement, about which Salmond repeats that he has no regrets.

So, if there is no change there, is there any change in his attitude to coalitions after the revelation that Tony Blair and Paddy Ashdown appear to have done a deal on a Lab–Lib coalition before the last UK election?

'Whether it was a whole pact, half a pact, a whole loaf, half a loaf or even a few slices of bread, it's still an indication that the London leaderships were anxious to stitch up the Scottish parliament.

'Paddy Ashdown and Tony Blair were engaged in a project, the endgame of which is to merge the Liberal and Labour parties.

'I don't think Liberal activists in Scotland would be too enthusiastic about this prospect and I don't think Liberal MSPs in the new parliament will be.'

So is it now 'let's call the whole thing off' between the SNP and the Liberal Democrats despite having a lot of policies in common? 'No, I'm going to wait until after the election and see what the verdict of the people is, and take it from there.'

Has he spoken to Wallace about this pre-election deal? Salmond laughs again. 'I might give him a ring and ask for clarification. No, I'll invite him for a pint.'

Does he believe that Wallace is moving towards a Lab–Lib coalition? 'If that's what he wants to do, he is perfectly able to do it. That's his entitlement but I just think he should tell people beforehand.'

What if they could form a coalition and Wallace offered a deal where they could implement policies like extra funding for education, ending PFI or abolishing tolls on the Skye Bridge, but the price was the referendum? 'The independence referendum is not negotiable. I don't regard coalition politics as the minority party coming to the larger party and saying we're going to knock the following things out of your programme.

'I regard the way that coalitions are formed as the majority party or the largest party with the biggest mandate gets to implement its programme, keep its contract with the electorate and then asks the minority party if there are aspects of their programme they would like to see implemented as well.

'In the circumstances of having a referendum – that is winning the election – I think a popular administration would be well placed to win a referendum and ours would be a popular administration.'

If the SNP wins an overall majority, is that a mandate for independence? 'No. What you say is that it is an indication that there should be immediate negotiations. John [Swinney/Deputy Leader of the SNP] has said the timescale might be six months, that's based on the Czech and Slovak example, and I've said that the referendum would follow as soon as possible.

'The decision on independence is taken at the referendum, it ain't taken at the general election. The point of decision is the referendum. The reason for that is quite clear. In any election, whether it be a British or a Scottish general election, it is decided on a range of issues and not on a single constitutional issue, and the single constitutional issue will be put to the people on a straight question in a referendum and decided by the people.'

The SNP's strategy changed after the polls showed that there was a big gap between them and Labour. Salmond uses a golf analogy. 'I once said that we should play the ball where it lies, but we have shifted the ball and we have shifted the ball by changing the style of the campaign and, of course, by the launch of our paper which will run daily.'

Here his aversion to the press is clear. 'I don't care about editorials. That doesn't matter to me in the slightest. When editorial gets into the news columns I think it's a bit much.

'I don't expect a mass conversion overnight in terms of the ownership structure of the Scottish press which has provoked that position and therefore we've got to deal with that, and we have dealt with it by changing the style of our campaign and getting the impression across to people.

'This is not a moan or a whinge, this is a statement of fact on something we have done something about. We are getting a bit mad but we're also getting even by equalizing the odds by publishing our own daily paper.'

He reveals that he has stopped taking *The Scotsman* for the first time in his life because he disagrees with the opinions of Andrew Neil, the editor-in-chief. 'I haven't stopped reading it, I have just stopped buying it. That's my preference. I'm not advocating other people do that. I am not on a crusade to stop people buying *The Scotsman*.'

Although he has been working night and day on the campaign trail, Salmond says he sleeps like a log, but does he not have nightmares about the stories that his leadership is in trouble if he fails to secure at least forty seats? 'It never actually entered my head.'

Salmond is not a politician prone to flights of moist-eyed Caledonian rhetoric but ask him to define his nationalism and you get a rare glimpse of sentiment. 'I came into the Scottish National Party to achieve independence for Scotland; to achieve what that independence will achieve for Scotland – substantial economic progress matched with a keen sense of social justice.

'A rich country and a rich society, in that phrase we have borrowed from Ireland; a society not just rich in its material distribution but also rich in terms of its wider cultural, social, psychological impact and how it feels about itself.

'I think we can have that rich society. I think independence is necessary to achieve that. I shall pursue this independence cause and that Saltire shall fly in the wind.'

29 April 1999

Forget Big Tam, Big Margo is is the Nationalists' real star

GILLIAN GLOVER

Just one word: Margo. No other prospective MSP dares to campaign with only their first name on the posters.

But then there is no other potential parliamentarian quite like Margo, and adding the MacDonald is as unnecessary as saying Edinburgh, Scotland; or Paris, France.

That's not to say that more than twenty-five years in – and out of – Scottish nationalism has gifted Margo any exclusive little shortcut around the mechanics of pre-election toil. A landmark she may be, a fondly remembered, or sarcastically noted, 'blonde bombshell', a warrior queen, or just a gallus, brazen big-mouthed lassie from Hamilton, but this last lap towards polling day saw her with a diary creaking with good deeds, grave concerns and routine rabble-rousing.

If the Scottish rabble are for rousing, that is. Margo is no longer convinced on this point. 'All this guff about the settled will of the Scottish people. My husband considers he won the referendum. He urged people not to take part and 40 per cent of them answered the call, which, he says, was the biggest single return.'

She erupts into a big wheezing laugh which quickly tails off in a fit of furious coughing. She has a chest infection and has been advised by her doctor to take things easy, but the calendar and her own cussedness will not permit that, so by 9.15 on a wet, blustery morning she's heading for a nursery school in Edinburgh's south side, railing at nature and the manipulation of the media *en route*, like Lady Macbeth swapping the blasted heath for the blasted pavement.

'This election more than any other has made me start worrying about the quality of our democracy, and therefore the quality of our society,' she rasps. 'Folk don't have the time, or feel they don't, to consider the big issues of the day. They're all working harder, under more pressure. They may have better holidays, nicer houses, but the price has been strain on society and not enough time to reflect. That's why people want their information packaged and pre-digested. And I find that quite frightening, don't you?

'We have phone-ins on whether or not to bomb Milosevic. Line one for yes, line two for no. Does that not worry you? It worries the hell out of me. How can people come to big, moral decisions when everything's reduced to such simple terms, to slogans and soundbites?'

And so with a wheeze and a hefty shoulder to the door, we arrive at the repellently named Potty Place nursery school, where the owner, a pretty young woman of athletic physique and even more energetic commentary, addresses her parliamentary candidate about the flaws in government policy for educating the under-fives.

This is the perfect approach for an old pro like Margo. 'Excuse me, you're asking me to explain this government's policy. Well, if I could do that . . .' and she breaks into another laugh. She has quickly taken control of the conversation; asking question after question with polite intensity. 'I'm being deliberately hard on this point,' she says, 'because I have to understand your problems properly.

'Now why can't you just go to the bank with a business plan? How come you're having difficulties? So what is it, precisely, that you want? Is it a grant? Is it a loan? Or what?'

Margo mentions, repeatedly, that she has made enquiries and knows that this nursery is well run and popular with local parents. The young woman preens. She does not appear to notice that she has lost control of the debate. Her impassioned speech about a shocking lack of trained staff trails off and Margo moves majestically towards the infants' table where, to the slight anxiety of the staff, she perches on a tiny chair to help the children make scones.

'This is our baking project,' the nursery owner informs us unnecessarily. 'It gives them weighing, measuring and knowledge of the world.'

The scones go off to the oven for baking, we move outside to discuss the vexed question of taxation. 'I have a friend,' Margo is told, 'who has a big, big business and thinks he would have to move to England if the SNP got control.'

'What does he make, your friend?'

The young woman blushes, thinking Margo has thundered in and asked the unthinkable: an estimate of someone's salary. 'I wouldn't like to say,' the nursery owner falters.

'So he makes nothing. He's a service provider.' And she sweeps into a series of fine hypotheses about why anyone would believe the SNP would be so foolish as to drive someone like this rich and anonymous friend across the Border.

Back on the street Margo demands: 'Well, how do you think she'll vote? My guess is we haven't got her at all. She just wanted to see who would respond to her letter. I understand the Lib Dems didn't.'

She has lavished two hours on this 'legitimate constituency interest' and her next stop is the campaign HQ, a former butcher's shop in Causewayside. In keeping with its lineage, there are still large mammals displayed in the window: life-size chipboard figures of the area's SNP candidates. 'My big babies,' Margo beams, showing me a series of speech balloons which will be attached to each inert candidate's frozen smile. 'I'm sure they've made mine weer and fatter,' she grumbles. 'Look, I'm taller than this damn thing.' And she is. In all senses.

After a series of phone calls, she's off again, to Shelter this time, a a charity she has been involved with for more than twenty years. Then it's into the 'big noisy car' with her agent, Peter Warren, to tour the constituency. They have stalls set out on the main streets. 'Always either outside food shops or off-licences,' says Warren. 'Make of that what you will.'

Sitting behind this pair as they cruise the neat streets of Edinburgh's south side is like gatecrashing a rehearsal for the Goon Show. The loudspeaker on the roof blares out a few phrases. 'This is Alex Salmond. This is Alex Salmond.'

'Is that all he says?' I ask.

'Oh no,' says Margo. 'Every so often water will appear and he'll walk on it. But we've got big Sean as well.' And Connery's voice, sounding even more shlurred than ushual, filters into our sealed cocoon. Warren opens the sun roof to let me hear how loud the message really is.

'Turn it off a minute,' wails Margo as the car noses down a wide avenue in the Grange. 'These people are behind their big high walls for a reason. They'll no' want to be disturbed by the likes of us.

'Personally I think we should take requests. Country music, maybe. Or the Alexander Brothers . . . I'm nobody's child, no-o-body's child. Hey, look, there's a woman waving. Come on, practise that wave back. Is this the textbook wave? Ach, who am I to go waving at people? What a cheek.'

Next stop is Moredun, a windswept gritty street outside Scotmid, where Margo bars the exit of a skinny young girl in jeans. 'Are you dashing somewhere?' she asks. 'Aye,' replies the girl, increasing her pace. 'Then I'll dash with you, if you don't mind,' beams our candidate, and she takes off in pursuit, a sight so unseemly that the girl eventually stops and offers up a few minutes of her attention.

'Parking and access to the new infirmary,' Margo summarizes when she returns, breathing heavily. 'They're really worried round here. These roads are going to become rat runs.'

Just then a shopper sidles up and asks a question. 'The fact is, madam,' booms Margo, offering her a leaflet, 'we may be rogues and vagabonds every one of us, but we didn't create the problems you're complaining of, did we now? So why not take a risk? Give us a chance and see how much better things can be.'

The woman smiles, tucks the leaflet in her bag and shakes hands. 'Another happy customer,' concludes Margo. 'Back in the bus, everybody.'

28 April 1999

THE DENOUEMENT

The mature, radical choice

ELECTION '99 LEADER

History only rarely looks historic to contemporaries. For every obviously dramatic revolutionary moment there are many more slow evolutionary processes the centrality of which can only be perceived in retrospect. Thomas Hardy put it well when he reflected that '. . . war makes rattling good history; but peace is poor reading'. Scotland's parliamentary election campaign has fallen firmly within the peace category. The limited scope of the arguments on offer has been rendered still less tantalizing by the horrifying events unfolding simultaneously in Kosovo and in Brixton, Brick Lane and Soho. We yearned for greatness and discovered, like Camus before us, that 'politics and the fate of mankind are shaped by men without ideals and without greatness'.

So the battle for Holyrood has been punctuated by whimpers and no great resounding bang. It has been cautious and essentially negative. The vision which might have emanated from the engagement of Scotland's great men and women of letters has not surfaced because few of them have been motivated to become engaged. Alasdair Gray and Angus Calder made a bold attempt to enliven politics with ideas in a series of articles written for this newspaper. The parties ignored their radicalism. That is the nature of party politics.

And yet, beneath the froth of accusation and counter-blast, the mind-numbing cycle of assertion and rebuttal which has replaced ideology as the stuff of modern political activism, something truly significant has happened. Scotland has begun to understand devolution for what it is, not for what its enemies would seek to make it. The constitutional change which will become reality when our votes are counted in the early hours of Friday morning was not conceived as an ante-chamber to fully fledged independence. Though Labour itself began to talk the language of nationalism during the wilderness years of the Thatcher and Major governments, the shock of reality, of doing rather than simply talking devolution, has forced the party of government to focus. Belatedly but effectively it has started to articulate the case it always really believed.

That case was for the recognition of Scottish identity within the United Kingdom. It was formally expressed a quarter of a century ago when Labour's Scottish Executive first approved a report which asserted that 'there is a real need to ensure that decisions affecting Scotland are taken in Scotland ... A measure of devolution could perhaps give to the people a feeling of involvement in the process of decision making'. Donald Dewar and his colleagues came to describe it as filling the democratic deficit. It is a sensibly limited ambition but a valuable one. Only apathy remains to threaten it. There must be no excuses now. A low turn-out tomorrow would undermine all that has been achieved. It would challenge the legitimacy of Holyrood.

The eighties arguments about sovereignty, and the portrayal of devolution as a diluted version of a nationalist paradigm, are dead. They were a reaction to Conservatism and profound economic change. Labour had not suddenly become a revolutionary proto-nationalist movement. It simply found itself outflanked on the Right by a triumphant Conservative Party, which was forced by electoral reality to condemn devolution, and from the Left by an increasingly professional and united Scottish National Party.

That was then. This election campaign has not been fought under the shadow of Thatcherism but under a New Labour government with a spectacularly popular prime minister, a massive parliamentary majority and a reputation for economic competence. New Labour is certainly more popular in England than it is in Scotland. But that is because New Labour has, until recently, been a primarily English phenomenon. Throughout the first eighteen months of Donald Dewar's administration there were solid grounds to fear that Scotland was to be denied the benefits of the undiluted Blair/Brown project. The secretary of state appeared feeble in his support for change and his willingness to confront those who would preserve within Labour the tired old social democratic instincts of the seventies and eighties. The election campaign has changed that.

Labour has fought on a New Labour manifesto and with New Labour tactics. Gordon Brown's Budget has formed the heart of its appeal. It has spoken the language of confident modernity. It has been proud to portray itself as the Scottish wing of a successful British party. A new generation of politicians has emerged from its ranks offering real hope that Labour has the strength in depth to create a young and radical Scottish leadership cadre who will be both distinctively ours and simultaneously confident about their place within the larger Labour Party and the British constitution.

SNP misjudgement of the public mood

Is there an alternative? The Scottish National Party does not offer one. It has misjudged the public mood on tax and on Kosovo. Desperate to mark out clear territory to the left of Labour, the SNP has formed alliances of convenience with teaching and other public-sector unions which render it incapable of exercising the hard choices Scotland will inevitably require. By advancing the case for income-tax increases the SNP shamefully ducked an issue Holyrood is obliged to confront: Scotland cries out for greater efficiency in the use of public money, not fresh injections of hard-earned cash into the bottomless pit of complacency and incompetence.

The harder it has tried to present a coherent programme for government the more clearly the SNP has emerged as a single-issue campaign united only in its desire to rupture the Union.

The argument that the SNP is a one-man band has looked truer as the campaign has progressed. In fact it disguises the real picture. There are good minds in the Nationalist ranks, but they do not agree with the leader. Mr Salmond surrounds himself with unimpressive acolytes who have shown themselves barely adequate for back-bench roles but hardly the stuff of which effective ministers are made. There is only one reason for supporting the SNP. It is independence. Mr Salmond truculently insists independence is possible. This election has been about whether it is desirable. If the polls are remotely accurate, that question has been answered clearly and in the negative.

What of the others? The Conservatives have fought a brave and organized campaign against the formidable odds created by their own legacy. They have marked themselves out as a distinctively Scottish party, free from the ideological schisms which have rent asunder Mr Hague's parliamentary party. David McLetchie has been the surprise of the election. Intelligent, calm and willing to take risks in order to be noticed. The Tories have begun the long climb back towards real political influence. There is a lot farther to travel. The performance of their contingent at Holyrood will allow voters to judge whether they deserve complete rehabilitation. They must hope that voters in areas dominated by Labour constituency majorities will choose to exercise their second vote so as to inject a hint of diversity into parliamentary ranks.

Poor performance by Liberal Democrats

The Liberal Democrats have been the real failures, apparently willing to abandon principle with the alacrity of a stripper shedding clothes. While the Conservatives have outperformed their Westminster colleagues, Mr Wallace's team have done the opposite. They have behaved as if the advent of proportional representation gives them a sacred right to form part of a coalition government. The electorate will be entitled to take a different view, not least because the Liberal Democrats seem willing to promise everything and nothing simply to win a share of somebody, anybody, else's mandate.

In their desperation to build a new politics with the tactics of the old, Mr Wallace's uninspired little band has flailed and missed. Coalition-forming is a business which must be concluded when the votes have been counted and with due deference to the will of the electorate.

Tomorrow's election may not have inspired passion, but it is hugely important. It is an opportunity to confirm the value of devolution. If the nation chooses that road the result will come, in future years, to be seen as a turning point in British politics. It can be the moment when Scotland chooses the mature option of electing a New Labour government of its own. Such a government deserves a mandate to govern in a distinctive manner secure within the frontiers of the United Kingdom.

New Labour deserves that opportunity. Scotland deserves the chance such an outcome affords to put the relentless dullness of the constitutional debate firmly behind it. Great governments come to be seen as such because of the differences they make to the everyday lives of citizens.

Scotland has the opportunity to choose a distinctively better future. But distinctive and better must be defined as meaning that hard decisions will not be ducked, that consensus will no longer substitute for rigour and that hard choices will be pursued because they are right, not because they are immediately popular. Radicalism can be measured in scope but still profound in impact. For Scotland, the mature and radical choice to deliver that impact is New Labour.

5 May 1999

Parliaments and power games

ALASDAIR GRAY

I am glad a Scots parliament is happening, though with some exceptions to be mentioned later. I avoided the campaign leading to it. As a professional writer I am part of showbusiness, but the show made of politics by the papers and TV is mostly distractions from how we are ruled: more scraps of opinion and personal gossip than explanations of policy to choose from. Include this article in that criticism.

Visiting a friend's house a fortnight ago I had the bad luck to see a TV contest between Donald Dewar, Alex Salmond and a Liberal Democrat whose name I did not hear. There was also a chairman who did not make the first two obey debating society rules. They interrupted each other in ways that made reasoned argument impossible; only the Liberal sounded polite and sensible. I hope the Scots parliament is better conducted, though it seems Westminster parliamentary debates are equally bad.

Despite which today I am giving my first vote to the SNP, my second to the Scottish Socialist Party. If you have not voted yet do not, dear reader, follow my example. Give all your votes to the Scottish Socialists, or Conservatives, or Human Rights Party, or Greens, or SNP, vote for any party at all except the Labour Party. All the others now have ideas or ideals which can do good. The Labour Party's only aim is to keep power in Westminster. Let them keep it, but not in Scotland.

What follows is personal gossip and scraps of opinion in answer to questions asked me by TV and radio reporters in the past few days. They interviewed me because I have written pamphlets on Scots home rule, though my view of it is no more valuable than that of any sixty-four-year-old who has read some history, worries about politics and spouts about them to get them off his chest. The questioners worked for foreign broadcasting companies which I identify by nationality where relevant and by ANYONE where not. I gave hardly any of the answers below at the time but afterwards wished I had. The remarks and questions *in italics*, however, were put to me.

FRENCH – *The British prime minister and most of his Cabinet are Scottish. Why do the Scots want a separate government when they now rule the whole of Britain?*

You are mistaken in thinking that the Westminster Cabinet rules Britain. The Thatcher government enriched many people in south Britain at the expense of the rest by privatizing as much of it as possible, reducing public welfare and income tax for the wealthy, weakening trade unions and helping British money invest in foreign industry with the notable exception of arms manufacture. The Conservative leaders put Britain under the rule of the Stock Exchange and banks, for they had faith in these things. By adopting these policies New Labour is now in office but certainly not in power. The most powerful thing it can do is follow the advice of Britain's huge military establishment which, like the USA's, wants wars against folks who can't fight back in order to justify its existence, get rid of old weapons and order new ones. Yes, this (from a Conservative point of view) is a good time to have Scots Labour figureheads in Westminster.

ANYONE – *You sound like a socialist.*

Yes. I belong to a third generation who supported the old Labour Party. It was created a century ago by an alliance of trade unions and socialist professional folk, many of them civil servants. My dads were manual workers – semi-skilled labourers – who worked long hours for poor pay with bad housing and threats of unemployment which their employers and most professional folk did not suffer. The Labour Party wanted government to change that. Its earliest leaders were Scots who promised home rule for Ireland and Scotland too. But outside Scotland many Scots adapt so well to their surroundings that Scot and surroundings can hardly be told apart, except on Burns night, so in the 1930s a Scots Labour prime minister amalgamated with the Tory Party to found a National Coalition Party.

ANYONE – Yet your people still voted Labour?

It was possible then. Scotland still had an Independent Labour Party it called itself that) which rejected Ramsay MacDonald's National government. It only supported the coalition government when it started ruling Britain along socialist lines during the Second World War. Conservatives like Churchill knew Britain could not defeat Germany by fighting it for private profit, so they nationalized the whole of Britain and made allies of the trade unions by promising social justice and welfare for all when the war was won. This was the foundation of the welfare state which the old Labour Party created around 1950. They could not have done it if Tories then had not wanted it too. Butler, a Tory, brought in the student grants that enabled me and most of my closest friends through colleges and into professional jobs. I believe Margaret Thatcher also had that advantage. In those days I did not even tell close friends that I liked the notion of Scots home rule.

It seemed romantic and impractical. I voted for Harold Wilson's Labour Party because Scottish industries were becoming branches of international ones and closed down under Tory rule and I hoped for some more British socialism to help us.

ENGLISH – When and why did you start voting SNP?

When Harold Wilson explained that he could not deliver any socialism now because the banks and stock markets weren't healthy enough to stand it. When Labour Party cut-backs led local governments to sack park keepers and employees who did the most lowest-paid, most essential work and got in publicity men to advertise the virtues of their administration, etc. I thought then, this messy and amateurish Scottish National Party (for the first SNP members of parliament were not good professional politicians) is my only hope for a change in British politics that will give meaning to a democratic vote.

ENGLISH – *You think today's SNP is less amateurish?*

We shall see.

ENGLISH – *Do you not think nationalism is an evil thing? Has it not killed enough people this century?*

Any word with ism on the end is indefinite and therefore dangerous. I am for a Scottish nation – a land in north Britain that is electing its own government. I define the Scots as anyone who lives here, whether English, Pakistani or Irish. The most intolerant group in Scotland is the Orange Order, who are strong British Unionists.

NORTHERN IRISH – *Is there really no danger, in an independent Scotland, from the sectarian violence of the Rangers–Celtic matches?*

There will probably be as much danger, but I see no cause for more. That kind of beastliness only endangers good government when businessmen and bankers finance it, as happened in Germany between the wars, or when a foreign government finances it, as the USA did with fascist movements in South America and Iran. I doubt if any big businesses see advantages in financing the Orange Order. The nearest thing to a middle-class Scottish fascist party was the Church and Nation Committee, a group of Scots ministers and MPs who, from 1922 to 1938, tried to have all unemployed people born in Ireland sent back there. But there were too many working Irish in the trade unions and Labour Party for this clique to whip up much of a working-class following.

NORTHERN IRISH – *That suggests the Scottish Labour Party was a source of protection for Irish Catholics – it certainly gave*

Catholics their own local authority schools – yet you are asking them to abandon that protection and vote for other parties.

The kind of branch members and voters who worked with them have not left Scotland. They have joined or voted for other parties, and so have many Catholics.

The folk most in danger of unprovoked nastiness are minorities who can be recognized by skin colour. Scottish cities are not worse than English ones in that respect and all the main Scottish political parties have Indian and Pakistani members and candidates. Scotland was composed of many different races – Picts, Gaels, Norse, the Welsh in Galloway, Anglo-Saxons in Lothian, Scots from Antrim who gave the place its name – so only recent immigrants have a single root to hark back to.

GERMAN – *So what, exactly, is Scottishness?*

. . . Eh?

GERMAN – *Of what does Scottishness consist?*

Are you asking me what sentiment unites people in Scotland?

GERMAN – *Yes*

It is a reaction to Englishness. You know, of course, that all nations have been made from smaller ones, usually through warfare? I believe Germany got unity last century through a war with France.

The Anglo-Saxon kingdoms in south Britain were united through conquest by Danes and then Normans. North of the Tweed five different races and language groups united to prevent conquest by England, and succeeded until our government was paid to go south in 1707.

ENGLISH – *So Scottishness depends on hatred of the English?*

No no no no! The English are the least hateful of people in the world. They did not conquer a third of the globe because they hated the natives there, they did it to get more business, and territory, and sources of employment. A few bad-tempered English may have found hating the locals made them easier to deal with. I am sure they were never typical. In the same way hatred may strengthen resistance to rule from outside but is a sign of weakness. Scottish independence was lost because Scottish leaders preferred safety and quick money to keeping it. By argument and democratic voting we are regaining it. Nobody has been killed. I don't think anybody will be unless one of Britain's security forces (who used to keep their office secret but now work from a building as vast as an oil company headquarters on the Thames and are, I believe, semi-privatized) work hatred to destabilize Scotland by working through *agents provocateurs* on weak-minded enthusiasts.

GERMAN – *The sentiment for independence belongs to many people. Can you not give me a more local definition of Scottishness?*

Only by contrasting what I dislike in Scotland with what I dislike in England, but remember, please, dislike is not hatred.

I have been to parties where friends of mine – socialists with a wish for Scottish independence, intelligent thinkers and writers whose work I admire – have quarrelled bitterly and insulted each other over small points of difference. I am English on my mother's side, which may be why that upsets me. I have also been to parties in London where Conservatives, Labour folk and radicals have mixed in perfect friendliness, each lot telling the other comic tales against their own leaders and carefully steering clear of all political differences to show that, before everything else, they are all charming and tolerant people. As indeed they are. But I came to feel this consensus (as it is sometimes called) had something stifling about it. It certainly stifled British socialism. Of course my dad's parents were Scots.

ENGLISH – *The Scots are too quarrelsome and the English too bland?*

At times. The constitution of this parliament is devised to give place to as many small parties as possible so that Labour can dominate the rest. My hope is that the SNP, Liberal Democrats, Scottish Socialists and Conservatives will unite on the one point which they all agree and which puts them all to the left of New Labour – the student grants. Like any old Etonian I am sentimental about my early education, and feel now as most Etonians would feel if a government decree abolished English private schools. THE OLD SYSTEM MUST BE REINSTATED.

The Protestant Reformation in Scotland destroyed many fine traditions in art, music and literature that are only now being revived, but John Knox devised a system of parish schools, for children of every social class, and wanted grants that would let all those capable of university educations have equal chances of it. The Knox system did, for several centuries, give a good start in life to working-class talent. The Butler Acts completed what Knox had imagined. But when grants prevailed in Germany and most west European states the Tories decided to emulate the USA and do without them. To restore this precious piece of social equality would be so much to Scotland's honour – so good an example to the rest of Britain – that if the parties in favour combine to achieve that first I am sure some in the Labour Party would join them.

GERMAN – I notice that in Scotland many people are discussing such political issues.

Don't they do it in England?

GERMAN – No, these things are thought out of date.

I didn't realize England had got to that state.

GERMAN – I also noticed with interest, in following Mr Dewar around, that the Scottish Labour Party publicity agents are all English. Can you tell me why?

The Scottish Labour Party don't trust the Scottish natives. They feel the English do things better, even up here. Please do not interpret that as an anti-English remark. It is anti-Scots Labour Party.

ANYONE – How do you see Scotland in ten years' time?

I don't know and won't speculate.

ANYONE – Are you excited about this new parliament?

No. I'm just glad. This parliament is not a final achievement but the start of a different new period. As a great English historian said, 'Any change, even from a worse to a better state, is attended by inconveniences.' We should prepare for them. But the long steady political decline of Scotland since the 1920s will not continue quite so predictably. And for that I sincerely thank Tony Blair who, I am sure, is honestly ignorant of why the party he leads has such a quaintly irrelevant name.

6 May 1999

Scotland makes history

ALASTAIR McKAY

We have waited and yearned. Perhaps not since 1707, for there were times, long good times, when that settlement was not seriously challenged. But certainly for two decades. For long enough for children to grow into adults.

We have defined ourselves in terms of our right to be different, by reference to the hard facts which prove that, truly, we are a nation. Our legal and educational systems, our sporting and cultural life.

For too long it all looked like an impossible dream, an aching which could not be filled because, hard as we argued our case, often as we voted in overwhelming numbers for politicians who backed our project, the state to which we owe affection and loyalty was governed by an ideology that rejected our claim.

It hurt. Banging your head against a wall does hurt. We begged and pleaded for flexibility. Pious lectures were the response. Scotland was ungrateful. Scotland was infuriatingly wrong. Scotland had to grow up. Today it can.

This is it. This is where we are. This is the fine morning we have dreamed of, the day we demanded. It is the first day of the rest of our lives. If devolution is the settled will of the Scottish people there is one small thing to do which will show that we still care. Today we vote.

It has been so long coming that its arrival may seem like a disappointment. The momentum of the devolution campaign was gathered in the last quarter-century, but to focus purely on the recent past is to misunderstand the opportunities of the present. Devolution is a renegotiation of a constitutional arrangement that has lasted three hundred years. It is as important, as vital as that.

No one is sure where this process will lead, whether to a stronger Union, or independence. The one place it cannot be allowed to lead is towards apathy. Scotland has demanded the right to be viewed in the world as a nation, and we should not shirk the responsibility we have won for ourselves. We must not let the fearfulness that inhabits our psyche limit our imagination. We will need imagination in the months and years to come. That would be a very Scottish response – wouldn't it? – to want something, and then, just as the prize is about to be delivered, to think, well, it does not matter. It has been one of the curiosities of the campaign that such an outcome has seemed possible.

It has, it's true, been a curious campaign. At times it has seemed like a mini-referendum on independence, which is one of the many things that it wasn't. The concentration on the tortured arithmetic of nationalism has been Labour strategy, and it has kept the Nationalists on the back foot, since devolution is not what they are for, and to settle for it would be to deny the purpose of their existence.

But this wasn't – isn't – the end of the Union. It isn't even a trial separation. If we see the Union in terms of a marriage which is in the midst of some strife, the granting of devolution by the British (not English) state is a small, positive step. A problem acknowledged is a problem which can start to be unpicked. In our troubled Union, the weaker party is being sent for assertiveness training. If the course works, it should help with communication. Perhaps then our careworn lovers can, get over the sense of weary familiarity which has recently characterized their exchanges.

Positivity, then. Instead of grumbling quietly into her gassy beer, Scotland will be forced to learn to speak up for herself, to assert the things that she would like to do. This will be a frightening process, because there is something quite comforting about defining oneself in negative terms; glorying in what one is not. We will have to learn confidence, but a kind of confidence which fits; which does not seem like boastfulness. A country whose visage is pitted with Calvinism will have trouble with boastfulness.

Watching the performance of our politicians these past few weeks has been an instructive, but not a cheering experience. As Scots, we might feel bad about that if we allowed ourselves to believe that the shadow-play of party grudges which has passed for creative thought was as good as it could get. But perhaps we get the politicians we deserve. If we want better, we should demand it. The new electoral system allows for surprises.

In the confusion caused by Mel Gibson's folly, *Braveheart*, it is easy to forget that Scottish politics has undergone a Darwinian change these last few centuries. Today's political battles are not about blood and toil, not about life and death. Scotland is more of a timorous beastie than a rampant lion. And *Braveheart*, a Hollywood lie, is a long advertisement for face-painting.

The place we have come to is not about that. It is something more pragmatic. It is about a penny on or off tax. It is about the notional ownership of a hospital. It is about helping opportunity to knock. It is about all these small, dull things, and it is about everything else. The politicians cannot be relied on to think of the answers, or even the questions. We will have to dream them ourselves.

How does it feel, this settled will of the Scottish people? It feels fresh, raw, a little worrying. But there is continuity too. It feels a bit like what came before it, the unsettled will. History is a sneaky companion, never there when you need her, hanging around when you do not. Commentators tend to concentrate on the first half of the equation, the 'settled will', yet the whole drift towards self-determination has been about the other bit, the identity of the Scottish people. We can't have a settled will until we understand who we are, and the question of identity has been the thing which has long haunted us.

Somehow, we have come to think of ourselves as a people. The current wave of nationalism has been triggered by a number of things: North Sea oil, Mrs Thatcher, the poll tax. Perhaps it has also been aided by the sense that the world is smaller, that our possibilities are greater. We are no longer cowed by London, because a world ruled by multinationals has many capitals. But a sense of identity must be found closer to home.

But, admit it or not, we have chosen this path. It was not an accident. How we did it is baffling, and we will all take our own histories into the future. But we cannot flinch now. It is that banal, and that important. That's how it feels when destiny is no longer a stone.

6 May 1999

'The Scottish parliament, adjourned on the 25th day of March, 1707, is hereby reconvened'

IAN BELL

David Steel could not resist it. Five years to the day since the death of John Smith, nobody thought that he should. It was, said Sir David, Presiding Officer of Scotland's first democratic parliament, the start of a new sang. That and more.

Dr Winifred Ewing, sixty-nine, mother of the house, had already reminded us of what was being done. In the capital's grey Assembly Hall, just after 9.30 a.m., to a half-empty chamber, she uttered the simple, astonishing truth: 'The Scottish parliament, adjourned on the 25th day of March, 1707, is hereby reconvened.'

History is memory. This moment was memory reclaimed, a right restated, a truth reaffirmed. The nation of Scotland, with all its thrawn suspicions, numberless confusions, apathy, clumsy rivalries and disparate hopes, had remembered.

We began again on a May morning in Edinburgh, high on the Mound, with thirty-five white roses, a clenched fist, 129 members sworn in with a measure of honest dissent, a Labour Party honouring John Smith's promise and a strange kind of ease. This, said the language of ritual, is what we do, ours by right, and this is how we do it. The fact was woven in neat, white letters into the very uniforms of the hall's polite, patient staff: 'Scottish Parliament'.

But then, suddenly, many strands came together. The clenched fist was Tommy Sheridan's, affirming on behalf of the Scottish Socialist Party and a long tradition for a democratic socialist republic. The white roses were on the lapels of the Scottish National Party. The power was with Donald Dewar's Labour, the novelty with Britain's first Green parliamentarian, the democratic question with the Liberal Democrats, the new argument with the new Scottish Tories. Whatever else home rule may come to mean, it has already given articulacy to Scotland's diversity. We have not been here, or anywhere like it, before.

Hence, perhaps, the sense of relaxation. Whatever the tensions over pacts and deals, whatever the storms to come, the bitterness and the arguments, Scotland's parliamentarians seemed content yesterday just to celebrate, to be themselves.

Mr Dewar entered the forecourt of the Assembly Hall and, as usual, failed to co-operate with the photographers. Alex Salmond of the SNP was as ebullient as nature intended. By lunchtime David McLetchie of the Tories was in a pub in a Royal Mile close listening hard, as promised, to the people, in this case some young men from an Edinburgh housing scheme.

This is what we are; this is what we do. Mr Salmond spoke for the collective strength of the SNP when he said, before swearing the oath: 'For the Scottish National Party parliamentary group, loyalty is with the people of Scotland, in line with sovereignty of the people.'

Before that, Mr Dewar, following Dr Ewing, had seemed almost to efface himself, he whose creation this parliament had been. Jim Wallace of the Lib Dems took his place after Mr Salmond, but made no objection to monarchy or ordained allegiances. But then came Dennis Canavan, the socialist from Falkirk West that 'new' Labour could not silence, recording that he owed a duty first and above all to the people of Scotland.

It became what the glib call a defining moment: almost one-third of Scotland's first democratic parliamentarians put on record their belief that sovereignty resides, as old doctrine and the Claim of Right once supported by Labour says, with the people of Scotland, not with the Crown. Mr Canavan said it; the

SNP said it; Robin Harper of the Greens said it; Mr Sheridan of the SSP said, loud and clear, that he took his oath under solemn protest.

The maker's label in Mr Sheridan's dapper suit says 'Candidate'. Yesterday the democratically elected socialist amended the prescribed ceremony by affirming his vision, as he called it, of a democratic socialist republic. An open palm was raised towards him as he recited the oath to 'bear true allegiance to Her Majesty Queen Elizabeth, Her Heirs and Successors, according to Law'. In return, Mr Sheridan offered a clenched fist.

An antique gesture from another Scotland, in some books, but yesterday there seemed nothing odd in that. The reconvened parliament, for all the blond wood and desktop computers, the twenty-first-century procedures, the pagers and the mobile telephones, was itself an antique revived. The idea, if not the entity, had proved unkillable. Scottish Labour, under orders, male and female, to dress with due sobriety, finally seemed proud of itself. The SNP at last seemed a reality rather than a rhetorical device.

It was a haphazard day, nonetheless. The journalist Dorothy Grace Elder, the SNP MSP for Glasgow region, upset the parliamentary lawyers by infiltrating a mention of the people into the formalities involving the Queen and was obliged to say her piece again. Fergus and Margaret Ewing, Nationalist spouses and MSPs for Inverness East and Moray, made their declarations simultaneously.

When Mr Dewar trooped his parliamentarians *en masse* up the High Street after lunch, in an interval between showers of rain, it seemed more than symbolic that Mr Canavan followed, as though tracking them, twenty yards behind.

But business, such as it was, was conducted. After the MSPs had made their oaths and settled into their blue chairs, Sir David Steel was found to have won the Presiding Officer's job over the SNP's George Reid by eighty-two votes to forty-four. Mr Reid, a friend of Sir David's for more than four decades, duly became one of the PO's deputies. This is, was, remains, a small country – and what of it?

Yesterday in the Royal Mile the bewildered tourists wanted to know what was going on, and if it might be worth a souvenir snap. The journalists wanted to know whether the Lib Dems and Labour had reached an accommodation, and what it might be. A few local people looked on diffidently, with honest curiosity at this parliament suddenly reborn in its temporary home beneath the standing rebuke of John Knox's statue. If a historic thing can be done casually, without much fuss, this had become the Scottish way.

There were clues for that. Refusing Mr Canavan's considered and dignified demand that there be an open vote rather than a secret ballot for the post of Presiding Officer, for example, Dr Ewing confounded centuries of Westminster practice by calling a parliamentarian by his first name. In the Assembly Hall's black-and-white corridor, so called, that instantly became the parliament's lobby, political rivals mingled freely. The absence of pomp was almost disconcerting.

This was a small parliament in a small country, and none the worse for it. The spin-doctors were conspicuous, if not by their absence then at least by their silence. How to enlarge or diminish what was taking place? It may be sullied in the months and years to come but Scotland's parliament pledged itself into existence with what seemed, in the measure of these things, honest intent.

Mr Dewar is there for the sake of his own belief and for John Smith's promise. Mr Canavan is there for his principles, Mr Sheridan for his people, Mr Salmond for a new nation, Mr Harper for the planet, Mr McLetchie for the Union. Scotland is represented, male and female, from a sixty-nine-year-old to a twenty-five-year-old. In the closes, wynds and pends off the Royal Mile, new politics, a new democracy, came to an old city and an old country.

It is too easy, now, to be cynical. On the Mound yesterday something new did happen, just for once, without self-consciousness, from beneath the weight of history, with a sense of honest purpose. This process will take us only where we want to go. Just for once, we cannot say that we have seen it all before.

Yesterday, for a moment, Edinburgh was the only place in the world to be.

Under the television lights, the SNP's white roses had a yellowish hue, and we could not all remember every word they were meant to invoke. No matter. The flowers were a nationalist gesture that might, just once, have done for all. Hugh MacDiarmid (Christopher Murray Grieve) wrote of the little blossom sixty-five years ago, in another Scotland, in the same Scotland:

The rose of all the world is not for me. I want for my part
Only the little white rose of Scotland
That smells sharp and sweet – and breaks the heart.

13 May 1999

CONTRIBUTORS

Ian Bell was born and raised in Edinburgh. Educated at Edinburgh University, he was literary editor of *The Scotsman* before becoming Scottish editor of the *Observer*. He is currently a *Scotsman* columnist. A former winner of the Orwell Prize, and Scottish Journalist of the Year, he is the author of *Dreams of Exile*, an acclaimed biography of Robert Louis Stevenson.

Angus Calder read English at King's College, Cambridge, and received his doctorate from the School of Social Studies at the University of Sussex. In 1967, he was awarded a Gregory Award for his poetry. After writing the highly acclaimed *The People's War: Britain: 1939–45*, he spent three years lecturing in literature at the University of Nairobi. Before retiring to concentrate on writing, he was a staff tutor with the Open University. Among his other books are a study of T. S. Eliot, *Russia Discovered: Nineteenth-Century Fiction from Pushkin to Chekhov*, and *Revolutionary Empire*, an ambitious attempt to tell the story of British expansion from the 15th century to the 1780s.

Gavin Esler is a presenter on BBC News 24 and a *Scotsman* columnist. He began his career with the BBC in Northern Ireland and has worked as a radio and television journalist in Europe, Russia, China and the USA. He was appointed BBC Washington correspondent in 1989 and was made chief North America Correspondent a year later.

Gillian Glover was born in Glasgow and educated at St Leonard's school, St Andrews, Hutcheson Grammar, Glasgow, and the University of Manchester. She spent nine years as a feature writer with the *Sunday Post*, during which time she travelled to the USA, USSR and South America, as well as the more parochial polarities of hunt balls and homeless women's hostels. She joined *The Scotsman* in 1988 as a writer and subsequently edited the features page. She is now a senior features writer and the paper's restaurant critic.

Alasdair Gray, who is now 63, described himself six years ago as 'an elderly Glasgow pedestrian.' While undoubtedly true, there is much more to him. One of Scotland's foremost novelists, he was born and brought up in the east end of Glasgow. An artist as well as a writer, his breakthrough came in 1981 when he published *Lanark*, a novel of enormous scope and invention. Since then he has published prolifically, including *Lean Tales* (with James Kelman and Agnes Owens), *1982 Janine*, *Unlikely Stories Mostly*, a collection of poems entitled *Old Negatives*, and *Why Scots Should Rule Scotland*, a polemic. Since 1986 he has been working on *The Anthology of Prefaces*, a book of introductions to English vernacular masterpieces by their authors, which he plans to complete before the 21st century.

Robin Harris was born in 1952. Educated at Canford School and Exeter College, Oxford, he worked in the Conservative Research Dept from 1978–81 and was Special Adviser to the Financial Secretary to the Treasury 1981–83; to Home Secretary, 1983–85; and Director of the Conservative Research Dept, 1985–89. Since 1990, he has been Assistant to Baroness Thatcher.

Peter Jones was brought up in the north-east of Scotland and educated at the University of St Andrews. He worked for the *Aberdeen Press and Journal* before joining *The Scotsman* in 1984 as Scottish Political Editor, in which capacity he wrote leaders and commentary pieces as well as breaking stories. In 1994, he joined the *Economist* as its North of England and Scottish correspondent. He is one of the most respected and authoritative commentators on the Scottish political scene.

George Kerevan was born in Glasgow in 1949 and studied Economics at Glasgow University. From 1984–96, he was a local councillor in charge of Edinburgh's economic redevelopment, where he helped create the Gyle shopping centre, Edinburgh Business Park and Conference Centre and Science Festival. He was also Chair of the

Edinburgh Tourist Board. A lifelong supporter of the arts, he has served on the boards of the Traverse, Lyceum and 7.84 theatres, the Edinburgh Festival and Film Festival, Assembly Productions and Edinburgh Film House. In 1997–8 he was the SNP's environmental spokesperson. He is currently producing documentaries for American television.

Tim Luckhurst was born in Sheffield and educated at Peebles High School and Robinson College, Cambridge. He has worked in the House of Commons as Parliamentary Research Assistant and as a Press Officer to Donald Dewar, Scotland's First Minister. At the 1987 general election, he stood as a Labour candidate for the Roxburgh and Berwickshire constituency. In 1988, he joined the BBC, where he spent five years on Radio Four's Today programme, before moving to Five Live and spending a year as Editor, News Programmes, at BBC Scotland. He has covered the Romanian Revolution and the Gulf War for BBC radio and was posted to Washington DC in 1993. He is deputy editor of *The Scotsman*.

Alastair McKay is an assistant editor on the *Scotsman*, where he writes about popular culture, sport and current affairs. He has written more articles about Elvis Presley than is healthy or advisable, and has an unreasonable interest in the history of golf balls. He is a former editor of *The Scotsman's WeekEnd* magazine and chief feature writer and television critic of *Scotland on Sunday*. His career as a journalist began with a fanzine called *Alternatives to Valium*, and a stint at the *North Edinburgh News*, a community newspaper. He was educated in Aberdeen and North Berwick.

Peter MacMahon was born in Dublin in 1959. His family moved to Scotland when he was seven and he was educated at St Augustine's High School, Edinburgh, and St Andrews University, where he was on the Students' Representative Council. His career as a journalist began with the *Cambrian News Agency* in Cardiff after which he moved to the *Northampton Chronicle and Echo* and from there to become a lobby correspondent at Westminster, working for, among others, *Scotland on Sunday* and the *Sunday Mirror*. He is presently Assistant Editor (Politics) of *The Scotsman*.

Joyce McMillan was born and brought up in Renfrewshire, and educated at Paisley Grammar School, and the universities of St Andrews and Edinburgh. She has been a political and arts columnist for *The Herald*, political and theatre critic for *Scotland on Sunday*, and Scottish theatre critic of the *Guardian*. She is involved in Scottish and European campaigns for democracy and human rights, and was a member of the recent Scottish Office steering group on procedures for the Scottish parliament. Currently the theatre critic of *The Scotsman*, for whom she also writes a political/social commentary column, she lives in Edinburgh, from where she broadcasts frequently on Radio Scotland and Radio Four.

Robert McNeil was born in 1957 in Edinburgh. Educated at Broughton High School, he started work as a clerk at Scottish and Newcastle Breweries. Thereafter he was a postman and, for three days, a railway porter. In 1981, he enrolled at Paisley College of Technology where he did a degree in Social Science. He finally entered journalism in 1988, starting at the *Edinburgh and Lothians Post*. As a freelance, he worked mainly for the *Observer* until 1991 when he joined the *Shetland Times*. In 1996, he joined *The Scotsman*, contributing news features and an eccentric weekly column which has a cult following.

Iain MacWhirter started with BBC Scotland after leaving the University of Edinburgh where he was doing post-graduate research into regionalism and nationalism in Europe. He was a reporter on the social affairs documentary programme *Corridors of Power* before becoming the BBC's Scottish Political Correspondent in the late Eighties. He then joined the BBC's parliamentary unit in Millbank and has presented several programmes, including Scrutiny, Westminster Live and Scottish Lobby. Currently the *Sunday Herald*'s main political commentator, he has also worked for *The Scotsman*, *Scotland on Sunday* and the *Observer*.

Allan Massie was born in Singapore in 1938 and brought up in Aberdeenshire. He was educated at Glenalmond and Trinity College, Cambridge, where he read history. He lived and taught in Italy for a number of years. A prolific journalist and book reviewer, he contributes regularly to *The Scotsman*, the *Sunday Times* and *Daily Mail*. His many novels include *Change and Decay in All Around I See*, *The Death of Men*, *A Question of Loyalties*, which won the Saltire/*Scotsman* Book of the Year award in 1989, a sequence of novels centring on Ancient Rome. His non-fiction includes a historical study, *The Caesars*, critical assessments of Muriel Spark and Colette, and *Byron's Travels*. He lives in the Scottish Borders.

Andrew Neil was born in Paisley in 1949 and educated at Paisley Grammar School before taking a degree in politics and economics at the University of Glasgow. His first job was as political adviser to Edward Heath's Conservative government. As a journalist he has worked for the Economist, for whom he became American correspondent in 1979, and UK editor in 1982. He was the editor of the *Sunday Times* from 1983–94. A prolific columnist, he is currently Publisher of Press Holding, who own *The Scotsman*, *Scotland on Sunday*, the *Edinburgh Evening News* and *Sunday Business*. He is the author of *The Cable Revolution, Britain's Free Press: Does It Have One?*, and *Full Disclosure*, an autobiography. He is a familiar figure on the airwaves and has presented The Andrew Neil Show and The Midnight Hour. He was Chairman of Sky TV from 1988–90.

Sir Malcolm Rifkind was born and brought up in Edinburgh where he attended George Watson's College and read law at Edinburgh University; he became a QC in 1985. He was Conservative MP for Edinburgh Pentlands from 1974–97. In Parliament he frequently held a Scottish role and from 1975–6 he was Opposition frontbench spokesman on Scottish affairs and from 1979–82 Parliamentary Under-Secretary of State, Scottish Office. From 1986–90 he was Secretary of State for Scotland; 1990–92 Secretary of State for Transport; 1992–95 Secretary of State for Defence; and Foreign Minister from 1995–97. He is President of the Conservative Party in Scotland.

Alan Taylor is managing editor of Scotsman Publications. Born and educated in Scotland, he worked in London for the Civil Service before becoming a reference librarian with Edinburgh City Libraries. As a freelance journalist, he has written for most British broadsheets and many international magazines. He has edited the *Assistant Librarian* and *The List* and is a former literary and features editor of *Scotland on Sunday* and deputy editor of *The Scotsman*. He is the author of *Long Overdue: A Library Reader*, half of the Scottish team on Radio Four's Round Britain Quiz and a former Booker Prize judge. He is currently writing a biography of Alex Salmond, leader of the Scottish Nationalist Party.

ACKNOWLEDGEMENTS

The original idea for this book came from Tim Luckhurst, Deputy Editor of *The Scotsman*, who, along with Richard Neville, the paper's Assistant Editor (News), helped me select the articles and shape the content. As ever, the staff of *The Scotsman* library were unfailingly helpful. Peter MacMahon, *The Scotsman*'s Assistant Editor (Politics) kindly read the introduction.